Alexander von Humboldt

Letters of Alexander von Humboldt to Varnhagen von Ense

Alexander von Humboldt

Letters of Alexander von Humboldt to Varnhagen von Ense

ISBN/EAN: 9783742892072

Manufactured in Europe, USA, Canada, Australia, Japa

Cover: Foto ©Thomas Meinert / pixelio.de

Manufactured and distributed by brebook publishing software (www.brebook.com)

Alexander von Humboldt

Letters of Alexander von Humboldt to Varnhagen von Ense

LETTERS

OF

ALEXANDER VON HUMBOLDT

TO

VARNHAGEN VON ENSE.

"Your last favor doing me so much honor contains words about which I wish to prevent every mistake. 'You are afraid to confess yourself the exclusive owner of my impieties.' You may freely dispose of this sort of property after my not far distant departure from life. Truth is due to those only whom we deeply esteem—to you therefore."

ALEXANDER VON HUMBOLDT TO VARNHAGEN.
Letter of December 7th, 1841.

Contents.

		PAGE
1.	Humboldt to Varnhagen,	17
2.	Humboldt to Varnhagen,	18
3.	Humboldt to Varnhagen,	19
4.	Humboldt to Varnhagen,	20
5.	Humboldt to Varnhagen,	21
6.	Humboldt to Varnhagen,	22
7.	Humboldt to Varnhagen,	23
8.	Varnhagen to Humboldt,	25
9.	Humboldt to Rahel,	28
10.	Humboldt to Varnhagen,	29
11.	Humboldt to Rahel	31
12.	Humboldt to Varnhagen,	32
13.	Humboldt to Varnhagen,	33
14.	Humboldt to Varnhagen,	34
15.	Humboldt to Varnhagen,	35
16.	(No Address.)	35
17.	Humboldt to Varnhagen,	40
18.	Humboldt to Varnhagen,	41
19.	Humboldt to Varnhagen,	43
20.	Humboldt to Varnhagen,	44
21.	Humboldt to Varnhagen,	45
22.	Humboldt to Varnhagen,	46
23.	Humboldt to Varnhagen,	49
24.	Humboldt to Varnhagen,	49
25.	Humbold to the Princess von Pueckler,	51
26.	Humboldt to Varnhagen,	52

Contents.

		PAGE
27.	Humboldt to Varnhagen,	54
28.	Humboldt to Varnhagen,	56
29.	Humboldt to Varnhagen,	58
30.	Humboldt to Varnhagen,	59
31.	Humboldt to Varnhagen,	60
32.	Humboldt to Varnhagen,	61
33.	Humboldt to Varnhagen,	62
34.	(No Address.)	66
35.	Humboldt to Varnhagen,	67
36.	Humboldt to Varnhagen,	70
37.	Humboldt to Varnhagen,	73
38.	Humboldt to Varnhagen,	74
39.	Humboldt to Varnhagen,	75
40.	Humboldt to Varnhagen,	76
41.	Humboldt to Varnhagen,	77
42.	Metternich to Humboldt,	79
43.	Humboldt to Varnhagen,	82
44.	King Christian VIII. of Denmark to Humboldt,	83
45.	Humboldt to Varnhagen,	85
46.	(No Address.)	86
47.	Humboldt to Varnhagen,	87
48.	Humboldt to Varnhagen,	89
49.	Guizot to Humboldt,	93
50.	Arago to Humboldt,	94
51.	Humboldt to Bettina von Arnim,	96
52.	Humboldt to Varnhagen,	97
53.	Humboldt to Varnhagen,	100
54.	Humboldt to Varnhagen,	101
55.	Humboldt to Spiker,	104
56.	Humboldt to Varnhagen,	105
57.	Humboldt to Varnhagen,	106
58.	King Christian VIII. of Denmark to Humboldt,	108
59.	(No Address.)	110
60.	Humboldt to Varnhagen,	112
61.	Humboldt to Varnhagen,	115
62.	Humboldt to Varnhagen,	119
63.	Humboldt to Varnhagen,	120
64.	Humboldt to Varnhagen,	122
65.	Humboldt to Varnhagen,	127
66.	Humboldt to Varnhagen,	128
67.	Humboldt to Varnhagen,	130
68.	Humboldt to Varnhagen,	131
69.	Humboldt to Varnhagen,	138
70.	Humboldt to Varnhagen,	139
71.	(No Address.)	140
72.	Humboldt to Varnhagen,	141
73.	Humboldt to Varnhagen,	142

Contents.

		PAGE
74.	Humboldt to the Prince of Prussia.	144
75.	(No Address.)	146
76.	Humboldt to Varnhagen,	151
77.	J. W. T. to Humboldt,	154
78.	Count Bresson, French Ambassador, to Humboldt,	155
79.	Arago to Humboldt,	158
80.	Four Notes of Frederick William the Fourth to Humboldt,	160
81.	King Christian VIII. of Denmark to Humboldt,	163
82.	John Herschel to Humboldt,	164
83.	Balzac to Humboldt,	168
84.	Robert Peel to Humboldt,	169
85.	Metternich to Humboldt,	170
86.	Prescott to Humboldt,	171
87.	Madame de Récamier to Humboldt,	174
88.	Humboldt to Varnhagen,	175
89.	Leopold, Grand-Duke of Tuscany, to Humboldt,	175
90.	Humboldt to Varnhagen,	177
91.	Humboldt to Varnhagen,	178
92.	Humboldt to Varnhagen,	180
93.	Humboldt to Varnhagen,	182
94.	Humboldt to Varnhagen,	183
95.	Humboldt to Varnhagen,	184
96.	(No Address.)	185
97.	Humboldt to Varnhagen,	186
98.	Metternich to Humboldt,	188
99.	Jules Janin to Humboldt,	189
100.	Humboldt to Varnhagen,	192
101.	Humboldt to Varnhagen,	193
102.	Humboldt to Varnhagen,	196
103.	Humboldt to Varnhagen,	196
104.	Humboldt to Varnhagen,	198
105.	Humboldt to Varnhagen,	199
106.	Humboldt to Varnhagen,	201
107.	Humboldt to Varnhagen,	203
108.	Humboldt to Varnhagen,	204
109.	Humboldt to Varnhagen,	205
110.	Humboldt to Friedrich Wilhelm IV.,	206
111.	Bessel to Humboldt,	208
112.	Victor Hugo to Humboldt,	215
113.	Friedrich Rueckert to Humboldt,	216
114.	Alexander Manzoni to Humboldt,	217
115.	Thiers to Humboldt,	220
116.	The Princess of Canino, Lucien Bonaparte's Widow, to Humboldt,	220
117.	Duchess Helene d'Orleans to Humboldt,	221
118.	Duchess Helene d'Orleans to Humboldt,	222
119.	Duchess Helene d'Orleans to Humboldt,	223

Contents.

		PAGE
120.	Humboldt to Varnhagen,	223
121.	Humboldt to Varnhagen,	225
122.	Metternich to Humboldt,	225
123.	Humboldt to Varnhagen,	229
124.	Humboldt to Varnhagen,	229
125.	Humboldt to Varnhagen,	231
126.	Humboldt to Varnhagen,	232
127.	Mignet to Humboldt,	233
128.	Humboldt to Baudin,	235
129.	Humboldt to Varnhagen,	238
130.	Metternich to Humboldt,	240
131.	Prince Albert to Humboldt,	241
132.	Humboldt to Varnhagen,	242
133.	Humboldt to Varnhagen,	243
134.	(No Address.)	248
135.	Humboldt to Varnhagen,	251
136.	Humboldt to Varnhagen,	252
137.	Metternich to Humboldt,	253
138.	Humboldt to Varnhagen,	254
139.	Helen, Duchess of Orleans, to Humboldt,	254
140.	Humboldt to Varnhagen,	256
141.	Humboldt to Varnhagen,	259
142.	Humboldt to Varnhagen,	260
143.	Humboldt to Varnhagen,	160
144.	Humboldt to Bettina von Arnim,	262
145.	Humboldt to Varnhagen,	263
146.	Humboldt to Varnhagen,	266
147.	Humboldt to Varnhagen,	268
148.	Humboldt to Varnhagen,	271
149.	Humboldt to Varnhagen,	271
150.	Humboldt to Varnhagen,	275
151.	Humboldt to Varnhagen,	276
152.	Humboldt to Varnhagen,	278
153.	Humboldt to Varnhagen,	279
154.	Humboldt to Varnhagen,	281
155.	Humboldt to Varnhagen,	284
156.	Humboldt to Varnhagen,	286
157.	Arago to Humboldt,	287
158.	Humboldt to Varnhagen,	289
159.	Humboldt to Varnhagen,	289
160.	Varnhagen to Humboldt,	294
161.	Humboldt to Varnhagen,	297
162.	Humboldt to Bettina von Arnim,	300
163.	Humboldt to Varnhagen,	302
164	Humboldt to Varnhagen,	303
165.	Humboldt to Varnhagen,	304
166.	Varnhagen to Humboldt,	305

Contents. xi

		PAGE
167.	Humboldt to Varnhagen,	306
168.	Humboldt to Varnhagen,	308
169.	Humboldt to Varnhagen,	313
170.	The Princess Lieven to Humboldt,	316
171.	Varnhagen to Humboldt,	317
172.	Humboldt to Varnhagen,	318
173.	Humboldt to Varnhagen,	320
174.	Varnhagen to Humboldt,	321
175.	Humboldt to Varnhagen,	323
176.	Humboldt to Varnhagen,	324
177.	The Prussian Minister Resident, von Gerolt, to Humboldt,	325
178.	Varnhagen to Humboldt,	327
179.	Humboldt to Varnhagen,	329
180.	Humboldt to Varnhagen,	330
181.	Grand Duke Charles Alexander of Saxe-Weimar to Humboldt,	330
182.	Varnhagen to Humboldt,	331
183.	Humboldt to Varnhagen,	333
184.	Humboldt to Varnhagen,	334
185.	Metternich to Humboldt,	336
186.	Humboldt to Varnhagen,	338
187.	Humboldt to Varnhagen,	338
188.	Humboldt to Varnhagen,	341
189.	Charles Alexander, Grand Duke of Saxe-Weimar, to Humboldt,	343
190.	Jobard to Humboldt,	344
191.	Lines by Varnhagen on Hildebrandt's Painting of Humboldt's Apartments, and the Motto Attached.	346
192.	Humboldt to Varnhagen,	347
193.	Humboldt to Varnhagen,	360
194.	Charles Alexander, Grand Duke of Saxe-Weimar, to Humboldt,	351
195.	Humboldt to Varnhagen,	352
196.	Varnhagen to Humboldt,	354
197.	Varnhagen to Humboldt,	356
198.	Varnhagen to Humboldt,	359
199.	Humboldt to Varnhagen,	360
200.	Humboldt to Varnhagen,	362
201	Karl Alexander, Grand Duke of Saxe-Weimar, to Humboldt,	363
202.	Varnhagen to Humboldt,	364
203.	Varnhagen to Humboldt,	366
204.	Humboldt to Varnhagen,	368
205.	Humboldt to Varnhagen,	368
206.	Humboldt to Varnhagen,	370
207.	Charles Alexander, Grand Duke of Saxe-Weimar, to Humboldt,	371

		PAGE
208.	Humboldt to Varnhagen,	372
209.	Humboldt to Varnhagen,	374
210.	Charles Alexander, Grand Duke of Saxe-Weimar, to Humboldt,	375
211.	Thiers to Humboldt,	376
212.	Humboldt to Varnhagen,	377
213.	Humboldt to Varnhagen,	379
214.	Humboldt to Varnhagen,	382
215.	Varnhagen to Humboldt,	383
216.	Humboldt to Varnhagen,	385
217.	Humboldt to Varnhagen,	387
218.	Humboldt to Varnhagen,	389
219.	Prince Napoleon, Son of Jerome, to Humboldt,	390
220.	Varnhagen to Humboldt,	393
221.	Humboldt to Varnhagen,	394
222.	Humboldt to Varnhagen,	395
223.	Humboldt to Varnhagen,	397
224.	Humboldt to Varnhagen,	399
225.	Humboldt to Ludmilla Assing,	402

Preface.

———o———

THE following letters of Humboldt furnish a contribution of the highest importance to the true, correct, and unveiled representation of his genius and character. That they should be delivered to publicity after his death was his desire and intent, which have found their positive impression in the words preceding this book as its motto. Never has he spoken out his mind more freely and sincerely, than in his communications with Varnhagen, his old and faithful friend, whom he esteemed and loved before all others. In him he placed an unlimited confidence; with him he deposited those letters received by him, which he desired to be saved for their importance, while he used to destroy nearly all others. He presumed that Varnhagen, the junior of the two, would survive him.

Varnhagen, however, died first and transmitted the duty—a doubly sacred one—to me, of publishing this memorable evidence of the life, the activity, and the genius of this great man. In the accomplishment of this charge it was a religious duty to leave every word unchanged as written down. I would have thought it an offence to Humboldt's memory had I had the arrogance to make the slightest alterations of his words. For the same reason I did not think myself authorized to grant the request—however well-meaning it may have been—of the publisher, that I should make such alterations, nor could I accord the least influence to my own feelings or to personal regards. There was but one consideration to be obeyed—the *eternal truth*, for an adherence to which I am responsible to Humboldt's memory, to History and Literature, and to the will of him who enjoined this duty upon me.

And therefore the legacy, intrusted to my hands, will appear full and complete, as it was received. The interest of Humboldt's letters is sometimes pleasantly heightened by entries in Varnhagen's diary—they will indicate the verbal sentiments of Humboldt in addition to those written by him. Of Varnhagen's letters few only were preserved or could be found. In the little, however, which is known, the noble friendship, the constant, never-ceasing mental activity, the faithful fellowship in their mutual efforts in behalf of science and liberty, in all of which Humboldt and Varnhagen were so many years united, find a sufficient expression.

The letters of many other distinguished and celebrated persons, which are also added, will show Humboldt in his world-wide connexions, in his manifold relations to savans and authors, to statesmen and princes, all of whom approached him with reverence.

LUDMILLA ASSING.

BERLIN, February, 1860.

Humboldt's Letters.

1.

HUMBOLDT TO VARNHAGEN.

BERLIN, *September 25th*, 1827.

MY HONORED FRIEND:

Allow me to present you with the best copy of my essay* left me.

The end of it will, I hope, secure me your indulgence for the whole.

Tuesday.   A. v. HUMBOLDT.

* On the Principal Causes of the Variation of Temperature upon the Earth.

2.

HUMBOLDT TO VARNHAGEN.

BERLIN, *November* 1*st*, 1827.

You recollect having once uttered some affectionate words in acknowledgment of my endeavors to describe Nature vividly and truly (that is, with strict correctness as to what we do observe).

That your words have left agreeable impressions, you will perceive from this insignificant token of my gratitude.*

I have altered nearly all "the Explanations," and added "The Genius of Rhodes," for which Schiller has shown some predilection.

With friendship and the highest consideration,
Yours,
A. HUMBOLDT.

Is it not strange, that Koreff has never acknowledged what we did for him here?

---

* With a copy of "Views of Nature," new edition.

3.

HUMBOLDT TO VARNHAGEN.

BERLIN, *November* 21, 1827.
WEDNESDAY, AT NIGHT.

TRUSTING more to your friendship for me and to my memoranda, which always guide me in my lectures, than to the notes taken by the students, I send you herewith the entire fifth lecture, together with to-day's recapitulation. I am sure, you will not find anything anti-philosophical therein. You may make whatever use you like of them—except a copy for publication—please send them back before Saturday. That the memoranda were made for my own use only, you will observe by the confusion in their composition—the desire, however, to be always frank, makes me forget any consideration which vanity could suggest.*

A. HUMBOLDT.

---

* The memoranda were intended to be communicated to Professor Hegel, who was told that Humboldt had indulged in attacks on Philosophy in his lectures.

4.

HUMBOLDT TO VARNHAGEN.

BERLIN, *April* 15*th*, 1828.

WILL you allow me to disturb you for some moments between 2 and 3 o'clock this afternoon, that I may ask your literary opinion? My book shall bear the title: "Sketch of a Physical Description of the World."

I should like to embody in the title itself the occasion of these lectures, so as to make it understood at once that the book contains more and something else than the lectures. "From reminiscences of lectures in the years 1827 and 1828, by A. v. Humboldt," is considered, I am told, ridiculous and pretending. I do not insist on it; but "Souvenirs d'un cours de Physique du monde," or, "Souvenirs d'un voyage en Perse," seemed simple enough. How shall I arrange the title of the book? "Sketch of the Physical World, elaborated from lectures by A. v. H.;" or, "Partly treated from Lectures?" All that seems rather awkward. Adverbs will not do for titles. What if I add in small type: "A part of this work has *been* the subject of lectures in the years 1827 and 1828?" This is, however, rather long and then *the verb!* " *Occasioned by,*" &c., would perhaps be better. I trust to *your* genius! *You* will help me out of this labyrinth, I am sure! With the sincerest attachment,

Your obedient,
A. HUMBOLDT.

NOTE BY VARNHAGEN.—I had objected to the first herein mentioned title myself when I once dined at Prince August's, and Humboldt had heard it from Beuth.

5.

HUMBOLDT TO VARNHAGEN.

BERLIN, 3*d of April*, 1829.

I SHALL call and thank you and enjoy your being home again, and the good effects which the exercise of your new duties have everywhere had. And I will implore *pardon* of your gifted lady, so dear to me through the misfortunes that happened in my own family. It is never allowed to present a book to the King, not even by Prince Wittgenstein. It must go the usual way. But I will entreat Albrecht very, very fervently.* I am quite exhausted and will be off in a week.

Friday. A. HT.

* It was a book of Ranke (the Historian).

6.

HUMBOLDT TO VARNHAGEN.

Berlin, 26th of April, 1830.

I have just come home from Potsdam, and find your dear letter and your present, so very agreeable to me. The "*Zinzendorf*"* will delight me very, very much. He is an individual physiognomy like *Lavater* and *Cardanus*. The recent pietism, which *began* to break out at Halle, made me smile. I rejoice that you will kindly accept my "Cri de Pétersbourg"—it is a parody recited at Court—the forced work of two nights; an essay to flatter without self-degradation, to say how things *should* be. As you and your high-gifted wife, my ancient and kind friend, rejoice in anything agreeable that happens to me, I wish to say that the King sends me to the Emperor to attend the meeting of the Potentates. I shall probably go with the Crown-Prince, who will meet the Empress at Fischbach.

Yours,

A. Ht.

Zinzendorf's *letters* to the Saviour were rather more legible. †

---

* Biography of Count Zinzendorf by Varnhagen.—*Translator*.

† Humboldt wrote a very illegible hand, hence this allusion.—*Translator*.

7.

HUMBOLDT TO VARNHAGEN.

BERLIN, *July* 9*th*, 1830.

PLEASE accept for yourself and your highminded and excellent lady my sincerest thanks for your new present, so agreeable to me.* I was not personally acquainted with the man whose eccentricities you have so æsthetically described. He was one of those who shine by their personal appearance; their lives are of greater effect than their writings. A man who boasts that his recollections go back to the *first year* of his life (how differently the Margravine judged things, when she says: " J'étais un enfant très précoce—à deux ans je savais parler, à trois ans je marchais!"); a man who owns a guardian angel in a black cloak, like Cardanus—who makes love to old maids, without being drunk, only in order to convert the same to virtue and reading; a man, to whom the *fate* of German profes-

---

* Memoirs of John Benjamin Ehrhard, Philosopher and Physician. Edited by Varnhagen von Ense. Stuttgart and Tubingen. Cotta. 1830.

sors under German princes appears more tragical than that of the Greeks—such a man cannot but be admired —as a curiosity! The "Kirchen-Zeitung" will never inscribe his name in the list of "the faithful," and the Schimmelmanns will hardly thank you, my most honored friend, that the work recalls the Danish-Holstein saturnalia of sentimental demagogism.

I am very much gratified that you will take "Hardenberg" in hand. It is a difficult but satisfactory task, if you be careful to separate the *epochs*, and provided his life be judged without party hatred, which seems to have subsided at last, with regard to Hegel in the Academy.

Thankfully yours,   A. HUMBOLDT.

We find in Varnhagen's diary the following entry referring to the above: "Alexander von Humboldt said to Gans, after the July revolution, when he heard him express very exalted hopes of the new government, 'Believe me, dear friend, my wishes go as far as yours, but my hopes are very feeble. I have seen changes of government in France for forty years. They always fall by their own incapacity; the new ones give always the same promises, but they never keep them, and the march to ruin is renewed. I was personally acquainted with most of the men in power, some of them intimately; there were distinguished, well-meaning men among them; but they did not persevere; after a short time they were not better than their predecessors—nay, they became even greater rascals. Not one of all the governments there has kept the promises made to the people—not one of them has subordinated its own interest to the welfare of the country. And until this be done, no power can possibly take a lasting root in France. The nation has always been deceived, and will again be deceived; when it will punish the treason and the perjury of its rulers; for it is strong and mature enough to do this at the proper time.'"

8.

VARNHAGEN TO HUMBOLDT.

BERLIN, *January* 23*d*, 1833.

CERTAINLY it was I who met your Excellency some time ago at the sunny hour of noon and who recognised you too late, as I was recognised too late by you. How I should have liked to run after you, but it would not do, the distance was already too great. I would have liked to have told you something concerning Mr. von Bulow at London, which I had just got from the best authority, and which I thought would be new to you, as it was to me. It was about the danger in which that bold ambassador was for some time, and which, according to a declaration of the King, had passed over. Since then your Excellency has heard it from other sources, and my information will be but stale.

Now we Prussians are also gratified at last by a general representation of the people, or, to speak more correctly, we had it a long time ago, only we did not know it! Bishop Eylert has lifted the veil from our eyes. He is the first to speak out the great truth, like a second Mirabeau, in clearness of thought and boldness of words. I can vividly imagine how the "Rittersaal," nay, the whole palace, was shaken to its foundation, when he thundered that powerful truth to the assembly, that the representation of the whole people, of all the classes and interests, ought to be found in that solemn lodge of the Order of Knights! I bend my head in deep reverence to such a colossal boldness, to such a new unheard-of combination, by which *other miserable institutions, until now regarded as national representations, as for instance Parliaments, Assemblies, Cortes, and the like, were annihilated and blown into nothingness! I have listened to the orator from the silent mouth of the official gazette only; but your Excellency was present without doubt at the solemnity and pitied me, to be sure, and will say, what in ancient times was said when a speech of Demosthenes was read: "Oh! had you heard it delivered by him!" And the smiling approval, the gracious satisfaction of the high audience, the amazement of all present at the wonderful discovery, how much the impression must have been heightened by all that!

Oh, our Protestant parsons are on the best road, they promise to leave behind their Catholic brethren as they were when in the most flourishing condition of their priesthood. Such hypocritical black coats make us the laughing-stock of the world. Representation of the people or no representation, may we have it, or may it be denied, I care little about it just now, but that such a scoundrel should assume to call the meeting of the Knights of an Order a national representation, is an attempt which should be rewarded by the lunatic asylum or the State prison. And there is not even a song, a street ballad, a caricature, to make merry of such a monstrosity—all is silent!

But as this is the time of sleep, I will go to bed and wish you and myself good night and sweet dreams.

With the highest respect, &c.,

V.

See A. v. Humboldt's note to Rahel, Varnhagen's wife, of the 1st of February, 1833.

9.

HUMBOLDT TO RAHEL.

BERLIN, *February* 1, 1833.

My speedy reply has no good foreboding, my dear friend. When anything is to be done in this country, it wants fourteen months' maturing—after that there is hope. The inclosed letter, which, however, you are entreated not to leave in the hand of your lady friend, explains all. I was listened to in my words and letters kindly and promisingly. This morning, however, the drawings—those beautiful drawings—were sent back. The underlined word in the accompanying note might give some hope; but I like better to give myself up to illusions than to nourish them in others, and the firmness with which Beuth, who alone has to decide in the matter, sticks to his will, bars all prospects. That I have done my best in the matter, as you yourself have desired it, does not require further words—this should be a sort of *historical faith* with you. Please send me a word of comfort about my dear Varnhagen—the only brilliant star in the literary world of our country—*that* country in which, as the bishop *with the drawn sword* says, even the *most eminent talents*, as such, ought to have no distinction whatever! I do not wonder that such things are spoken out, but what depresses me is the vileness of the society in which we are here living, and which is not even aroused by such contemptible assertions. May both of you preserve your nobler selves.

A. Ht.

10.

HUMBOLDT TO VARNHAGEN.

Berlin, 3*d of Feby.*, 1833.

I am eternally grateful and affected by your noble letter. Grace and euphony of language should always be joined to purity of character and gracefulness of manners.

My brother was here for two days, but almost always under the shock of the waves, dashing from the Court. Princes have the right to pray without ever being deprecated. He ordered me to tell you, dear friend, how very sensible he is to the flattering nature of your offer; but he is just now so much occupied with the publication of the quarto edition on the affinity of Asiatic languages with the Sanscrit, that he cannot accept

what he considers, nevertheless, as highly important.
He desires, in honor of the celebrity of the great
departed one,* that *you* should undertake the task. I
am painfully concerned to hear that you enjoy, together
with your ingenious friend, but a small bit of health,
which you kindly lend each other—something of a
mutual self-instruction, or Azais-compensation, which
afflicts me very much. I have received a long letter of
Mrs. Cotta. It seems she will assume the editorship of
the *Allgemeine Zeitung*, an anti-salique enterprise alto-
gether. Is it not strange, how, at certain epochs, a
certain principle seems to penetrate all mankind? Resuscitation of reverence for the past, not-to-be-disturbed
love of peace, distrust in the possibility of amelioration,
hydrophobia against genius, religious compulsion for
unity, mania-diplomatica for protocols. . . . . Cardi-
nes rerum.

NOTE BY VARNHAGEN.—I had replied in Rahel's name, who was
prevented by sickness, to the note of the 1st inst., directed to her, and
in a postscript had expressed the desire Minister de Humboldt
should write the critique of *Faust*, just then to be published for the
Jahrbücher der Kritik.

* Goethe.—*Translator.*

11.

HUMBOLDT TO RAHEL.

BERLIN, *February* 9*th*, 1853.

I have seen Beuth once more, to remind him of his ancient friendship with L. His opinion is, that it would be advantageous for the family to separate the architectural subjects from what belongs to landscape merely, and also to leave out the engravings. Only the architectural drawings were of any use to his institute, and if the family wanted the money, he would be enabled to purchase to the amount of some hundred Thalers (perhaps four to five hundred?). However uninviting such an offer may be, I thought it my duty, dear friend, to impart it to you. In case of acceptance, Beuth wishes to deal forthwith with some agent, who should come and see him in his house.

May the sun of gentle spring give you both warmth, cheerfulness, and vigor! The "Byzantine empire" (ours I mean) is seriously divided into two parties about "Bunsen's Psalm Book," and "Elsner's Collection of Hymns!" The military power and the adjutants are in favor of the "Collection of Hymns." As for myself, I have not yet made up my mind.

Saturday. A. HT.

12.

HUMBOLDT TO VARNHAGEN.

SATURDAY, *March 9th*, 1833.

To a mind like yours, noble friend, solitude and calm are necessary. You draw only upon yourself. Think, that I received the painful news* only last night by Prince Carolath. You know what a warm-hearted, long-proved, and kind friend I lost in her, the honor of her sex! how amiable she was, when lately she instructed me to transact the little business with Beuth. So experienced in all the vicissitudes and illusions of life, and yet so cheerful, and so gentle! With such an intellect, so full of soul, and so true of heart! The world will appear to you a solitude for a long time, but the consciousness of having imparted to such a lovely woman, until her very last breath, all that genius, and heart, and gracefulness of intercourse like yours can afford, will be a balm to your wound, dear Varnhagen. I conjure you, take care of your health!

A. HUMBOLDT.

* Of Rahel's death.

13.

HUMBOLDT TO VARNHAGEN.

BERLIN, *December* 3, 1833.

PARDON, a thousand pardons, for not sooner returning the classical studies of Friedrich Schlegel. I studied them diligently and I am convinced that many views of Grecian antiquity, which modern authors ascribe to themselves, are buried in writings dated from 1795 (a deucalionic time of yore!). Angelus Silesius, whom I have but now learned to appreciate, has also gratified me and my brother very much. There is a piety in the book, which breathes on the mind like the balmy air of spring, and the mysterious and hieroglyphical marks of your departed wife, render your gift doubly dear to me.

Spiker,* very curiously mistook the genitive in the " astronomical observations *of* Alexander von Humboldt," for my signature, when he informed the public of Oltmann's death. I will pass it over, however, without correction.

With everlasting affection, yours,

A. HUMBOLDT.

---

* At that time editor of the Haude and Spenersche Zeitung in Berlin.—*Tr.*

14.

HUMBOLDT TO VARNHAGEN.

BERLIN, *December* 9, 1833.

I ENCLOSE you, most honored friend, some words of the lovely Duchess of Dessau. Anything honoring the memory of our departed lady friend must be dear to your heart.

Sunday.   A. v. HUMBOLDT.

DESSAU, *December* 1, 1833.

ACCEPT my best thanks for the books you sent me. Each in its way interested me very much. I am sorry not to have been personally acquainted with Rahel. Her mind now lies so clearly before me, that I should have been happy to have been acquainted with her exterior appearance, that it might suggest to me the intellect within.

FRIEDERIKE, Duchess at Anhalt.

Yet full of admiration for R. the book of all books. May I ask you, my honored friend, for Friedrich Schlegel's works, third volume?

15.

HUMBOLDT TO VARNHAGEN.

BERLIN, *December* 19, 1833.

I HAVE been prevented by the irksome and noisy Court-life from inquiring personally after the dear health of my friend. I am sorry that I must request you, by the present note, to return me the letter of the Duchess of Dessau, containing the amiable words concerning our sainted friend.

Tuesday.   A. V. HUMBOLDT.

16.

BERLIN, *Oct.* 24, 1834.

I BEGIN the printing of my work (the work of my life). I have the extravagant idea of describing in one and the same work the whole material world—all that we know to-day of celestial bodies and of life upon the earth—from the nebular stars to the mosses on the granite rocks—and to make this work instructive to the mind, and at the same time attractive, by its vivid language. Every great and sparkling idea must be nóticed, side by side with its attendant facts. The work shall represent an epoch of the intellectual development of mankind in their knowledge of nature. The prolegomena are, for the most part, ready. They are my amended "discours d'ouverture" as they were delivered from memory, although immediately afterwards carefully written down; the picture of physical nature—incentives to the study of nature in the spirit of our age—these latter are threefold: 1. "Poesie descriptive" and vivid description of natural scenery in modern works of travels. 2. Landscape pictures, sensitive description of an exotic nature—when it originated, when it became a necessity and a pleasure to the mind; the reason why antiquity (too passionate) could not feel it. 3. Plants—grouping of them, according to the physiognomy of plants (no botanic gardens).—History of the physical description of the world. How the idea of the world—of the connexion of all the phenomena, became clear to the nations of the world in the course of centuries. These prolegomena are the most essential. They contain the general part of the work, which is followed by the special part, the particulars of which are arranged in systematic order. I send also a part of the tabular register; space of the universe; the whole physical astronomy; our globe, its interior, exterior; electro-magnetism of its interior; vulcanism, that is, the reaction of the interior of a planet upon its surface; organization of the masses; a concise geognosy; ocean; atmosphere; climate; organic matter; vegetable geography; animal geography; human races and languages; the physical organization of which (articulation of sounds) is controlled by the intellect, the product and manifestation of which is language. In the special part all numerical results, the most minute, as in "*Laplace's* Exposition du Systéme du Monde." As these particulars do not admit the same literary perfection of style as the general combinations of natural science, the simple facts are stated in short sentences, arranged in tabular order. The attentive reader will find condensed in a few pages all results on climate, magnetism of the earth, etc., which it would take years of application to learn by study. The intimate relations of the fundamental details, for the sake of literary harmony with the general plan, are effected by brief introductory remarks to each chapter. Otfried Mueller, in his ably written "Archæology," has very successfully pursued the same method.

It was my wish that you, my dear friend, should get a clear perception of my undertaking from myself. I have not succeeded in concentrating the whole in one single volume, however magnificent the effect of such conciseness would have been. I hope, however, that two volumes will contain the whole. There will be no notes under the text, but at the end there will be notes appended, containing solid erudition, and minuteness of detail; these, however, may be left unread.

The work is not what is commonly called "*Physical Description of the Earth.*" It comprises heaven and earth—everything existing. I began to write it fifteen years ago in French, and called it "*Essai sur la Physique du Monde.*" In Germany I thought first of calling it "*The Book of Nature;*" a title already adopted in the middle age by Albertus Magnus. But all this is too vague. The title shall be "*Kosmos,*" *Sketch of a Physical Description of the World, by A. v. H., enlarged outlines of his Lectures in* 1827 *and* 1828. Cotta, Publisher.

I wanted to add the word *Kosmos*, and to force people to call the book by this name in order to avoid their calling it "Humboldt's Physical Geography," which would throw the thing in the class of Mittersacher's writings. "Description of the World" (formed after History of the World) would, as a designation seldom used, always be confounded with "Description of the Earth." I know that "Kosmos" sounds rather pretending, and the word is indeed not without a certain "Affetérie;" but this title says in one and the same striking word, "*Heaven and Earth,*" and is quite opposed to "*Gaea,*" the title of that rather imperfect description of the earth by Professor Zeune. My brother is also for the title "Kosmos." I myself hesitated for a long time. Now, grant me a favor, my dear friend. I cannot prevail upon myself to send away the commencement of my manuscript without entreating you to cast a critical eye over it. You possess such an eminent talent for style, and you have at the same time so much genius and independence of judgment, that you do not quite discard the style of others because it differs from your own. Please read the "Discours," and put in a little sheet on which you write—without giving any reasons.—"So .... I would better like, so .... instead of ...." Do, however, not condemn without *assisting* me! and do also ease my mind as to the title.

With the utmost confidence, yours,
Monday.   A. v. HUMBOLDT.

The principal faults of my style are an unhappy inclination to hyper-poetical forms, long constructions upon participles, and too much concentrating of manifold views and sentiments in one and the same period. I think, however, that these radical evils, founded in my individuality, are somewhat lessened by a grave simplicity and generalization, enabling me to contemplate my subject with a complete mastery of its details, if I may be permitted so much vanity. A book on nature should produce an impression like nature itself. I have been always careful, as in my "*Views of Nature,*" and in that work my manner is quite different from that of Forster and Chateaubriand. I have always endeavored to describe faithfully, to design correctly, and to be even scientifically true, without losing myself in the dry regions of knowledge.

17.

HUMBOLDT TO VARNHAGEN.

BERLIN, *October* 28*th,* 1834.

You have encouraged and cheered me by your amiable letter, and your still more amiable solicitude. You have quite entered into the spirit of my efforts. But the expression of my affectionate confidence in you [a manifestation of the acknowledgment of your talent in the Humboldt family] has rendered you too considerate and inclined to praise. Your remarks have a degree of refinement, of taste, and acuteness, which makes emendation a highly pleasant task. I have adopted all, or nearly all—more than nineteen-twentieths. Some obstinacy, however, must always be allowed an author. I beg a thousand pardons for sending you some sheets, in which (towards the end of the Discourse) I had not corrected the newly-annexed parts. Some sentences were really confused. You will permit me to call one of these days, and thank you personally. I will then show you the emendations at the end of the discourse. How happy I would have been to have laid some of these travels before her, the dear departed one!

Yours gratefully,
A. v. HUMBOLDT.

I would there were in Germany as excellent a book of synonyms as the inclosed one, which, I am sure, you did not see before now. Abbé Delisle has advised me to use it, and indeed it spares much time; if a similar word is wanted, one finds it at once. I shall come and take the book back.

18.

HUMBOLDT TO VARNHAGEN.

BERLIN, Sunday, 6 o'clock A.M.,
April 5th, 1855.

You, my dearest Varnhagen, who are not afraid of grief, but who trace its phases through the depths of sentiment, you should receive at this sorrowful time a few words expressing the love which both brothers feel for you. The release has not yet come. I left him last night at 11 o'clock, and I hasten to him again. The day, yesterday, was less distressing. A half lethargic condition, frequent, though not restless, slumber, and after each waking, words of love, of comfort; but always the clearness of the great intellect, which penetrates and distinguishes everything and examines its own condition. The voice was very feeble, hoarse, and thin, like a child's—leeches were therefore applied to the throat. Full consciousness! "Think often of me," he said the day before yesterday, "but always with cheerfulness! I was very happy; and this day also was a beautiful one for me; for 'Love is above all.' I will soon be with mother, and will have an insight into a higher order of things." I have no shadow of hope. I never thought my old eyes had so many tears! It has lasted near eight days.*

* Wilhelm von Humboldt died on the 8th of April, 1835, at Tegel, at 6 o'clock in the evening.

19.

HUMBOLDT TO VARNHAGEN.

Berlin, May 15th, 1835, Tuesday.

My time is, unfortunately, so much occupied by the many princely strangers, and I am so affected by the cold, though not at all bracing weather, that I can scarcely find leisure to thank you, dear friend, for the "Bollmann"* and the biographical sketch of him, in which I recognised at once *your* pen, and also the "retouchings," when the "Staats Zeitung" fell into my hands. One should not undertake to speak of distinguished men in such papers; it is a difficult task, even for a man of your genius, to keep the proper course between the family, the censor, and the cold, indifferent public.

The name of "Mundt" has recalled to me some remarkable pages of his "Madonna," on the tendency of the Germans to sentimental lucubrations. There is

---

* Bollmann, a German who resided a long time in the United States, and who is known by his bold attempts to liberate Lafayette from the prison of Olmutz.—*Translator.*

much truth in these observations, and I thought to read my own sentence in them. So much, dear friend, on this world, to us, now unhappily deserted.

Always gratefully,   A. HUMBOLDT.

I feel some sorrow, nevertheless, that you refuse to see the Grand-Duchess.

20.

HUMBOLDT TO VARNHAGEN.

BERLIN, *May 6th*, 1835.

I SEND back the communicated sheets, as they might interrupt the series. I was personally acquainted with almost all those whom Bollmann describes so vividly and faithfully. One perceives how he rises as he enters into more important situations. What a strange course of life, "Médecin de Sauvetage!" I have now a better impression of him, thanks to you; for, without being capable of divining the true cause, I noticed some coolness towards Bollmann in Lafayette's family, for some years past.   A. HT.

21.

HUMBOLDT TO VARNHAGEN.

BERLIN, *Saturday, 23d of May,* 1835.

If the " Morgenblatt" of the 18th of May should fall into your hands, dear friend, please glance at a rather offensive article therein, entitled " Wilhelm von Humboldt's Funeral." My brother is said to have died abandoned by his family. I take but little notice of such misrepresentations. I should wish to know, however, is " that other thing" which my brother was " ignorant of, besides music, and which one dare not name"—is it God, or some lewdness ? I do not know what it possibly can be ! Please, dearest one, to find out how this assertion is explained by the public. The cause of my brother's retiring from public life is also so world-known, that it is singular to intimate that one did not know whether it was by his own fault. I call with pleasure on your acuteness and affection. Supply my deficiency in the first.

Most thankfully yours,   A. HUMBOLDT.

22.

HUMBOLDT TO VARNHAGEN.

BERLIN, *March* 28*th*, 1836.

A MIND like yours, my generous friend, understands, in its mildness and fortitude, how to discover some justification for everything. I do not fear, therefore, to appear this morning again before you as a petitioner, after a winter distracted by the dashing court-waves and festivities. You are the only one in this harmony-barren, genius-deserted city who possesses a harmony of style and a sense of moderation in the utterance of painful sentiments. May I beg you to cast a critical glance over the inclosed sheets?* The variations played on the praise-chanting lyre for forty individuals were a tedious, style-spoiling necessity. It was arranged who should be invited to the great table. As for me, I think I came out not quite awkwardly, by some individual characteristics, and by a sort of graduation in my praise. Allow me to call to-day, about eleven

---

* Preface to Wilhelm von Humboldt's work about the Kawi language.

o'clock, to receive the sheets, which are much wanted by the printer, together with your verbal remarks at the same time. I can alter, if necessary, *sous votre dictée*, at your home. It would be humane in you to receive me in bed.

Respectfully yours,

Monday.   A. HUMBOLDT.

At eleven o'clock I shall be with you.

Varnhagen made, on the 11th of May, 1836, the following entry in his diary:

"Very early this morning, Alexander von Humboldt came to see me, and remained an hour and a half. The principal subject of our conversation was the French princes, who arrived here to-day. The embarrassment of the King is very great; he would like to show the greatest attention to the strangers, while at the same time he desires his attentions should have the appearance of insults at St. Petersburg. State Secretary Ancillon had not courage enough to advise the Crown-Prince for their coming here as a certainty. He trusted to chance to acquaint him with it. Our princes got into a violent passion, and complained bitterly of the unwelcome visit. The Princesses Augusta and Maria, who showed themselves pleased with it, had hard words to hear. It was said that there would be a demonstration in the theatre: some would applaud, and a greater number would hiss, it was hoped. At Treves, something of that sort had already happened, on their way through that city. No doubt, however, that our Princes, notwithstanding their ill-feelings, will behave very civilly, as the King has expressed his wishes in this respect too positively. The Queen of the Netherlands, who is just now here, and who was believed to be the most violently opposed to them, leads the way with a good example, and declares that she will receive the strangers. The Ambassador, Mr. Bresson, and Mr. von Humboldt, at first disapproved of this excursion. That it is carried out notwithstanding is owing to Prince von Metternich, who desiring to secure the influence of France in the Oriental affairs, and at the same time to preserve the friendship of Russia, puts Prussia in the foreground, whose conduct in receiving the French Princes will form a precedent which must necessarily be followed at Vienna. The thing is, indeed, an event of great importance, and must tell effectively on public opinion. It is a fact, and, as such, speaks to every one. Every one will say that our Court has not the principles it pretended to have, or that it is too weak to avow them openly, and is driven, therefore, to try hypocrisy. A bad thing either way!

23.

HUMBOLDT TO VARNHAGEN.

BERLIN, *May* 31*st*, 1836.

[Concerning the article in the Allgemeine Zeitung, against Raumer,* written, it was said, by Major von Radowitz.]

THE correspondent had, it seems, little to fear from the mendacious declaration of this "defloured." In the general view on the shallowness and dough-facedness, of the *great* historian, I am of his opinion. Moreover reading Herr von Raumer's books is like being "whipped," and that I neither suffer nor pardon.

24.

HUMBOLDT TO VARNHAGEN.

Monday, April 24*th*, 1837.

IT is very consoling, that both brothers in this intellectually desolated city (how brilliant it was when Rahel was in her zenith) live in the memory of the only one, to whom have remained good taste, refined manners, and gracefulness of style.

* Professor of History at Berlin.

All my researches concerning the separate print of the essay were in vain to-day. I have not even the single volume of the Academical Proceedings of 1822, because at that time I lived in Paris. Yet, in a few days, I will bring you this one. I will then also show you a list of all the remaining works of my brother, which I have made with great care, and which you may perhaps increase. Cotta will print all of them; also, the eight hundred sonnets, and likewise the hitherto unprinted ecclesiastical poems from Spain. I make the preparations for this edition in a spirit of sincere piety that I may not die regretting its non-completion.

How could I ever suspect, dear friend, that you would let me become a Madame Sontag, at the house of the excellent Princess (as in the saloon of the Princess Belgiojoso), and make an exhibition of myself! I will read with pleasure in a small circle of twelve or fifteen persons, certainly not otherwise, because Berlin is a small illiterate town and more than malicious, in which people would find it ludicrous, if I, in addition to two alas! already so *public* theatres were to offer a third entertainment. But happily, I certainly am no Madame Sontag in Berlin, and the lecture can therefore well remain a secret de comédie. You are certainly sufficiently humane to understand all this, and not to blame me.

With all reverence, yours,   A. v. H.

25.

HUMBOLDT TO THE PRINCESS VON PUECKLER.

I ARRIVED this very night from Potsdam, and I accept with pleasure the amiable offer of Madame la Princesse for to-morrow, Wednesday night, at eight o'clock precisely, for the spectacle lasts one hour. I feel some fear in fixing it for Thursday, considering the planetarian perturbations. Any persons selected by you will be agreeable to me. I would only beg Madame la Princesse not to invite Rauch, Gans, and Mr. and Mrs. Ruhle, because they have already been bored by this affair. Mr. de Varnhagen may add whomever he pleases. This tact in selecting only those who will have some indulgence in listening to me is unsurpassed.

Thousand respectful and affectionate devotions.

A. HUMBOLDT.

THURSDAY, 2d *May*, 1837.

26.

HUMBOLDT TO VARNHAGEN.

I CAME, dear friend, for two purposes: 1, to bring you the opinions of Minister Kamptz (*casus in terminis*, only twenty-five copies printed), which you, perhaps, had not seen before, and which has elicited a vehement reply from Herr von Oertzen, the Minister of Mecklenburg-Strelitz, burned in the Lord. Read (p. 30 and 32), how one can whitewash a person. I would beg of you not to laugh at me, when you are invited to-morrow to a lecture at the Princess's. I can assure you there is less vanity, from which, by the bye, I am not at all free, than weakness of character and good nature in it. Thus, I believed that I owed this satisfaction to the Princess; the daughter also pressed me, and she showed me a harmless list of ten persons. If you will propose or bring with you one or more persons, it will be agreeable to me; only bring no one who has heard me already. Your friends are mine; from yours I may expect indulgence. I insist upon it, that a man is not without merit, who after spending his life with cyphers and stones, has put himself to the trouble of learning to write German.

Yours,

A. Ht.

I hope also to procure for you the vehement "opus" of the Strelitz Minister, which is by far more spirited than might be expected.

Varnhagen remarks in his Diary, under May 3d: In the evening, at the Princess of Pueckler's, the long-promised lecture by Herr von Humboldt. The lecture was very fine, and made an excellent impression. I had a conversation with General von Ruhle on Humboldt's genius. He totally agreed with me, saying, "When he shall have died, then only shall we understand well what we have possessed in him."

Herr von Humboldt was with me yesterday, and brought me the little note of Minister Kamptz, of which twenty-five copies only were printed, "Casus in terminus," in which he puts the best face on the French change of rulers, and in which he justifies the Mecklenburg marriage. So much in contrast with his old principles, that I could exclaim: "If he could only cut himself in two, he certainly would put one half in prison." There is still no opposition wanting against the marriage. Duke Charles of Mecklenburg-Strelitz has formally intrigued against it, and tried to form in the Mecklenburg and Prussian dynasty an alliance, a covenant and obligation, against all marriages with the house of Orleans. There was even talk of a formal protest. All this is the most vehement opposition to the expressed views of the King. Duke Charles is now really sick from annoyance and trouble, not only in this but also in other things.

27.

HUMBOLDT TO VARNHAGEN.

BERLIN, *May* 10*th*, 1837.

AT last, my dear friend, I can send you the volume of the Academical Proceedings, which contains the important treatise on history. I shall soon exchange this borrowed volume for another, which you may keep. It seems that there never were separate copies made of this essay. You disappeared so quickly after the last performance, that I fear very much your appearance on that fated day was only a sacrifice to me. I move eternally like a pendulum between Potsdam and Berlin. To-morrow again to Potsdam, where we expect, on the

16th, the amiable Princess,* who has set at variance the whole hellenic camp, and whom they will now be happy to find "by far not beautiful enough."

Most gratefully yours,

WEDNESDAY. M. HUMBOLDT.

I knew long ago that General Bugeaud did not speak French. I now see that his real language is Mongol. What a Timurid proclamation of the "armée civilisatrice."

The essay of thy brother is one of his most perfect works as to style. "God governs the world (p. 317); the task of history is to trace these eternal mysterious destinies." This is the essence of his production. I have sometimes discussed with my brother, not to say quarrelled about that. This result certainly is analogous to the oldest ideas of mankind, expressed in every language. My brother's treatise is a commentary developing, explaining, praising, this dim perception. In the same manner the physiologist creates so-called vital powers, in order to explain organic phenomena, because his knowledge of physical powers, which act in what they call lifeless nature, does not suffice to explain the play of living organisms. Are vital powers demonstrated by this? I know that

* Helene, Princess of Mecklenburg-Strelitz, afterwards Duchess of Orleans.

you will be angry with me, because you divine that the fundamental idea of this wonderful treatise is not entirely satisfactory to me.

28.

HUMBOLDT TO VARNHAGEN.

WEDNESDAY, *May* 17*th*, 1837.

You have prepared for me, my highly esteemed friend, a delightful pleasure. I hope that these remarks upon the composition of history will hereafter form a part of your miscellaneous writings! The mind certainly becomes dizzy in contemplating the abundance of material which springs copiously from every fresh source. You point out how this material may be moulded by a man of genius. In the approaching millennium everything will be simplified—the individual life of nations is preserved, in spite of warlike expeditions over continents. Since the great epoch of Columbus and Gama, who made one part, one side of this planet known to the other, that fluctuating element, the ocean, has established the omnipresence of one kind of civilization (that of Western Europe). Its influence breaks through the rigid barriers of continents, and establishes new customs, new faith, new wants of life even in the most unorganised parts of the earth. The South Sea Islands are already Protestant parishes; —a floating battery, a single vessel of war, changes the fate of Chili. . . . .

Princess Helene, by her charming grace and intellectual superiority, also yesterday made many conquests over the raw and obstinate material which had opposed her. It was ludicrous to see how some persons tried to appear serious, dignified, and—silly. That she leaves in good spirits for her new country, I am much rejoiced. Would that she passed the Rhine with less retinue! Her mother is good and refined, but of retired habits; but some other members of her suite had better remain on this side of the river. Fortunately, people in the great French world are entirely free from the paltry gossip and fault-finding that rule in Berlin and Potsdam, where they subsist for months, in thoughtlessness, upon the self-created phantasy of a weak imagination.

I made Privy Councillor Mueller, who knows how to estimate you and your genius, participate in my joy. But he also, as a jurist, strayed away to the first sheet, No. 63 (Criticisms on the Provincial Law, by Goetze). Will you not, dear friend, send me, for Mueller, the commencement of that criticism?

Most gratefully yours,   A. v. Humboldt.

29.

HUMBOLDT TO VARNHAGEN.

MONDAY, *May* 30*th*, 1837.

You can, my revered friend, dispose entirely of the volume of the Academy until I shall procure you a copy for yourself. I am particularly pleased with the communication to the ingenious Gans. The historical studies of Hegel will interest me particularly, because, until now I nourished a wild prejudice against the idea that each nation individually is bound to represent an idea. In order that the prediction of the philosopher may be fulfilled I shall nevertheless read it attentively, and gladly abandon my prejudice.

Yours,

A. V. HUMBOLDT.

30.

HUMBOLDT TO VARNHAGEN.

Saturday, *July 1st,* 1837.

To-morrow to Tegel,* and on Monday I depart for the eternal spring,† at which the sight of the Prince of Warsaw will not lessen my sadness; I cannot, therefore, thank you personally. Sophie Charlotte‡ and Hegel's Philosophy of History will accompany me, and both will delight me greatly. My soul rather turns to you. I shall certainly find a torrent of ideas in that Hegel, whom his editor, Gans, in so masterly a manner has not deprived of his great individuality; but a man who is as I am, like an insect, inseparable from the earth and its natural variations, feels himself uneasy and constrained at an abstract assertion of totally unfounded facts and views on America and the Indian world. At the same time I appreciate what is grand in the conception of Hegel.

* Tegel, Humboldt's country-seat near Berlin.—*Tr.*
† Toeplitz, a Bohemian bathing-place.—*Tr.*
‡ Biography by Varnhagen.—*Tr.*

With you all is profound and subdued, and you possess what is wanting in the other, unceasing grace and freshness of language.

A. HUMBOLDT.

I have badly arranged my life; I do every thing for becoming prematurely stupid. I would gladly abandon "the European beef," which Hegel's phantasy presents as so much better than the American, and I could almost wish to live near the weak inanimate crocodiles (which, alas! measure 25 feet). Pp. 442-444, are certainly made more palatable to me by our noble friend.

31.

HUMBOLDT TO VARNHAGEN.

BERLIN, October 4th, 1837.

You delight sometimes in arresting fleeting events, and in preserving what the winds usually carry away. I therefore send you, dear friend, the little speech, which the papers have published in such a mutilated form. The sense of it will please you, although its neglected style might be better. *Political* Hanover I found, as you supposed; and private conversations with King Ernest, which at the same time express wrath and fear, confirm the view. Leist of Stade with his report, which lasted five hours, has lately done harm by his flattery.

Yours,

A. Ht.

Stieglitz, Wilhelm's oldest friend, and who once saved his life in the Leine river (my brother cried out to him, with unexampled stoicism; "I die, but it does not matter,") was to me a serious apparition of a ghost. The effect of his spirit upon me is uncomfortable.

32.

HUMBOLDT TO VARNHAGEN.

SUNDAY, October 22d, 1837.
Six o'clock, A. M.

I FIND after a week's residence in Potsdam, which has very much discouraged me, your amiable souvenir. Receive, revered friend, this very evening, my warmest thanks; you have praised me for my most cherished aim, which is, that I may not become a fossil, as long as I move, and cling to the belief, "that nature has put her curse upon stagnancy and inertia." Youth is the symbol of progress, and those, who rule now (the Berlin world's elephants) sont des momies en service extraordinaire.

> Good night,
>
> A. Humboldt.

33.

HUMBOLDT TO VARNHAGEN.

Berlin, Tuesday, *November 7th,* 1837.

The commencement of my letter is weak, the end of it more reasonable. But you should not lose the dramatic effect of the whole.

What you ask, my dear friend, is very perilous, for the question is not about my feelings, but about a family who anxiously *interpret*. The more striking and spirited your delineation is, particularly p. 10–15, ("He started from ideas." ... "That which many deny to him entirely.") ... it impresses me uncomfortably, the more because it is in so short an essay, and because it would appear less harsh in the description of a whole life which was, in a literary and political point of view, not unimportant. But this more complete description is impossible now; therefore, my wish is incessantly to secure his renown by the publication of his literary works. To leave out anything, or to alter anything in this fine essay of yours, would rob it both of its charm and vigor. You have written the whole in the noblest mood; but there are points (Reineke Fuchs, the relation to Frau von Humboldt), which it is not pleasant to allude to just now. Since you only demand of me to enumerate individual impressions, I will give you these. Often they are merely doubts. P. 5: "Foreign to abstract thinking." The term "Conservative philosophy" points, I believe, to Kant, to whom he adhered most. He just believed that metaphysics, ante-Hegelian, had been the chief study of his youth. I only wished a more decided expression. P. 6: "In the proper sense not productive." Philosophy of language according to entirely new views, genius of antiquity, treating of history, deep understanding of poetry—in all these branches he produced nothing that was not of importance. P. 8: "Style all ice;" make it somewhat milder. You do it yourself (p. 30), where the word "warms." P. 13: "Thus the call is soon decided, and the name is Mephistopheles or Reineke." One would wish the two significant names left out, since all is said before in the happiest, liveliest style. "Mephistopheles" reminds one of Duke Charles.

P. 14. The question about tender feeling, and the saying of Talleyrand, which I did not know before, and which can have a sense only by secondary relations of political irresolution, are not agreeable. "C'était un des hommes d'état dont l'Europe, de mon temps n'en a pas compté trois ou quatre," was an expression heard from Talleyrand.

P. 15. "What many denied to him entirely," very ingenious and fine. Old Princess Louise said of you: "You are most to fear when defending."

P. 18. My brother often narrated that Stieglitz saved him; but those words, which would have sounded vain-glorious coming from his lips, I only just now learned from Stieglitz. They are very characteristic and true. Therefore, I wished only an explaining word, to prevent misunderstanding.

P. 23. That he admired Rahel infinitely, is very, very true!

P. 28. "Constitutional principles." If you ever make use of these sheets, my dear, please add, at any rate: "Although he afterwards, in other essays, pressed in the most distinct manner the necessity of a general representative constitution." This limitation is necessary. I myself had in my hands his plan for a constitution, and for the mode of election, and he died with these ideas.

P. 31. In place of "avarice," say too great economy.

I read once more, with more peace of mind. I consider this your best effort.

Pp. 6, 7, 10-12! 13-20, 24-27, 30!! all—almost all; and you have treated with infinite consideration those things which you yourself, here and there, hardly approved of.

"Il n'y a rien de maudit," said the great painter, Gérard, "que de consulter la famille sur la ressemblance du défunt. Il y a de quoi se prendre, telle est leur exigeance! Ils auraient fait bon marché du parent vivant." Thus you will speak of me. I now ask myself, at the close, whether I am not depriving the brother whom I loved so tenderly and so *watchfully*, of a great renown, by asking you in the beginning not to print your article?

Certainly *I would deprive him of renown*, for who will ever write of him so very truly and eloquently. Therefore, what I wish to sacrifice, what I dare to beg, is so trifling, so easy to change with your versatility of style! It refers to the few lines, which I underlined, pp. 13 and 14, Rahel's opinion, pp. 14 and 15, not included; for she always is mild and just and charming.

Take my warmest, most heartfelt thanks, my revered friend! Do not answer me. I shall call on you to-morrow morning, about twelve o'clock.

Yours,   A. Humboldt.

34.

BERLIN, *June 9th*, 1838.

I AM very happy, revered friend, that I can offer to you as a present the only volumes of the great Russian poet hitherto published. Shall I come to you to-morrow, Sunday, at one o'clock, that my eyes may see the beautiful eyes which have enticed you (for our literary benefit) into the Slavonian lingual labyrinth?

I called twice at Mr. K.'s; but, as he was not in, I left cards. Moreover, I wrote him a tender letter, with offers for Petersburg (concerning his journey to Geneva) —but I have not heard a word from him since. Such conduct in a young man, who without me would still sit in Orenburg as a Cossack clerk, is difficult to understand.

Most gratefully yours,

SATURDAY. A. HT.

Do not answer, if you permit me to come.

35.

HUMBOLDT TO VARNHAGEN.

BERLIN, *August* 3d, 1838.

You are for me, my dearest friend, the standard of refinement as well as my authority in matters of elevated taste. I have written two articles (not heretofore published) for Cotta's "New Quarterly," with which his advisers are very much delighted, viz.: a natural description of the Plateau of Bogota, and on the fluctuations in the production of coin since the middle age. He sends me for them (they fill four printed sheets) an exchange for fifty fredericksdor's, or more than twelve fredericksdor's per sheet. I have a mind (although very much in need of money) to return one half the sum. Before carrying out, however, the resolution, I thought it best to ask, what at the present time may be considered as a maximum of an author's payment for such articles? Is it six, eight, or ten fredericksdor's? I would then return only in proportion. It may be of some importance hereafter to me. Excuse the prosaic question, and send me some word of answer one of these days. I am going to the Island to-day.

HT.

In Varnhagen's Diary is the following entry, dated August 9th, 1838. Humboldt told me in a long visit the news of Toeplitz. The King of Prussia and the Emperor of Russia have both avoided meeting each other alone, each of them fearing the embarrassment of a tête-à-tête. The Emperor spoke on several occasions quite contemptuously of the present French Government, and still worse of the King Louis Philippe himself. Prince Metternich's conduct was frivolous, light-minded, and without fear for the present; he is not alarmed, though haunted by the gloomy thought that at Louis Philippe's death things must take a new turn, and that then war will become inevitable. Does he think to make people believe this, I ask? With Metternich one always ought to examine first, how far an opinion adapts itself to the position of the moment.

Under date of April 9th, 1839, Varnhagen wrote in his Diary: "Humboldt called quite unexpectedly and made the greatest excuses for not having called on me before. And then he opened his newsbag and recited a thousand stories from Paris and Berlin—at least for two hours. Things in France bear a very gloomy aspect, he thinks; and he has lately written about it to Prince Metternich. The crisis in France is yet a latent one—but to-morrow it may burst forth, and how needful it would then be, and, in this event, how necessary, that Germany should be strong and united, and the farces at Cologne and Hanover be settled!

Under 19th of April, 1839, Varnhagen says in his diary: "I saw Humboldt to-day, who told me many things, and showed me a beautiful portrait of Arago, which pleased me very much. He talked much about the difficulties between Russia and England, as to their interests in the East Indies and in Persia, and repeated what he had heard about it from the Russian Emperor himself. The Czar was in a great passion against the English, and thought it highly important to oppose their supremacy in Asia. Humboldt agrees with me that the English have nothing serious to fear for the next fifty years from Russia in the Indies, but that fear and jealousy may engender a quarrel in Europe prior to any conflict in the East, although conflicting parties will certainly think twice before allowing it to come to that pass."

Under date of May 25, 1839, Varnhagen wrote in his diary:

"I met Humboldt 'unter den Linden:' we had a long talk together. He told me that the death of Gans had been the object of the meanest slander at court by all except the King, who never speaks ill of the dead, and the Crown-Prince, who had even uttered a word of sorrow. The other princes were delighted, and the Princess of Liegnitz showed herself very ill-natured."

36.

HUMBOLDT TO VARNHAGEN.

BERLIN, MONDAY, *June* 3d, 1839.

THE book which you lent me, dear friend, is delightful,* as everything must be called which characterizes the individuality of men. My brother's letters are excellent indeed. His opinion of the State Chancellor does much credit to his character, and the conclusion, which seems to take away something from the praise bestowed on him, is full of a deep political meaning. He alludes to some other result of greater magnitude, which the development of the world-wide events in question might have produced.

What pleases me most is the acknowledgment of *your* talents, of *your* power of writing; the praise of the high-mindedness exhibited in *Rahel's* letters (to the few who can appreciate them). Adam Mueller's aristocratic fancies and coarsely but naturally sensual princess,† a

---

* Dorow's Memoirs and Correspondence, 3d vol.
† Sophia Wilhelmina, Princess of Baireuth.

little lewd—no doubt from being hunchbacked—afford the most striking contrast of political and human filth. "To save the country," says Gentz, in his Primary Political Position, " means to restore to the nobility of Prussia their ancient privileges, to liberate all the noblemen from taxes, so that they may spontaneously, after some negotiation, offer their ' don gratuit' to the monarch. To enable them to do this the peasant must be indissolubly bound to the soil." How charmed " the Montmorencys of the Ackermark " must have been to see what, until then, was uselessly concealed in their miserable souls, expressed in refined language by a talented writer, and moulded into such systematical dogmas. This narrow spirit of caste knows neither place nor time. Like a threatening spectre it will reappear when I shall be no more. I frequently ask myself whether Adam Mueller could not, at the present time, again canvass for votes among the " cross-bearers," who, like Homerian heroes, take their repose stretched on their bags in the wool market? Benjamin Constant has exquisitely pictured this aristocratic idea of self-importance in the parable of the Shipwrecked. He cries, " Grand Dieu, je ne suis pas assez indiscret pour vous prier de nous sauver tous! Sauvez-moi tout seul!"

If you have a moment's leisure, please read in the 3d volume of my "History of the Geography of the Middle Ages," what I have said of the natural views and the style of Christopher Columbus, vol. iii. p. 232. This dream, p. 316, was the object of a lecture at Chateaubriand's and Madame Récamier's, and had a good effect, as the utterance of sentiment always will have, on the barren fields of minute erudition. I hope to offer you shortly the five volumes that have already been printed. The negligence of the publisher prevents my doing so now.

A. Ht.

On the 9th of June, 1839, Varnhagen writes in his diary: "Humboldt agrees with me in the assertion made by me at different times, that too much cannot be inferred from the silence of the historians. He refers to three highly important and undeniable facts, which are not mentioned by those whose first duty it should have been to record them. In the archives of Barcelona, no vestige of the triumphal entry held there by Columbus; in Marco Polo, no mention of the Chinese wall; in the archives of Portugal, nothing of the travels of Amerigo Vespucci, in the service of that crown." (History of the Geography of the New Continent, part iv., p. 160, *sq*.)

37.

HUMBOLDT TO VARNHAGEN.

FRIDAY, *Sept.* 13*th*, 1839.

Mr. PIAGET has made a very favorable impression on me. In my opinion, he would be most useful as "Professeur de Litterature ou d'Histoire" at the "College Français." A pedantic examination, however, stands in his way. I will try my best with Mr. von Werther. I have, however, some fear that the rather illiterate-looking mustaches, and the long, straight, South Sea hair, will be found a little odd in that quarter.

Ever with the same attachment,

A. v. HUMBOLDT.

Is it not remarkable that the Neufchatel Councillors in the cabinet, have tried to dissuade Mr. Piaget—" par jalousie de métier?"

38.

HUMBOLDT TO VARNHAGEN.

BERLIN, 29*th Dec.*, 1839.

IT is kind in you, and very *humane*, dear friend, sending me that little pamphlet,* which otherwise would certainly have escaped my attention. The praise which you bestow on it is of great weight, as you understand so well sketching a life-portrait and adorning it gracefully, without discoloring its characteristic traits. Kries is one of my earliest friends. We were students together in Heyne's Seminary.† I will return the print very soon.

In great haste, A. HUMBOLDT.

* Fr. Jaco's Jubilee Oration for Kries, at Gotha.
† At Göttingen.

39.

HUMBOLDT TO VARNHAGEN.

WEDNESDAY AFTERNOON, *Feb. 26th,* 1840.

I DEEM myself unfortunate, dear friend, in having missed you. I have been suffering from a miserable little boil on my foot, and went to-day (for the first time) to my neighbor, Leopold von Buch. Best thanks for Sesenheim.* You certainly were right in snatching the little work from oblivion, a work which possesses a German character in the highest degree, and derives a tender interest from your preface. There is in this little work a nice appreciation of what must ever be important and sacred to a German in his literature. The author searches Sesenheim and Drusenheim as others do the Troade. The proper names, alas! are less poetic. The passages (p. 12 and 13), are written in a charming style; afterwards the philologist becomes heavy and doubtful about what he only half examined; doubtful, as if he had superficially read an old code. Whether the sisters

---

* Pilgrimage to Sesenheim. By August Ferdinand Nacke. Published by K. A. Varnhagen von Ense. Berlin, 1840.

of Friederike, "of whom one has not to care at all" (p. 48), whether the Catholic clergyman who, according to some, caused, and according to others, did not cause, and then did cause her fall, will rejoice at all this, I do not dare myself to decide. About the Troade and the Skamander, they never could exactly determine, and Helen had to suffer much from Hellenic gossip.

In old friendship most gratefully,

Yours,   A. v. HDT.

40.

HUMBOLDT TO VARNHAGEN.

MONDAY, *March 9th,* 1840.

THE Crown-Prince, to whom I brought, this morning, your thoughtful "*Lebensbuch,*" has ordered me to express to you, revered friend, his "most friendly thanks." It reminded him, at the same time, of your "Sophie Charlotte," your "Seydlitz," your always delightful language, and your skill in portraying difficult relations of life. The liberal passage on Grimm I read to him. It pleased him much, and brought on a conversation on Hanover. He expressed himself very sensibly in regard to it. "The King of Hanover does not understand how to treat Germans: he does not know how to win them, by availing himself of their loyal emotions. On the day when the news of the final election in Göttingen arrived in Hanover, I would have sent an aide-de-camp or a civil officer to Göttingen, to thank the professors, and ask them whether they would like to have the whole seven professors reappointed." These are words flowing from a noble soul. Of your article on Niebuhr, I do *not* speak to the Crown-Prince, though I entirely agree with you regarding it.

With old attachment,

Yours, A. v. HDT.

41.

HUMBOLDT TO VARNHAGEN.

WEDNESDAY, *March* 18*th*, 1840.

AN insipid polemical book of Mr. Gretsch, against Melgunoff, and against the book of Koenig, which is entirely unknown to me, full of Siberia, strangulation, secret funds, and Russian patriotism—an insufferable rehash! Will you read it, my dear friend? For you alone understand it entirely. The book might almost reconcile me with Mr. Melgunoff, against whom I have felt some anger. I have, it is true, neither a recollection of him nor of my conversation with him; but he must have strangely interpreted and translated into his own language, what I said to him, when he represents me as condemning one whose great talents and delightful style and manners I praise everywhere. How is it credible that I could have spoken unfavorably of you in the only conversation I ever had with a man who brought me a letter from your own hand? Who recognises in me such careless, Orinoco manners?

Marheineke also has made a campaign in the "Kritische-Blätter," more against Savigny than against Stahl. There is a good deal of acrimony in the air, and the black-coats are not merciful. The conclusion of the philippic is very eloquent, in the climax from the rationalists, *viâ* St. Hegel, to Galilee. It is a pity that the preceding twelve pages are so indifferently written—in the most mediocre style.

Goerres and Schelling understand coloring better. I thus feel only interested in what is dramatic and in the talents exhibited, or not exhibited, therein. Caesareopapacy, territorial system, nay, even "the authority of a *distinctly positive doctrine, and marked physiognomy,*" for which Marheineke (p. 41) has a tendency, are abominations, and are mere carnival buffoonery to me. Both parties are mere compressing machines of different kinds, and a philosophically proved Christian dogmatism of "marked physiognomy," this seems to me the most offensive of all strait-waistcoats.

Raumer (Carl) has published "Crusades"—crusades against the geognosts. The Saracens are Leopold von Buch (your newly converted one), and myself.

A. Ht.

And Sintenis at Magdeburg and the State's Council at Neufchatel, "who have prohibited the deluge!" And all that in the year 1840! Three comets are not enough!

I received a letter from the Marquis Clanricarde, at St. Petersburg, on the 5th of March, stating, "that nothing was heard for four or five weeks from the expedition to Chiwa. It is purely an attack upon the Khan, whom they propose to dethrone, and to put his brother in the place." You see that he wishes to appear very tranquil! What meek politics!

42.

METTERNICH TO HUMBOLDT.

VIENNA, 29*th of March*, 1840.

MY DEAR BARON—Though I do not doubt that the Crown-Prince, to whom I had the honor of replying to-day, will inform you of my declaration, I refer you to my letter to his Royal Highness. You will see that I have placed myself at his disposal, with a reservation, however, prescribed by my ignorance of archæology. To my ignorance upon this point must be added my ignorance upon another—I mean the duties of the Presidency. I desire to state, at all events, what I think of the relations of a single member with any scientific association. There are three sorts of men—some are true savans; the number of these is small: others are friends of science in general, or of some branch of it; these are more numerous: the third class—the largest of all—comprises the narrow-minded, the barren in spirit, the "*viveurs*," to whom, though often they are very good fellows, art and science are quite superfluous. I enrol myself in the second of these classes. My brethren and I can be of some service to mental cultivation, provided we do not meddle too much with details. When I feel that I can do a good work, I consider it my duty to devote myself to it. In the present case, however, I can only throw my good will into the scale.

My confession of faith is set forth in the explanations given to the August Protector; and to what I took the liberty of stating to him, I also take the liberty of referring you.

It is so long, my dear Baron, since you paid us a visit, that when you feel inclined to judge for yourself, you will be more than gratified by the real progress we have made in the departments of which you are the acknowledged master. The place of Jaeger, whose loss was greatly to be regretted, is well filled by Endlicher —a man of eminent genius; Baumgarten and Ettinghausen, are savans of great distinction. The Polytechnic School goes on admirably and is training up savans, and thoroughly educated mechanicians. Roesel is the best optician of our time, and the young Voigtlander follows in his footsteps.

The establishment of Baron Charles Huegel has opened a new and vast field to botany. The arts and sciences advance quite to one's liking; all that is wanted is a supervisor like yourself.

You complain, my dear Baron, at finding yourself the oldest of the foreign members of the Institute; this indeed is a dreary lot, but it is inevitable and quite natural—provided one does not commit the folly of going off before the others. I have the same feeling— and that in a field which is certainly the greatest of all fields. Of all the Kings and the Ministers of State in office, between the year 1813 and the year 1815, the King of Prussia and myself are the only survivors! And yet the time does not embrace more than a quarter of a century—so true is it that twenty-five years are quite an historical epoch. Let us not lose courage at such trifles, but go on as if they were nothing at all.

My sincerest homage, dear Baron.

METTERNICH.

43.

HUMBOLDT TO VARNHAGEN.

Thursday, *April 9th*, 1840.

Here are two Salamanders. The *black* (black bordered) king of Denmark is not only a Norwegian constitutional, but also a mineralogical king, who has written pretty good memoirs on Vesuvius. The predecessor having been an astronomical king, who proposed prize questions on comets, presented *great* men like General Mueffling and myself with chronometers, and died of a comet on the night of the discovery of Galli's comet, the Danish astronomers were, probably, rather anxious for *their heavenly* pursuits under the reign of such an *earthly* (or rather subterranean) monarch. I was called upon to remind the King of his old predilection for me. I therefore resorted to the pretext, never before made use of by me, of congratulating him on his accession to the throne. This is the cause of the black drama. The letter is plain and sensible.

A. Ht.

Please read in Mr. Quinet's the passage on Goethe and Bettina, and return the venom to me.

44.

KING CHRISTIAN VIII. OF DENMARK TO HUMBOLDT.

COPENHAGEN, *the* 13*th January,* 1840.

MONSIEUR LE BARON DE HUMBOLDT:

Of all the letters received on the occasion of my accession to the throne, none has afforded me so sensible a pleasure as that which you addressed me under the date of the 17th of December last.

Your remembrance is of the highest value to me, and I recall with the greatest interest, Monsieur le Baron, our conversations many years ago at Paris. Since that time you have enriched science by new discoveries. Siberia, explored by you, as you before explored America, offers to natural science new views for which, Monsieur le Baron, it is entirely indebted to you. Really—I shall be happy at some future day to converse with you on these new researches.

The natural sciences are constantly presenting fresh interest, and I shall certainly not neglect to do everything that depends upon me for their advancement.

The astronomical and geodesical labors of your distinguished friend Schumacher, certainly deserve my patronage. He has acquired a European name as a savan, and I appreciate his rare merits. As to the magnetic observations after the method of Gauss—I am occupied in amplifying them here at Copenhagen, where an observatory, established since 1834 near the Polytechnic School, is about to be removed to a more suitable place on the outskirts of the city. It will be provided with two different "emplacements," one for "observations on declination," and another for experiments in "inclination." The establishment will be under the superintendence of the celebrated Oersted.

I esteem myself happy, my dear Baron, in being able to speak to you of the advancement of natural science in my own country, and you must consider it a proof that I shall not neglect any occasion of justifying the good opinion you entertain of my interest in the sciences and in everything which can tend to the enlightenment and happiness of my subjects.

I hope, Monsieur le Baron, that you will frequently find leisure to communicate with me, and I shall endeavor, upon my own part, to cultivate relations so agreeable to myself.

The Queen charges me with her compliments to you, and I embrace the occasion of assuring you of my highest consideration, Monsieur le Baron Humboldt.

Your most affectionate,

CHRISTIAN.

45.

HUMBOLDT TO VARNHAGEN.

SATURDAY, *April* 11*th*, 1840.

THE Crown-Prince would like very much to see that interesting letter of Prince Metternich to you. Could not you send it to me before half-past seven o'clock to-night, my dear friend?

A. HT.

In regard to the said letter, Varnhagen says in his diary, under date of April 2d, 1840: "When returning home, found a letter from Prince Metternich—a long one, under his own hand. He declares my picture of the Congress of Vienna to be a perfectly faithful one, a few points excepted, which ought to be corrected. He himself corrects, in detail, the description of the effect of the news at Vienna, that Napoleon had left Elba. It is a letter of historical value."

Under date of the 5th of the same month, Varnhagen mentions again the Metternich letter. "In the afternoon," he says, "Humboldt called. He had heard of the letter from Wittgenstein, who had spoken of it to

Count Orloff and others, as a most remarkable production. Humboldt also was astonished and delighted. He showed me a letter which Prince Metternich had addressed him, as to the position of several naturalists at Vienna, and the presidency of the Archæological Society at Rome. Humboldt tells me of dark tendencies of the Westphalian nobility, which the Crown-Prince favors. They think of establishing a great Catholic seminary for young noblemen—a proper nursery for Jesuits. On Humboldt's remarking that the Crown-Prince, perhaps, out of absence of mind, had not reflected on the important consequence of the King's illness, Minister von Rochow made the following reply: "Oh, certainly he has thought of it! And he has prepared various things, which he means then to propose. But to his views and commands in ecclesiastical matters I should be highly opposed."

46.

April 13*th*, 1840.

THE Crown-Prince has expressly charged me to offer you, dear friend, his thanks for such an interesting communication. Count Alvensleben was present. Every one considered the letter a gratifying testimonial to you and to your description of the Congress, and praised it for the noble simplicity in which one of the most remarkable events is recited. " Et tout cela prouve que ma fille est muette," and that a talent like yours (in advising, in describing, and in knowledge of mankind) is allowed to be idle, so that after your death, as after my brother's, people will express their astonishment at your not having been employed in time.

A. Ht.

I am quite "turned Quaker." Mrs. Fry and William Allan—little sermons in the penitentiaries (the most horrible ones which the Quakeress has ever seen), and little tracts against brandy-drinking!

47.

HUMBOLDT TO VARNHAGEN.

FRIDAY, March 29th, 1840.

DECIDE, master of eloquence and euphony: I had it thus, "As far as humanity (civilisation) extended on earth!"

Now, it pleases me better to put: 1, "It has influenced rulers and nations equally, as far as civilization and commerce extend" (extend, not extended, which latter

I abhor); or, 2 "As far as civilization and commerce ennobled mankind;" or, 3, "Made mankind susceptible;" or, 4, "United mankind."

Would No. 4 (the last), not be the better?" Perhaps you have an inspiration. Put clandestinely, to-night at Staegemann's, a bit of paper in my hand. Perhaps the first conception is the best.

A. HT.

"Humanity" I give up at any rate, having just read so many mockeries regarding it in the last volume of Campe's dictionary.

"Sed quamquam, primo statim beatissimi sæculi ortu, Nerva Cæsar *res olim dissociabiles miscuerit*, principatum ac libertatem; augeatque quotidie felicitatem imperii Nerva Trajanus." Tacitus in Agricola, cap. 3. Also, of the same old Nerva (noble and gifted with literary taste):

"Quod si vita suppeditet, principatum divi Nervæ, et imperium Trajani, uberiorem securioremque materiam senectati seposui: *rara temporum felicitas, ubi sentire quæ velis, et quæ sentias dicere licet*." Tacit. Hist. I. 1. I, of course, in order to avoid all detail, shall give only the numerical quotations, sic: Tacit. Vita Ag. c. 3 Hist. I. 1.

HT.

48.

HUMBOLDT TO VARNHAGEN.

BERLIN, TUESDAY NIGHT, *Oct. 27th,* 1840.

IF I have delayed so long in coming to you, my dear friend, both before and after my campaign to the North, it is only because there are impossibilities in life against which we battle in vain. Immediately after the festivities in this city I intended to hasten to you, but the uncertainty whether I should go to Paris (I refused, because then it would not have been honorable either to me or to the king, if Prussia did not dare to act independently!) the approaching departure of Bulow, the arrival of the sick General von Hedemann and his family, together with a rheumatic fever, which kept me in the house for six days, spoiled all my intentions. Tomorrow morning, at 8 o'clock, I have to move over again to Sans Souci; but (I hope) only for some days. I, therefore, now take up my pen to chat with you. First my best thanks for your talented and noble treating of the rather mediocre "*Erinnerungen von M. Arndt!*" I certainly had observed his hostility towards you. The tone of your criticism is the noblest kind of revenge.

The man, whom I never knew personally, was raised by the great events of his time and not by himself. Strange enough that the government attached to him in these latter days, in the evening of his life, an importance not arising merely from a simple love of justice.

Since you like everything individual, I shall answer your kindness with another very small one. I make you a present of a letter of Guizot, which he wrote to me to Koenigsberg, not without design. The underlining belongs to me, as you would guess yourself. I showed the letter to the King. It was written when the Belgian (the King of Belgium), Bulow, and Guizot had been in Windsor, and when his affairs looked promising, as they do now again, as Thiers at once shows himself so weak and yielding, and Palmerston so dogmatical and defying. But do not let the letter out of your hands.

For the news about the brothers Grimm I thank you most cordially. It is very important to me to keep "au courant" with the course of passing events. In the months during which I lived on the "historical hill,"* I moved uncontrolled in the same direction, though surrounded by conflicting elements.

Respecting the brothers Grimm, the King had given orders to others, not to me; but up to the return from

---

* Sans Souci, the King's residence near Potsdam.—*Translator.*

Königsberg, nothing was done. I therefore addressed a memorial to the King on the actions in Königsberg of the Provincial Diet, and on the necessity of acting authoritatively in things which interest all hearts, in order to secure their affections—and therefore to bestow a professorship upon the brothers Grimm, Albrecht, and Dahlmann. There is little hope for Dahlmann. Albrecht received a call, but refused it, giving as a reason his gratitude to Saxony. It would have been a satisfaction to the seven professors, could Albrecht have become professor in Berlin.

They certainly will at least hear in Hanover that the King has called the "Elbinger." In respect to the brothers Grimm, the King insists upon his plan, that minister Eichhorn should offer to them a place in the Academy, with a pension to both, as they live like husband and wife. That the King wants these things to be arranged with tact, you may see from the negotiations with Tieck. For librarians, although excellent men, they are very unfit. Whether Wilhelm Grimm, as a correspondent of the Academy, lectures or not is also very irrelevant. The chief thing is to get them. Of "smuggling them in," "a debasement," "to think of them so late,"—dans un regne de cent jours—it is nonsense to talk! It does honor at least to the administration of Ladenberg, that I was able to propose Dahlmann in due form, and in flattering terms for the university of

Breslau, where there was a vacancy. I have cleared the way as it was my duty to do, but the appointment itself is not in my hands. As soon as I return from Potsdam, I shall trouble minister Eichhorn, to settle this patriotic affair officially and at once. The interference of many in these things is injurious, although it can be pardoned where the interest is so natural. I know not, my dear friend, whether you will be able and willing to read these lines, the sense of which is more blameless than the style. I need not conjure you, the diplomatist, not to read my letter to the " child,"* but she ought to hear how these matters stand, respecting which I have neglected nothing.

A. Ht.

An inexpressible misfortune has happened in the death of the only son of my friend the astronomer, Bessel, only twenty-five years old, a young man of the most eminent mathematical talents. He died yesterday of nervous fever.

* Bettina von Arnim. Bopp's critique is to me a source of great pleasure.

49.

GUIZOT TO HUMBOLDT.

LONDON, *August* 24, 1840.

MONSIEUR LE BARON:

It was very amiable indeed in you to have thought of sending me the two new volumes of your brother's works. I thank you not only for this gift, in itself so very valuable, but also for your remembrance which is at least equally dear to me. I hope that notwithstanding all our affairs, for they are yours as well as mine, I shall manage to read something of this great work. I should like to employ my time in so complete and varied a manner as you occupy yours. Preserve a little of it for the advancement of a good and a wise policy, which though it already owes you much, still needs you.

I envy Baron von Bülow the pleasure of seeing you. I regret extremely losing his society in London. Conversation—genuine conversation—profound, pregnant, and free, is very scarce among us. His I shall miss very much. I should like to go some day to see you at your home, to visit your country, in which, beyond all others, human intellect acts the greatest part, and to see your new King, who is worthy, it is said, of such a country. In the meanwhile, Monsieur le Baron, pray preserve for me your old kindness and believe in the lasting sincerity of the sentiments which long ago I conceived for you.

GUIZOT.

NOTE OF HUMBOLDT.—Received at Königsberg during the festivals.
A. VON HUMBOLDT.

50.

ARAGO TO HUMBOLDT.

PARIS, *March 12th*, 1841.

I MUST not, I will not, believe that you asked me seriously whether I should look forward to your journey to Paris with pleasure. Could it be that you ever doubted my invariable attachment? Be it known to you that I should consider the slightest doubt upon this point a most cruel offence. Beyond the immediate circle of my own family you are, without comparison, the person whom, of all others, I love the most dearly. But you must be resigned to the duties of this position, as you are of my friends the only one to whom I would look in my difficulties.

I am truly happy in the anticipation of spending some evenings with him to whom I am indebted for my taste in meteorology and physics. There will be a bed for you at the Observatory.

Poor Savàry is in a lamentable state. The physician assures me that the disease of his lungs leaves no hope. What a calamity!

You will arrive at Paris at the opening of my course of astronomy. My new amphitheatre is got up with a profligate luxury.

I am charmed with the news of poor Sheiffer's* recovery (is it true?). Your good heart has always secured you a numerous family.

Adieu, best of friends. My attachment to you will only cease with my life.

Fr. Arago.

Note of Humboldt.—I had asked whether he thought it possible that the difference of our political wishes [war with Germany] might disturb our intercourse.

Note of Humboldt.—To his highly gifted friend, Varnhagen von Ense, with the most earnest request to avoid all publication of this autograph before Arago's death.

A. Humboldt.

* Probably Seiffert, Humboldt's servant.—*Tr*

51.

HUMBOLDT TO BETTINA VON ARNIM.

[A copy in Varnhagen's handwriting.]

SATURDAY, *November* 21, 1840.

How could you doubt, most honored Madam, my being thankful for the news of the real situation of those noble men, who after so many undeserved sufferings, and after so long and so shameful a neglect, are at last to be placed in an independent position. I thought that, to have given them such a situation in Berlin, three thousand thalers would be a sufficient salary for both, and with this view I have continued my efforts. The King has adopted it as a principle never to issue an order in financial matters on his own account; like all princes, he has no standard by which to measure the wants of learned men. The superior intellects with whom we wish to surround ourselves have wants as prosaic as their inferiors. Whoever wishes to obtain the end must also be willing to employ the means, and especially in an affair which attracts every eye and which touches the honor of the country. The minister Eichhorn, upon whom everything now depends, is happy in the arrival of the two Grimms. He was formerly on the most friendly terms with Jacob Grimm. I called on the minister an hour ago in order to support my view of the matter. He declares that by-and-by he will arrange the affair in the best manner, but that we must confide in him, and allow him to act without obstruction.

Receive, gracious Madam, the expression of my veneration and of my sentiments of gratitude.

A. HUMBOLDT.

52.

HUMBOLDT TO VARNHAGEN.

BERLIN, *August* 22d, 1841.

YOUR letter has done me an immense deal of good. I see that we feel ourselves both equally attracted to each other, and that you attributed my long, and to me very gloomy, seclusion, only to the distracted state of my life, and to the application of my faculties, to an aim which they never can reach. Towards the close of a much troubled life which has but imperfectly realized its aspirations, it is a happiness to remain secure in, and to possess the esteem of those to whose mind and intellect and wishes we are irresistibly drawn. I shall personally thank you, and this very afternoon apply for Mr. L. to the Princess of Prussia, and beg her Imperial Highness to assist me with all earnestness. With old veneration and love, yours,

A. v. HUMBOLDT.

At the request of the King I took the opportunity of reading to him Schelling's discourse on nature and art. (Philosoph. Werke, tome 1st, 1809.) The passages concerning Raphael, Leonardo da Vinci, and about the possibility of a resuscitation of the arts, are the most pleasing in our language. This lecture produced on the King the effect of a beautiful song. But the bird is now sixty-seven years old, and goes from one golden cage to another.

Varnhagen says in his diary, under date of April 28, 1841: "Humboldt came and remained more than an hour and a half; I found him looking ill, but lively, cheerful, and more communicative than ever. He praises the King for his disposition and his intentions, but thinks that he is no man of action, and that whenever he acts, he does it by starts, without system or method. Whether it be from kindness or timidity, at all events, he often does not dare to do what he most wishes and could do quite easily; thus he expects impatiently that the minister Von Werther will resign, and asks of Humboldt, whether the minister has given no intimation of it."

On the 30th April, 1841, Varnhagen says: "Humboldt has a great many enemies, as well amongst the savans as at court, who are constantly seeking an opportunity to malign him, but the moment he is praised all vituperation ceases—for it is all vituperation. It is seldom that anybody is able to maintain it. Some time ago a gentleman said to me, that he did not know what to think of Humboldt, and that he could not come to a conclusion concerning him. I answered: 'Think always the best of him, believe him always capable of the best action, and you always will be nearest the truth.' Another said, same day, sneeringly: 'Humboldt was a great man before he came to Berlin, where he became an ordinary one.' Moritz Robert remarked that Rahel had already said several times: 'Nothing holds its ground in Berlin, everything has a downward tendency; indeed, if the Pope himself came to Berlin, he would not continue long to be Pope, he would sink into the 'commonplace,' down perhaps to the standard of a groom.' What Rahel said is true, and I remember that she said so, but had made no note of it. This peculiarity of Berlin ought to be examined closer; it indicates a strong stratum of undeveloped greatness, and may, when positively brought forth to a point, bring the highest honor on Berlin; but if allowed to act negatively, it will, of course, become a shame to this city. 'The Berliners are such a daring race of men,' said Goethe, once. That is much the same definition."

53.

HUMBOLDT TO VARNHAGEN.

SATURDAY, *April 24th*, 1841.

A DISAPPOINTMENT, dear friend, not to have found you. Correct this title-page for me; I have to send it away. As it is necessary to state, "that this is not the lecture of 1828," I thought of having the long sentence printed on the title-page, in small type, like an aphorism. It may look strange *after* the name, but I hope you will be able to approve of it.

HT.

" Kosmos. Sketch of a Physical Description of the World, by A. von Humboldt. From Sketches and Lectures delivered in the years 1827 and 1828, enlarged and corrected according to the latest researches.

"' Naturæ vero rerum vis atque majestas sin omnibus momentis fide caret, si quis modo partes ejus ac non totam complectatur animo.'—*Plin. Hist. Nat., lib.* 7. c. 1. Stuttgart."

54.

HUMBOLDT TO VARNHAGEN.

WEDNESDAY, *April* 28*th*, 1841.

BE very kind and indulgent in reading my work. I am anxious that you should get a complete idea of the composition of it. In A, I have made large corrections. Notice especially p. 37 and the notes; Schelling's name, pp. 37 and 68; Hegel, p. 66. The positive declaration at p. 64, that it is not the creator of Natural Philosophy whom I accuse, will, I hope, make my biting severity at the "gay Saturnalia," *le bal en masque* of the craziest of all natural philosophers, seem more pardonable to him. "Il faut avoir le courage d'imprimer. Ce que l'on a dit et écrit depuis trente ans." It has been a lamentable period, in which Germany has sunk far below England and France. Chemistry, without so much as wetting one's fingers.

The diamond is a pebble arrived at consciousness. Granite is ether. Carus.

The side of the moon turned towards the earth is of a different convexity from the reverse. The cause of it: the moon fain would stretch out her loving arms—she cannot, but gazes at the earth, and protrudes her lower jaw.

The granite blocks on the rocks are the convulsions of nature.

It is well known that the forests are the hair of the earth-animal. The swelling equatorial region is the belly of Nature.

America is a female figure, long, slender, watery and freezing at 48°. The degrees of latitude are the years woman gets old at, 48 years. The East is oxygen, the West hydrogen; it rains when clouds from the East are mixed with clouds from the West.—*Schelling.*

Petrifactions in rocks are not the remains of former living beings. They are the first attempts of nature at making animals and plants. In Siberia some dogs lived for years on such an experiment—a stinking elephant at the mouth of the Lena.

These are the Saturnalia! Cast your eye particularly on the notes, *en masse,* of which I inclose a few. P. 40–49; p. 55–57.

I wish to give to the work the greatest generality and breadth of views, a lively and, if possible, graceful style, and to replace all technical terms with well-chosen, graphic, and descriptive language.

Correct freely, my friend; I gladly follow where I can. Some not very common erudition I intend to banish to the notes. This book should be the reflex of my own self, of my life, of my own very old person. This freedom of treatment enables me to proceed more aphoristically.

More will be suggested than elaborated. Much will be well understood by those only who know thoroughly one special branch of natural history; but I think my style is such as to confuse no one, not even the superficial. My real aim is to hover over those results which are known in 1841. *Mens agitat molem*, may the mind still be there!

That such a work cannot be finished by one born in the comet-year, 1769, is as clear as daylight. The separate fragments will appear in parts of twelve to fifteen sheets each, so that those who may see me buried will possess in each fragment some one subject complete. Thus of the "Prolegomena," there will be No. 1–4; My "incentive," descriptive poetry, which you have not yet seen, is a chief feature of the work on which I rely a good deal.—No. 5. The history of man's conception of the world, which is quite finished, will form the entire second book. Plain scientific description will always be intermingled with the oratorical, like nature itself. The glittering stars fill us with joy and inspiration, yet in the canopy of heaven all bodies revolve in mathematical figures. It is essential to preserve a dignified style, so that the impression of nature's greatness will not be wanting. I hope you will not find fault with my quoting (C) in a note the passage from Shakespeare which is but little known.

All the notes are to be printed in very small type at

the end of each chapter, never at the bottom of the page. I had said that a knowledge of nature is not absolutely necessary to enjoy it, but that it increases the enjoyment. Pardon this hasty writing. I leave to-morrow morning with the King for Potsdam, to stay there six or seven days. With thanks and friendship, your illegible

A. v. HUMBOLDT.

55.

HUMBOLDT TO SPIKER.

(C.)

[*Biron speaks to the King of Navarre.*]

"These earthly godfathers of heaven's lights,
That gave a name to every fixed star,
Have no more profit of their shining nights,
Than those that walk, and wot not what they are,
Too much to know, is to know nought but fame;
And every godfather can give a name."

SHAKESPEARE, Love's Labor Lost. Act I. Scene 1.

BE so kind as to send me back this page. I make use of your fine translation in a note which is now being printed in my *Kosmos*. You will permit me to say:

"according to Spiker's translation." It will give me pleasure to do so. Shall I excite the ire of the Marquis August von Schlegel or of Tieck Acorombonus? Please tell me whether they have also translated that passage? Many kind regards.

HT.

NOTE OF VARNHAGEN.—Unfortunately Spiker's translation is bad in every respect.

56.

HUMBOLDT TO VARNHAGEN.

MONDAY NIGHT, *May* 3, 1841.

I AM afraid, my dear friend, that I shall be obliged to go to Potsdam again on Thursday, and thence to Paris on the 10th or 12th. I am to send Cotta more copy before I go. Let me not be suspended so long between condemnation and indulgence. Pray send me a few words with the parcel.

Yours,
A. v. HUMBOLDT.

57.

HUMBOLDT TO VARNHAGEN.

Tuesday, May 4th, 1841.

My Dear Friend:—Even after deducting the kind expressions written expressly for my tranquillity, there still remains more than enough in your letter of to-day to comfort me. The penance,* therefore, which I assign you is to receive me to-morrow morning at 11 o'clock, for a few moments, to accept my thanks. The "*schmeichle mich*" must be a clerical error; as for me I am unconscious of it. The false use of the accusative case at p. 44, you will have to show me. It cannot be "*Einsicht in den Zusammenhang?*" because it is looking *into*. I shall expunge Mr. Spiker. I had a presentiment of the end, and would rather even omit the English as well, which, after all, is rather a praise of ignorance, than indicative of the increase of enjoyment to be derived from science.

I see that you give me full liberty concerning the "Saturnalia." Speaking of the Dane, you say: "I only mention, I do not object."

---

* The 5th of May was a day of penance.

I did not wish to mention Steffens, however much he might deserve a reproach for his utter barrenness in experimental science, and for his vain and criminal idleness. "Saturnalia" I call that merry but short farce, of which lately I gave you some specimens, but which are not from Steffens; they are by some of his worshippers several degrees lower down. Were Steffens a poor savan, oppressed by the powerful, I would be more careful; but as you are an amateur of autographs, I will give you one from which you will see how northern kings believe that there exists in Berlin a Steffensian philosophy, which is consoling to the theologians, *et qui n'est pas celle de Hegel!* Steffens will believe that he is included among those deep and powerful thinkers, whose advice has been disregarded. Besides the dangerous passage is immediately followed by another: "Abuse of youthful talents; for serious minds, devoted equally to philosophy and to observation, have kept aloof from those Saturnalia." Such a sentence is a *défense*, a *fort detaché*, and Steffens certainly thinks that he, too, devoted himself to observation, when he once descended into a mine at Freiburg. By softening anything I should spoil the whole, and we ought in writing to show the same courage as in speaking, but should do both in the same easy and cheerful manner.

Did you find out from Steffens's tiresome biography,

with which I was bored at Sans Souci, how his pietism and aristocracy is explained by the twofold inoculation of his old grandparents, performed by an archbishop and a king,—*ce sont des heritages!*

A. v. HUMBOLDT.

53.

KING CHRISTIAN VIIL OF DENMARK TO HUMBOLDT.

MONSIEUR LE BARON—I am doubly obliged to the illustrious counsellor Dieffenbach for his attention in presenting me with a copy of his work on the cure of strabism and stammering, since it was the cause of your dear letter of the 9th February. Introduced by you, Monsieur le Baron, any one is sure of success. In the present case, the reputation and the works of the author could have dispensed with all further recommendation; but you only do justice to the great services which Counsellor Dieffenbach has rendered to mankind, and I hasten to acknowledge them by bestowing my Danebrog Order on that distinguished savan. My letter to him on this subject will be remitted by the Envoy Count de Reventlau, and I shall particularly recommend to Chevalier Dieffenbach any Danish surgeons going to

Berlin to learn the art upon which he has thrown so much light.

The bearer of the present, whom I beg leave to recommend to your protection, is the theological candidate, Bornemann—a young man of talent and knowledge, whom I send to Berlin to study Philosophy under the guidance of my countryman, Steffens—not precisely that of Hegel, who has disciples enough in our University; but *that* philosophy which may assist in rectifying the sometimes rather extravagant doctrines of our modern thinkers. Steffens is kept at Berlin by a sacred tie, the gratitude he owes to the King; but I desire that his genius and his knowledge may not be lost to us, and that this young scholar may profit by his light before it ceases to shine, and to enlighten all those coming in contact with my illustrious countryman, who, in my opinion, is in himself worth an entire academic faculty.

I follow with the greatest interest, founded on sincere friendship and on the mutual relations of our respective positions, which I fully appreciate, all that your excellent King does and projects for the happiness of his subjects, for German nationality, and for the preservation of peace. May his efforts be blessed by the Almighty; his people will then enjoy an increased and steady prosperity, which will materially contribute to the welfare of their neighbors.

The King has shown more kindness to my son than I can thank him for. I look forward to a most happy future for him, based on his marriage with the amiable Duchess of Mecklenburg Strelitz.

I appreciate the good wishes which you address me on this occasion, and remain, with the highest consideration, Monsieur le Baron de Humboldt,

Your affectionate
CHRISTIAN R.

59.

BERLIN, May 17th, 1841.

[Written at Varnhagen's. With the preface to Wilhelm von Humboldt's works.]

I AM very sorry not to be enabled amid the annoyances of to-morrow's departure (first to Potsdam, then to Paris, until October) to bid you farewell. I appeal to you once more as the source, until Rückert's arrival, the only source of good taste, of pure language, and of a delicate appreciation of the appropriate sense. Tell me with all indulgence what I ought to strike out from the enclosed preface, but give me also your advice wherever you find fault. I wrote the two pages at night in a gloomy frame of mind. They show perhaps a too sentimental disposition to praise.

Page 1, line 2, "yet" because it happens during my life time. Line 10, "The highly gifted *souls*," perhaps displeasing. Should it be *men?*

A. v. HUMBOLDT.

On the 21st of November, Varnhagen wrote down the following about Humboldt:

"I read to-day the dispatches which Al. von Humboldt addressed to the King from Paris in the year 1835. They are not like Humboldt! Any body else could have written *such* dispatches—nay, what is still worse, nobody could have written them otherwise! Thus it is, however, with political business—it consists of mere trifles, not at all important in themselves, but becoming important because everybody has agreed to consider them so. Thus the established hypocrisy of forms, presumptions, and exaggerations drown the truth. I looked into myself and confessed that were I engaged in such affairs, I, too, would follow in the beaten track; and yet people wonder that in England and France editors of newspapers become ministers, as if it were not infinitely more easy to write the usual dispatches than good newspaper articles."

60.

HUMBOLDT TO VARNHAGEN.

FRIDAY, 3*d December*, 1841.

OF all that I have had to thank you for, dear friend, I like Hormayr's manly letter best. Le style est tout l'homme. *He* is not like the people who surround us, the better ones of whom lose themselves in reticences, temporizations, in trimming, excitements, and irresolution. His belief in Muenster's liberalism is perhaps only a misconception of Muenster's motives. No doubt Count Muenster has nobly contributed to the liberation of Germany—but assuredly he never did it in order to open the path to "that light" which, even to-day, is feared like a spectre. "Bruno" (Bauer) has found me out to be a præadamite convert! When I was a boy the court preachers reasoned in this way: I was confirmed by one of them, who told me that the biographies of the Evangelists were finally manufactured out of memoranda made by themselves during their lifetime. Many years ago I wrote: All positive religions contain three distinct parts—First, a code of morals, very pure and nearly the same in all—next, a geological dream—

and thirdly, a myth or historical novellette; which last becomes the most important of all. I enclose the pamphlet of Baron Seckendorf. He also calls for a "representation," namely the "re puro," the incarnation of the people, all explained in philosophical terms. It must be acceptable, for without being assured of this he would not have dared to publish it. Such people must not be left in doubt about our real opinions. I told him (he is vice-president) that I would read his essay attentively, although our political principles on popular constitutions differed very much.

The political atmosphere is to me thick, dark, and foreboding.

With the same old attachment, yours,

A. v. HUMBOLDT.

On the 2d of December, the day before the above letter, Varnhagen wrote in his diary: "Humboldt called yesterday. Talked about Paris. How he finds things here. He thinks seriously of retiring. He knows that his name alone is of any value to the King, and that his active usefulness has long been superseded by that of others. Thiers told him, in Paris, that France is much talked about as being revolutionary; but he thought Prussia was pretty well agitated, too. A letter from Guizot to Humboldt spoke much in praise of the King; and when Humboldt read it to him, and came to the word '*success*,' the King interrupted him with the words, 'Ah me! there is not much of that; on that point we had best be silent.' And really Humboldt thinks the public feeling here dreadfully changed for the worse. The King has enemies, and in the highest circles! Minister Eichhorn is generally hated, and makes but a poor figure at court. There seems scarcely a doubt that Bunsen will be Ambassador to England. Count Stolberg is almost the only one who speaks openly against Bunsen. Humboldt sneers at Bunsen's little tract, 'The Week of Meditation.'"

The 3d of December, 1841, Varnhagen observes: "I just received a note from Humboldt, inclosing a pamphlet of President Seckendorf's, which also calls for a 'representation'—the 're puro,' an incarnation of the people. Humboldt observes: 'Must be acceptable, for without such an assurance he would not have dared to publish it.' He concludes with significant melancholy: 'The atmosphere to me is gloomy and foreboding. It is hard to be Humboldt, and to be obliged to confess this, at the summit of honor, and in the fulness of glory.' Indeed, he has but little pleasure, and his satirical humor alone can make life here at all supportable to him!"

61.

HUMBOLDT TO VARNHAGEN.

BERLIN, MONDAY NIGHT, *Dec. 7th*, 1841.

I HAVE not the leisure, dear friend, to thank you as I ought to do for your spirited and historically thorough biography of Schwerin.* A deep penetration into the individuality of this great man pervades the whole. Simplicity is the essential, vital element of description. A hasty word of advice to ride off, and the winning of the battle by himself alone,† were constant stumbling-blocks in the path of this hero during his life. His end, the standard in his hand, amid the bloody massacre of thirteen thousand unsympathizing men, is a striking conclusion to the life of the old soldier, who, like Columbus, was at the same time great and unromantically avaricious. What does much honor to your talent as historian, and what is probably overlooked by

---

* A Prussian Field Marshal, killed at the battle of Prague, 1757.—*Tr.*

† Allusion to the battle of Mollwitz, 1741, which was won by Schwerin alone, who, indignant at the blunders of the King, ordered him to ride off, and assumed the command himself, which Frederick the Great never forgave.—*Tr.*

many is, that you do not allow Schwerin's death to interrupt the narrative of the strife of battle. I will bring you the "Collected Works" myself, and beg the second volume of Hormayr's exquisitely spicy production. Your last favor, doing me so much honor, contains words about which I wish to prevent every mistake. "You are afraid to enjoy the exclusive possession of my impieties." You may freely dispose of this sort of property after my not far distant departure from life. Truth is due to those only whom we deeply esteem—to you, therefore. A. HT.

On the 18th December, 1841, Varnhagen writes in his diary: "I heard to-day the quite incredulous, mysteriously-whispered story, that the King would go to England for the baptism of the Prince of Wales; that it had been agreed upon quite secretly, and that this flattering communication had contributed a great deal to make Bunsen's appointment as Ambassador agreeable to the Court of St. James. The latter part of the story makes me suspect the truth of the whole. This is by no means the real diplomatic state of things. Should, however, the journey have been decided upon, or even only be under discussion, there can be no doubt that Bunsen had a hand in it; and then important events would result therefrom, and very dangerous events, too, in my opinion. A near alliance with England would in itself be hazardous; but to enter into close connexion with the Anglican Church and the Tories, sure ruin! And all Prussia, all Germany, all Europe would take it for granted that such a connexion was really established, even if it were not; and the supposition alone would damage us in a thousand ways; the king would lose more in the loyal attachment of his subjects than he can now afford. I hope the whole story will turn out a fable. Humboldt says the spirit of discontent, which he calls the howling mania, has largely increased here. When he left, a few were howling; but now they all howl. His sharp and witty remarks are really refreshing in our spiritless society."

Before his departure for England Humboldt called on Varnhagen to take leave. On this occasion the following entry was made in the diary, on the 14th of January, 1842: "Humboldt called to take leave,—he starts to-morrow night. He came from Count Maltzan's of whose life but little hope is left to-day. 'His death will bring Canitz here—not Buelow', said Humboldt dolefully. I comforted him with the suggestion, that Canitz too might be dropped, 'And whose turn would it then be?' 'Bunsen's.' 'That would be too frightful! But as it is, he accompanies the King on his return. That is already decided upon.' Humboldt dislikes Canitz and cannot understand how I am not more afraid of him—of this arch-aristocratic, utterly bigoted —(and consequently preposterous, nay, stupid)—fanatically anti-French Canitz, with his malicious and vulgar sneers. 'But then you are a Tory yourself!' he added. 'As to that,' I replied, 'that is still somewhat doubtful—but as for Canitz, he is honest, strict, and straightforward; he will do much, and as for the rest, business and circumstances will control him.'"

After Humboldt's return, Varnhagen writes on the 24th of February, in his diary: "Humboldt gave me some very interesting descriptions of England. At court the greatest magnificence; the mode of living, however, plain and easy; conversation unrestrained; the tone very pleasant and cheerful, even between gentlemen and ladies of adverse parties. Peel pleases him as little as ever; looks like a Dutchman; is more vain than ambitious, and narrow in his views. Lord Aberdeen is invincibly taciturn, without being able to convince people that his taciturnity covers anything worth saying. Bunsen has shown the greatest want of tact; every one is against him, except the King, who likes him better than ever." The whole visit of the King was an intrigue of Bunsen, and was so understood even by Englishmen.

"Our affairs here are the subject of much conjecture. As minister of foreign affairs the pious Arnim will, for the present, be recalled from Brussels; at some later day Canitz will be appointed,—or Bunsen, say I. Count Alvensleben is to go to Vienna; Radowitz first to Carlsruhe, until the embassy to the German Diet become vacant. Perhaps there is hardly courage enough as yet to take Bunsen and remove Buelow. Every month, however, every week must improve the courage, and then both these appointments will be done. There is no hope that Maltzan can recover; the better days have again been followed by the worse, and light gives way to renewed darkness. Sad state of things.

62.

HUMBOLDT TO VARNHAGEN.

BERLIN, MONDAY, 28th *February*, 1842.

I AM anxious to hear a few words about your health, dear friend.

I have succeeded in procuring a pension of three hundred thalers, a miserable sum, but it is only a beginning, for the impoverished but talented poet Freiligrath at Darmstadt, involving no obligation on his part, and allowing him to live out of the country. Can you lend me his poems?

A. HT.

NOTE BY VARNHAGEN.—On Tuesday Humboldt wrote me with the feuilleton of the *Journal des Debats*, in which Philarète Chasles, in the most vulgar manner, abuses the literature of Germany, and sneers at the most distinguished German authors.

And this miserable fellow has been appointed under Guizot's ministry Professeur des Langues du Nord (litt. anglaise, allemande) au College de France.

You need not return the silly, spiteful trash.

A. HT.

63.

HUMBOLDT TO VARNHAGEN.

BERLIN, 16*th March*, 1842.

BE comforted about the mishap. The King purchases Italian, but, under no circumstances whatever, French pictures. The portrait of Cherubini is, indeed, very fine, and if I remember aright, I saw it in Cherubini's own house. As the author is not dead, and Ingres very rich, I cannot conceive how the portrait can be for sale? You can tell the sprightly "Child"* that you sent me the feuilleton.

In the last number of the *Journal des Débats* there is

* Bettina von Arnim.

a strong and very fine article against the abominable Jew Bill, with which we are threatened, and against which I have already protested in very impressive words.

Ever grateful, yours,

WEDNESDAY.   A. HT.

It was intended in the preamble of the law to speak of "the miracle which God performed in preserving the Jewish race amid other nations;" "of the will of God to keep the Jewish race separated." I have replied thereto, that the bill is a violation of all the principles of a wise policy of unity; that it is a dangerous arrogance in short-sighted man to dare interpret the primeval decrees of God. The history of the dark ages ought to teach us what abnormities such doctrines lead to.

I live in apparent outward luxury, and in the enjoyment of the fanciful predilection of a generous Monarch, yet in a moral and mental seclusion, such as can only arise from the monotonous dulness of a country (a real steppe) which, though it is not wanting in erudition, is torn asunder by the opposing influences of similar "poles," and becomes more and more contracted in its Eastern proclivities. May you be content with him, who, though standing alone, has the courage to avow his own opinions.

64.

HUMBOLDT TO VARNHAGEN.

BERLIN, *March* 21st, 1842.

My dear friend, so happily restored to me! It is a source of infinite joy to me to learn, from your exquisite letter, that the really very delightful society at the Princess's has benefited you physically, and, therefore, as I should say in my criminal materialism, mentally also. Such a society, blown together chiefly from the same fashionable world of Berlin (somewhat flat and stale), immediately takes a new shape in the house of Princess Pueckler. It is like the spirit which should breathe life into the state; the material seems ennobled.

I still retain your "Christliche Glaubenslehre,"* I who long ago, in Potsdam, was so delighted with Strauss's Life of the Saviour. One learns from it, not only what he does not believe, which is less new to me, but rather what kind of things have been believed and taught by those black coats (parsons) who know how to

---

* A celebrated work on the Christian Dogma by Friedrich David Strauss.—*Tr.*

enslave mankind anew, yea, who are putting on the armor of their former adversaries. I shall gladly copy the passage concerning Spinoza. Will not the late date of the second volume of the "Glaubenslehre" (1841) be urged against it by these men who pretend to teach from ancient manuscript? It would seem to me a better plan to have published the wonderfully conflicting chronology with some remarks on the new faith in the whole "*roman historique*" of the apostolic collectors of myths. He who teaches so publicly has to subject himself to the publicity arising from the defence of those who differ from him in creed. A private statement, clothed in the mild language of complaint, makes the subsequent public one very difficult, and elicits only patronizing smiles and a denial. It is not the mishap of Spinoza, but this degradation of the noblest intellectual faculties in the service of the narrow doctrines of dark ages, that is really painful to me. The man* himself had certainly nothing attractive for me, but I had a kind of predilection for him, because everything enthrals and enraptures me, in which, as in his lecture on Art, the gentle breath of imagination warms and enlivens the harmony of lan-

---

* Humboldt refers here to *Schelling*, the philosopher, who had just received from the King of Prussia a call to Berlin, and who, in a penitent spirit, endeavored to reconcile Christianity and philosophy, thus recanting his former views. Humboldt was quite exasperated at his conduct.—*Tr.*

guage. Now we are separated. In his last speech, not the one on art, amid the glare of torchlight, he spoke of his departure like a well-paid artist who had just accomplished a musical tour—probably only a sentimental figure of speech to frighten his listeners.

Now for an answer to enquiries for the biography, of which, after all, I think with some fear, not on account of its political contents, but on account of family considerations. I rely on your promise. The man certainly cannot want to afflict so many!

Wilhelm was born in Potsdam, because his father was Royal Chamberlain, and at the same time acting Chamberlain to the Princess Elizabeth of Prussia. He left Potsdam when the Princess was sent to Stettin. My father remained in high favor with the Prince of Prussia, who visited him frequently at Tegel. This explains to you the passage in the English despatch, running thus (I believe very early in 1775? Raumer's Beitraege zur neuern Geschichte, vol. v., p. 297) :—" Hertzberg, Schulenburg could form a ministry, but those have the greatest chance of success, who, although not of the same kind, are considered favorites of the Prince. Among the first of these stands Herr von Humboldt, formerly an official in the allied army, a man of sense and fine character; Herr von Hordt, an enterprising genius. . . . ." The expression "official" is a strange mistake. My father was major and aide-de-camp to Duke

Ferdinand, of Brunswick: after long service in the Finkenstein dragoons, he was frequently sent to Frederick II., during the gloomiest period of the Seven Years' War; thus Frederick II. writes in his letters on the Wedel disaster :—" I told Humboldt everything that can be told at such a distance."—(Manuscript letters quite recently bought by the King in Eastern Prussia.)

My family comes from Northern Pomerania. My brother and I were for a long time the last of our name. My mother's maiden name was Colomb, cousin of the Princess Bluecher, and therefore niece of the old President in Aurich (Ostfriesland). She was first married to a Baron von Holwede. From this marriage sprung my step-brother Holwede, formerly in the regiment of gensdarmes. To my mother belongs the merit of having procured for us, at the instigation of old privy-councillor Kunth, a thorough education. Wilhelm, for the first years, was educated by our tutor Campe. The foundation of his profound attainments in Grecian lore was laid by Loeffler, the author of a liberal book on the New Platonism of the Fathers of the Church ; he then was a chaplain in the army, and afterwards chief ecclesiastical counsellor at Gotha. Fischer, of the Graue Kloster, instructed Wilhelm in Greek for many years ; he had, what is little known, a profound knowledge of Greek, besides that of mathematics. That Engel, Reitemeier, Dohm, and Klein lectured to us for a long time on philosophy, jurisprudence, and political science, is known to you. When at the University of Frankfurt (for six months) we lived with Loeffler, who was Professor there. In Goettingen, both of us were members (for one year) of the Philological Seminary of Heyne.

To my father belonged Tegel (formerly a hunting chateau of the great Elector, and it was consequently only a leasehold property. Wilhelm first possessed the place in fee-simple, as a manor; therefore Schinkel added to it four towers, in order to preserve the old tower erected under the great Elector). Besides this, he owned Ringenwalde, near Soldin, in the Neumark. Ringenwalde afterwards belonged to me, then to the Counts Reeden and Achim Arnim. Wilhelm, at the time of his death, possessed Tegel, Burgoerner, and Auleben (acquired by his wife, as the fiefdom of the Dacheroeden family had been abolished), Hadersleben, in the Magdeburg country, and Castle Ottmachau, in Silesia, the dotation given to him after the Paris peace.

The Sonnet I., 394, refers to a second child, I believe, which Frau von Humboldt lost when at Rome. One was buried in Paris.

I conjure you do not mention to the author anything as coming from me. He would inevitably state it in the preface, and then I should become responsible for a great many things which I dread.

Pardon the stercoran-like* loquacity.   A. Ht.

NOTE BY VARNHAGEN.—He probably had just read of the Stercoranists in Strauss's "Glaubenslehre." Hence this allusion.

65.

HUMBOLDT TO VARNHAGEN.

THURSDAY, 31*st March*, 1842.

On my return from Potsdam with the King I received the "Loa-Tseu," a work with a peculiar flavor of ante-Herodotian antiquity. Your note accompanying the Chinese philosopher impresses me painfully. I find that you have not yet received the courage arising from a consciousness of restored physical strength. That the vigor of your intellect never suffered is shown in each of your letters. I think I have not lost any of them. About a week ago I wrote you a long one of four pages about that "Christianly-dogmatising philosopher," and my reply to the inquiries of the "Biographer," who pestered me with his pietistic curiosity. Did that letter come to hand safely? It contained also much chit-chat

---

* The Stercoranists are those who believe that the Host is subject to digestion.—*Tr.*

on my brother's first erudition. You don't make any mention of my talkativeness. I trust it will not be a source of trouble to me. We have succeeded with Buelow. He may be here next Saturday. It may be the beginning of something good; or the end of it—*le bouquet*—the stage effect of foot-lights. I met with Tholuk and Bekedorff yesterday at Potsdam at dinner. No other occasion would have favored me with their *apparition*. With constant devotion yours,

A. HT.

66.

HUMBOLDT TO VARNHAGEN.

BERLIN, *April 6th*, 1842.

SINCE the inquisitorial sentence against Bruno (Bauer) has been so presumptuously published, I deem it my duty to retain your Strauss no longer. I return you that remarkable book, which caused me to indulge in much meditation. Accept my best thanks. The method of the author is excellent; it makes us acquainted with the whole history of the faith of our time, particularly so with the jesuitical trick of so many people who declare publicly their belief in and their adherence to all the dogmas of the Christian mythology, after the fashion of Schleiermacher, and after having "drained the chalice," are followed to the grave by a solemn cortege of court equipages, although in fact they had always discarded the orthodox belief and substituted for it pseudo-philosophical interpretations.

What displeases me very much in Strauss is his frivolous manner of speaking of natural sciences, which makes him accept without hesitation the formation of organism from inorganisms, and which enables him to easily believe in the origin of man as springing from the primitive sod of Chaldea. That he seems to think very little of the blue regions on the other side of the grave I might cheerfully forgive him; the more so, as we are the more agreeably and willingly surprised when we expect little. As for you, you fortunate man, it could have caused no surprise. How purely Spanish and revolting in the present inquisitorial formula was the sentence that "The culprit would *admit* himself." Neque aliud aut qui·eadem saevitia usi sunt, nisi dedecus sibi atque reges illis gloriam peperere.

I send you a copy of "Don Juan." It shows beauty of language, also a rich imagination. I am anxious to hear how you are pleased with it.

The constitutional Roi des Landes* *repeatedly* said yesterday at dinner in the presence of forty people: The professors of Goettingen had talked of their patriot-

---

* King Ernest August of Hanover.

ism in an address to him. Professors, he said, have no country at all. Professors, prostitutes, and dancers may be had every where for money; they go to the highest bidder. What a shame to call such a fellow a German Prince!

With faithful attachment, yours,   A. HT.
WEDNESDAY NIGHT.

67.

HUMBOLDT TO VARNHAGEN.

BERLIN, *April* 7*th*, 1842.

OUR unknown friend is very amiable. I have lost all apprehension. *You* have a balm for every wound. I will show you, with pleasure, the few lines, which fell, as it was intended they should, into the King's hands on the following morning. I chose that circuitous way, because it enabled me to write more freely, and to openly show my dissatisfaction. The thing is now in a better way, but it is not yet irrevocably dismissed. I must entreat you, therefore, most fervently, not to give the lines in question out of your hand. They would irrevocably be inserted in the papers, and that would seriously injure my efforts in a good and important cause.

The King sent for me at a very early hour; and his

thanking me very cordially for my frank exposition does him much honor.

I did not go to Potsdam to-day, because I wished to advocate in the full board of the Academy the election of Mr. Riess, the Jewish philosopher, as a member. His election is very honorable to the Academy. There were only three black balls.

To-morrow I shall be with the King till Sunday. I will try to hunt up some interesting autograph—something poetical (by Wilhelm von Humboldt)—for Stuttgart. All that I possess are unfortunately but *copies*.

Take care of your health, dear friend, it is not firmly restored.

Yours,   A. v. HUMBOLDT.

THURSDAY NIGHT.

68.

HUMBOLDT TO VARNHAGEN.

BERLIN, *June* 24*th*, 1842.

YOUR kind remembrance, honored and gifted friend, was very beneficial to me—the more so, as I have returned from Sans Souci rather unwell, affected by a cold; and as I am involved in all the miseries of moving into a detestable house in the Siberian ward of the city, the Oranienburger Strasse, I have not even an inkstand on my table.

At present, nothing more than my best thanks. I have told Marheineke myself how dear he is to me. A thunderstorm, in the form of a cabinet order, suddenly growling through the papers, and exhibiting a few flashes of censorial absurdities, would be preferable to that impracticable law, the assigning of a Grand Inquisitor to the liberty of the press. We have so much to say to each other, I hope to see you yet before your departure. Think only of the enlivening presence of four Crown-Princes and throne-successors—one lame in the knees, and pale; the other a drunken Icelander; the third blind, and politically raving; and the last capricious and infirm in intellect. And this is the approaching generation of the monarchical world.

Yours,   A. Ht.

I accompany the King to the Rhine. That I had no mind to become a mere color-stand at Petersburg will be understood by you. The Chancellor has always the pleasure of being the subject of vulgar recrimination on the part of those who are either not invited or refused admittance to the banquet. What an excitement glass beads, peacock plumes, and ribbons can stir up among men!* . . . .

---

* Allusion to the new order—pour le mérite.

NOTE BY VARNHAGEN.—Marheineke's article on the Anglican church in the "Jahrbuecher fuer wissenschaftliche Kritik," with a couple of censorial blunders.

On the 26th June, 1842, Varnhagen writes in his diary about the new order :—"Humboldt tells me much about the foundation of the new order. The King had at first composed a list, in which he had written the names with Sanscrit letters. This list was referred for advice to Humboldt, Eichhorn, Savigny, Thiele; then it was altered many times; new names were added and others stricken out—the indecision lasted six weeks. Originally the King had decided for forty-six members, to correspond with the number of years embraced by the reign of Frederick the Great. Afterwards he thought of adopting forty, but was afraid of doing so, on account of the 'plaisanteries' about the number 'quarante' in the French Academy; at last he limited the number to thirty. All was managed by the King in his own way. Arago was originally placed on the list by the King. He insisted upon Metternich as his particular choice. Rumohr was abandoned. Steffens was, in the opinion of the King, not deserving 'enough—neither as philosopher nor as a naturalist.' Liszt was decidedly favored by the King, and no objections could prevail. Spontini was thought of, but Savigny and the cabinet counsellor, Mueller, succeeded in displacing him. Moore was objected to as having written satirical verses on

Prussia. 'That is not at all my business,' said the King. Melloni was opposed as being a Carbonaro, and having been at the head of a revolutionary Junta. 'I do not care the least about that,' said the King. 'I would confer the order on O'Connell, if he possessed such scientific merits.' The King proposed Raumer and Ranke. Eichhorn and Savigny assented only to Ranke, and thereupon both were dropped. Notwithstanding the view taken in Melloni's, Moore's, and Arago's cases, Schlosser the historian was rejected on account of his political views (?). Metternich had railed at the 'bishopric of Jerusalem.' Now to insure the new order against the same fate, he was to be nominated a member of it—this is deemed the 'secret motive,' in Humboldt's opinion. And for Metternich's sake Uwaroff was left out, for with him the other would not have been the sole representative of his species. Link was weighed, but found wanting."

On the 27th June, 1842, Varnhagen makes the following addition to his notes of yesterday: "Humboldt told me he had informed the King in advance of the intention of the Academy of Sciences to elect Mr. Riess, a Jew, one of their members, and that the King had replied he would confirm the election unhesitatingly. 'I will hope,' he added, 'your brother has not committed the folly of writing in the by-laws a clause against Jews becoming members of the Academy?' Minister Eichhorn knew that the King would not create any difficulty in the matter, but he himself disliked it, and he thought it likely that Thiele, Rochow, Stollberg, and others, would also be displeased at it; therefore he left the application of the Academy, to have their election confirmed by the King, unattended to for six weeks, and then wrote a letter, by which he inquired of the Academy, whether they were aware that Riess was a Jew? The Academy, indignant at this inquiry, replied unanimously, that they were only ruled by the by-laws, in concurrence with which the election had taken place, and they therefore repudiated the minister's inquiry as inappropriate and impertinent. Eichhorn pocketed the insult, and reported the application to the King, who at once confirmed the election; feeling, however, a little disinclined to approve, at the present day, what Frederick the Great had refused. Frederick the Great had declined to confirm the election of Moses Mendelssohn, out of regard, as it is believed, for the Empress Catherine of Russia, who was a member of the Academy, and who was presumed to be averse to such a colleague."

On the 30th of August, 1842, Varnhagen remarks in his diary: "Humboldt tells me miserable things of Eichhorn. Talks also much of the King, his amiability, good humor, jocoseness. He thinks, however, he will not relinquish his favorite views, even when he seems to abandon them. The King was more satisfied with Count Maltzan than with any one else of his ministers; he placed full confidence in him—believed him capable of anything. We had a dispute about the signification of the word 'ingenious,' and how far it could be applied to the King. Humboldt thinks the King intends going to Greece, and to extend his journey to Jerusalem. It was to be feared, however, that the parsons would at last get control of him, and destroy his cheerfulness. Humboldt goes to Eu on business, with the King of France; then to Paris. Will be back at Berlin in December."

Varnhagen speaks of a call made by Humboldt after his return from Paris, in his diary of the 18th March, 1843, as follows: "Humboldt came to see me; he looks much older since I last saw him, but his spirit and courage are fresh. In Paris he was happy and gay; here his spirits sank at once. Things here were going on miserably, he says; the old beaten track—treating matters of dangerous character in a spirit of childish frivolity. And besides that, he is overrun with applications and requests; every one wishes to secure his influence! 'Influence!' said he; 'nobody has any! Even Bunsen and Radowitz, the King's favorites, have none. All that they are capable of is to anticipate the weak fancies of the King, and obey them. Should they attempt anything beyond this, their overthrow is certain. The *King* acts just as he pleases. He follows the impulses of his early received and firmly rooted impressions, and the advice which he may now and then think worthy of hearing, is nothing at all to him. He speaks contemptuously of Eichhorn and Savigny, as hypocritical menials, who receive the word of command from Thiele, from Gerlach, and from Hengstenberg. The King has relinquished nothing whatever of his cherished designs, and may, at any time, come out again with them, as with his designs regarding the Jews' observance of the Sabbath, the Anglican ordination of the bishops, and the new institutions of nobility, etc. He has projects which it would take a hundred years to accomplish. He contemplates immense constructions, outlaying of parks, enterprises in matters of art. There is already the question of going to Athens; in the background a pilgrimage to Jerusalem may be looming; triumphant promenades *à la* Napoleon; peaceable ones to London, to St. Petersburg, to the Orient; conquered scholars and artists, instead of countries. Love of art and imagination upon the throne, fanaticism and deceit all round, and hypocritical exaggeration in matters unworthy of attention. And with all this, the man is really ingenious, is really amiable, and inspired by the best intentions. What will come out of all this at last?"

69.

HUMBOLDT TO VARNHAGEN.

BERLIN, *April* 3d, 1842.

IF I have appeared slow in thanking you, my dear friend, for your delightful present, it is because all my leisure time at Potsdam was absorbed by the perusal of your biography, beginning with your early youth and terminating with your description of the Congress of Vienna. To have had such a development as yours is a gratifying advantage. It is instructive to follow the career of men like you and to behold them acting before our eyes.

How unjust we once were in our opinions of the men who undertook to rearrange Europe at that great Congress—I mean to say how much more did we then exact in our unjust views, while at present, on comparing the members of that Congress with the mediocre creatures of to-day, they appear great in our recollection. In their place we have now court-philosophers, missionary-devoted ladies of state ministers, court theologians, and sensation preachers......

Minister Buelow complains that you never came to see

him *en famille* between the hours of 8 and 9. He will hold his public reception to-morrow, Tuesday evening, and you would be an ornament to his circle. He never sends letters of invitation to those who know how welcome they are to him.

MONDAY.   A. V. HUMBOLDT.

70.

HUMBOLDT TO VARNHAGEN.

TUESDAY, *June* 13*th*, 1843.

EXCUSE me, dear friend, for being prevented by the absence of Reimer, by my own eternal distractions and pendulum-like movements, as well as by some little preparations for an excursion to Pomerania, from sending you the two new volumes of Wilhelm's works. I know that you are little pleased with the commentary on Hermann and Dorothea. It would have been preferable, to be sure, had he extended it into a pamphlet on epics; but you perceive even in the Kawi book how that great genius always deduced general law from special instances. The sonnets are full of grave pathos and depth of sentiment. I shall call to embrace you, and to ask you the surest way of sending a copy to Mr. Thomas Carlyle?

A. seems unreliable, and Buelow's despatches cannot be overloaded. I shall thank Mr. Carriere personally. The "fossil" minister, I am told, has given evidence of his vitality by an amiable letter to you! My life is also described " dans les biographies redigées par un homme de rien," in which I am pictured as a socially-malicious beast. Such things will not kill, nor will they improve a man either.

Always faithfully yours, A. v. Ht.

71.

BERLIN, *June 26th*, 1843.

I AM sure, dear friend, to afford you some enjoyment by communicating to you (to you *alone*) a fragment of a new volume by Eckermann. Remarkable adoration of youthful vigor as the divine source of productiveness. This is simply the adoration of an old man. Napoleonic worship unrestrained by moral considerations. I most fervently entreat you, not to show the sheet to our *child*, also not to talk with Brockhaus about what Eckermann has confided to me. It might possibly damage him, and he is already unfortunate. I am confident the two last volumes will have come to your hands through Buschmann. The weather was very favorable for our journey north. Such journeys are the best means to deceive princes regarding public opinion. I have made a little speech, out of a window, to the young men upon "The intellectual ties"—which independent of "space" beget a just interpretation of liberal ideas, and an unfading confidence in the advancement of humanity. You may read the speech in the Staats Zeitung, as I wrote it down after delivery, a necessary precaution, as my daily increasing friends would have perverted it. I read a part of "Custine" to the King. He is infinitely ingenious and magnificent in style. I have read but two volumes, and of these I prefer the first, which portrays a modern greatness of tragical events in a masterly manner.

With devotion, yours,

A. v. HUMBOLDT.

Please send me back Eckermann.

72.

HUMBOLDT TO VARNHAGEN.

TUESDAY, *June 27th,* 1843.

I AM afraid, my dear friend, that you might come to Tegel next Thursday and find nobody at home. Buelow will take leave of the King to-night and expects to start to-morrow—Wednesday—for Schlangenbad. His wife and two oldest daughters are going with him. I write this in view of the impossibility of my embracing you before your departure. The torchlight procession at Düsseldorf could shed light on many a thing. I enclose the little speech for you, as you like to preserve everything concerning your friends.

Yours,
A. HT.

73.

HUMBOLDT TO VARNHAGEN.

SANS SOUCI, *August 27th*, 1843.

How could I be, my dear friend, otherwise than alive to the duty of thanking you at once for your precious gift, and for the affectionate souvenir of one whose life is gradually vanishing? I know nothing more graceful in composition, in sympathy of conception, in elegance of language, and in appropriate scenic surroundings, than your "*Lebensbilder*," which serve at the same time as correct commentaries upon all the valuable literature of our time. How generous you are when you mention me, and even my most insignificant words! I have often followed you through the three volumes, over those beaten, but still delightful paths; but nothing pleases me more in this "sylva sylvarum" than your dignified and just remarks on the historical blunder as to the "truly Germanic" distinction of political classes, ii., p. 256–272.

You will observe that my political "ire" is still the same; that I am always very much attached to this life, having learned from you that, according to Kant's doctrine, there is not much to boast of after our dissolution. "The budding twig starting up in the regions of northern empires" (I am satirical now) has been but poorly acclimated; and I have little time to spare, having already waited fifty-three years. . . . . . . The Germans will yet have to *write* many more books on liberty.

The card-playing man—ii., p. 157—will again cause some excitement in the environs of my "hill." I believe I have discovered some "moderation," which, however, one does not like to mention. The words, "that miserable fellow," are no longer heard. You see how much I love to read your writings—and not through fear. A. v. H.

We have not yet talked of Custine's book. The first volume is an eloquent and sprightly description (of dramatic scenes), and is the best done. What a startling effect such a book must have, even on those who detest justifying themselves. "Il y a des longueurs de déclamations,"—something of rhetorical blackening, which is tiresome. I find the publication of the hypertragical letter (of Princess Trubetzkoi) very wrong. Were it not for the irritation necessarily caused by the publication of this letter, we might have looked for some salvation from a new petition. What justification is there for risking so much, even for murder? I am also disgusted by the worship of those literary trifles by Mad. de Girardin and Mad. Gay. Such worship could, perhaps, be allowed in a beautiful Grand-Duchess.

That the "Saint-Simonism" was invented by a Prussian business-man, amuses me very much. As it concerns Königsberg, I will keep it secret.

74.

HUMBOLDT TO THE PRINCE OF PRUSSIA.

BERLIN, *Dec.* 29, 1843.

YOUR ROYAL HIGHNESS:

I HAVE the honor, most humbly, to inform you that the box containing the universal siderial clock of the inventors, D. and H. v. A———, together with your gracious orders, has duly been delivered to me. I shall do in the matter what will be agreeable to you. The two officers, in a letter dated Temesvar, 13th of December, gave me notice of the arrival of the instruments, naively adding "That I should try to procure for the inventors some military decoration from His Majesty the King 'the *universal physician*,' of all arts and sciences."

To obtain, however, such a "universal panacea," from the "universal physician," the gentlemen must address his majesty a few words themselves. The so-called universal siderial clocks had much reputation in the middle ages; in the present state of astronomy, however, they are never used in observatories, where the astronomer makes the calculations himself. Such graphic inventions in that line cannot therefore be recommended as deserving reward unless the inventors address themselves in person to the monarch. These rules are observed even when books are presented, which meet with no acknowledgment unless accompanied by a letter.

Under these circumstances I hope that your Royal Highness will approve of my writing to Lieutenant H. v. A., thanking him for his confidence, and requesting him, for his own sake and that of his friend, to write some letters to his majesty the King, in which he may refer to me. To secure the delivery of the letter at Temesvar your Royal Highness will gracefully be pleased to direct it under your seal to the ambassador, General von Canitz. I shall have the box opened at the observatory in the presence of Professor Enke, and charge him, as is usual in such cases, to make a report for the private cabinet. Although the word "*ingenious*" cannot be applied to instruments the construction of which is not strictly original, I will nevertheless try to obtain, through my representations, a small dose of "the universal panacea."

In deepest devotion, I remain
  Your Royal Highness's
   most humble servant,
    A. v. HUMBOLDT.

75.

MONDAY, *Jan.* 1st, 1844.

I AM in haste to tell you, as the Potsdam train is about starting, dear friend, in spite of your incognito, that the King, previous to the soap bubbling, lead melting, and to the angelic chorus in the cathedral, and the entrance of the watchman,* received and enjoyed very

---

* The usual festivities in family circles on New Year's night in Germany.—*Tr.*

much the charming gift. It is a group full of grace and sweetness of composition; it is heaven reflected in earthly love. The King instantly guessed it to be the work of those young fairies, Bettina's cygnets, and would like to offer his thanks.

A. v. Ht.

Privatissime.—I expressed some doubts about that hieroglyph distinguishing the male swan from the female. The King thinks me, however, quite "arrièré" as to the changes which art-life has made in modern education.

NOTE BY VARNHAGEN.—Bettina von Arnim had given me a delicate and beautifully executed drawing, representing a naked girl and a naked lad standing under a tree, in the foliage of which a nightingale is singing, which she requested me to send anonymously to Mr. v. Humboldt, asking him to present it also anonymously to the King as a New Year's present. The nakedness of the male figure might indeed appear rather shocking, although it would have been pardonable in one *like Bettina*, but that the King could suppose it the work of her daughters is rather too strong, unless by this pretence he meant to convey a rallying correction to Bettina.

On the 1st of April, 1844, Varnhagen wrote in his diary: "After a long interruption, a visit from Humboldt at last. He told me all that occupies his mind. He is striving to do what he can, but this is not much, and after all, the man of seventy-four years is but a man of seventy-four. He himself refers significantly to his advanced age. His manifold duties are a heavy charge upon him, although he is reluctant to abandon them. The Court and its society are to him like a tavern of habitual resort, where one is wont to pass one's evening, and to drink one's glass. The King, says he, busies himself with nothing but his whims, and these have, for the most part, a spiritual, nay, an ecclesiastical, tendency—worshipping, building churches, concocting missions. He cares very little about earthly affairs. It seems immaterial to him whether Louis Philippe's death causes a crisis; what may happen after Metternich's death, or how Russia behaves with us. To all this he is indifferent; he scarcely thinks of it. Whoever has secured his favor and nourishes his fancies plays a sure game. Bunsen, Radowitz, and Canitz stand highest in his favor. Stollberg comes only in the second rank. Besides, there exists the greatest carelessness and distraction. Rueckert had congratulated the Queen upon her recovery, in some very beautiful stanzas. They were found delightful; but the propriety of acknowledging such an offering by a word of thanks was overlooked, until at last it occurred to the Queen. Rueckert was then sent for, but had been gone some three weeks. Schelling is received scarcely once a year by the King. Having secured him, he cares but little for him. Steffens, too, whom he likes, is seldom invited. Reumont belongs to the exceptions; he secures a small share of the favoritism of Bunsen and Count Bruehl. There is much sneering at . . . . about his dancing, &c. Humboldt said once, he was green, if not quite yellow, whereupon the King answered: 'At . . . . every one had that complexion.' Bunsen has not grown much wiser: he proposed to the King to purchase California, to send missionaries there, &c. He strongly supports the schemes of Madame von Helfert; he had a mind to send his own son with her, and to contribute £12,000 of his own means for the establishment of settlements in the East Indies (!), with the view, of course, to open a field for missionaries; he withdrew, however, his offers when he saw that the King's co-operation was doubtful. In the meantime Mrs. Helfert could not obtain more than ten thousand thalers from the King. Minister Rother succeeded in frustrating her plot; he could not help, however, sending two agents to examine and to report on the state of the possessions of Mrs. Helfert in the East Indies. It was also attempted to induce the King to take part in the colonization of Texas—always in connexion, of course, with religious interests. Humboldt had written previously to Bunsen, in strong terms, advising him to warn Eichhorn, and to point out to him the hatred which his actions awakened, and which also reflected upon the

King. When he met Bunsen here he expressed himself in the same way, arguing in forcible but fruitless language. Bunsen, who talked with him with great interest on Egypt for two hours, did not answer a word, but rose and went away. Humboldt believes him vain enough to accept a ministry. It seems to me that Humboldt is much too familiar with Bunsen, and shows him too much friendship. The Queen, says Humboldt, has no Catholic tendencies; on the contrary, she is an arch-Protestant, and even more of a fanatic than the King himself, whom she is constantly urging in this direction. She would have more influence if she better understood the management of matters.

In the evening Humboldt sent me the work: 'Russie, Allemagne et France,' par M. Fournier, Paris, 1844, with a very amiable letter, inclosing eighteen precious autographs by Arago, Metternich, Peel, Stanley, Récamier, Balzac, Prescott, Brunel, Herschel, Bresson, Helene d'Orleans, Duchesse de Dino, and four confidential good-humored notes of the King. A brilliant present!"

76.

HUMBOLDT TO VARNHAGEN.

BERLIN, *April 1st*, 1844.

I HAVE a mind, my noble friend, to impart some enjoyment to you to-night by a few insignificant gifts, accompanying the horrible Ruthenic venom beneath enclosed.* I know that I am personally flattered in all the inclosed letters with the exception of that from Solingen; but this cannot prevent my offering what may be interesting to you. You will find the following letter from

1. Lord Stanley, the present minister, to whom I had recommended the cousin of our Dieffenbach, the author of a highly commendable journey to New Zealand. This traveller was implicated in the rebellion at Frankfort, wherefore it was difficult to get him an engagement in Germany. If travelling were still a business of mine I could not desire a better companion.

2. The "Presumption" from Solingen.

---

* The work of Marc Fournier: Russie, Allemagne et France. Paris, 1844.

3. A very interesting letter of Count Bresson, the ambassador of France, dated Feb. 6, 1839.

4. A very amiable letter from Arago, when I had dedicated him the " Examen de l'histoire de la geographie du 15 Siècle." I don't recollect having given you anything else of Arago.

5. A note written by the King, at a time when he assisted me in obtaining the pardon of young " demagogues." The note refers to the prosecution of young Hoeninghaus, for whom my efforts were successful. The letter of the Crown-Prince shows a noble indignation against Kamptz and his accomplices.

6. A letter of the Duchess of Orleans.

7. A letter of the King of Denmark. Simultaneously with Arago I had recommended Hansen, the great lunar calculator at Gotha, to the King. Our petition was granted. Arago received also a very amiable autograph from "Christianus Rex," once constitutional King in Norway.

8. Another note of the Crown-Prince, good-humored and witty. He wished very much to have Metternich accept the Presidency, *pour mettre la société en bonne odeur à Rome ou elle passe pour Bunsohérétique.*

9. A letter of the Duchess de Dino, now Duchesse de Talleyrand. She has been created Duchess of Sagan lately.

10, 11. Two good-humored letters more of the King. Le *Seehund*, the recommendation of a rather rough Danish sea captain, who declared his willingness to take two naturalists around the globe at the rate of 2500 rixthalers a head (a little high). The plan was a failure. *Le Seigneur Cados, ministre Sécretaire d'Etat* of the watchmaking *Duc de Normandie*, who addressed to the Crown-Prince a complaint about the indecent manner in which he was treated by the Staats-Zeitung.

12. From Brunel, the hero of the tunnel.

13. A letter of Sir John Herschel, full of flattering expressions.

14. Mr. de Balzac.

15. Sir Robert Peel. Somebody had written me, from Oxford, that Robert Brown, the first botanist of Europe, had got suddenly into money difficulties, and that Peel, on my intercession, would grant him one of the four only pensions accorded to savans by Parliament. I recommended him and was successful.

16. Mad. Récamier. I am sure you have already several letters from her.

17. A letter from Prince Metternich, to be added to the number of those which you have already from him.

18. The illustrious American historian, Prescott. In your hands all will be safe, even what I myself would destroy from wantonness. I entreat you, dear friend,

not to tell anybody that I gave you the King's notes, however insignificant they are. It would injure me.

With old veneration, yours,

A. VON HUMBOLDT.

MONDAY EVENING.

77.

J. W. T. TO HUMBOLDT.

HÖFGEN, NEAR SOLINGEN, *March* 12*st*, 1844.

YOUR Excellency will not be offended at the liberty I take of writing you. Some time ago I read in the newspapers that somebody of Koenigsberg is said to have written you about secrets of nature, referring to photographs taken in the dark. I presume, therefore, that your Excellency is a naturalist and has friends who are likewise so. As I also have made important discoveries in secrets of nature, which my present business will not allow me to pursue, I wish to have an opportunity of speaking with you about them. Perhaps we can be useful to each other. I am perfectly willing to make the journey to Berlin, in order to see you. May it please your Excellency to write me as soon as possible at what time I can call on you at Berlin, if you have no objection to my visit.

In hope that you will favor me with an answer, I am, with due respect,

    Your Excellency's most obedient,

                      J. W. T.

Mr. Gottfried H., merchant at Berlin, can give you information, if required, as to my standing and character.

NOTE OF HUMBOLDT.—The presumption of the writer, arising from the perusal of a newspaper, that I might be a naturalist, is a fact. I am guilty of having published some books on Natural History as early as 1789.

78.

COUNT BRESSON, FRENCH AMBASSADOR, TO HUMBOLDT.

                BERLIN, *February 6th*, 1839.

DEAR EXCELLENCY,—I am happy to be able to send you to-day an article worthier of you than that of yesterday. Keep this number "*Des Débats.*" I do not file them.

The remark of Mr. M. V. L—— on the "Nescio quis *Plutarchus*" is puerile. Besides, excepting this, his article is inspired by a just appreciation of your glory, which is ours as well, and which we claim as such.

Pray, dear Excellency, receive my affectionate and respectful homage. BRESSON.

P. S.—I had just finished this note when yours of this morning reached me. I shall keep it all my life, as well for its being a true historical monument, as for the precious title of friend which you deign to give me. It is true, alas! we shall see, if God grants us life, a great many things; but may it be His will that we shall never see again events like those which have already swept over our country, by sapping the power of the King. Yet the Coalition works in this direction with all its might. It is a fit of madness which reminds me of 1791. These plotters are Girondists in embryo, whom we would have loved; and they will be the first to be buried under the ruins of the edifice which they are undermining.

Does it, then, require a great effort of reasoning to perceive that the King is the cementer of all things, that he keeps us out of chaos, and that upon his living or dying the state of affairs wholly depends? Let us ask conscientiously, does our danger to-day come from him? Shall an order of things, acquired with so much trouble, established with so much labor—shall it be sacrificed to the renown of a few men, or to the vain theories inapplicable to France, serviceable at the best only in England, where they are consecrated by age, and, what is still better, administered by the enlightened upper classes. D., who is a man of sound intellect, writes me that he believes in the happy issue of the ministerial crisis. Mr. Molé has changed his determination not to resume office; he will do so if there is a majority of thirty-six or forty votes secured to him. The Jacqueminot party, which is rendering great service, is working for this.

Here are the adieux, the last ones of Mr. de Talleyrand at Fontainebleau, on the 2d of June, 1838: "Adieu, my dear Bresson, stay at Berlin as long as you can; you are well off there; do not try to be better off. There will be much commotion in the world; you are young; you will see it." I quote these words for you, because they agree with the spirit of your note, for which I thank you once more, and which will become a family title to me.

NOTE BY HUMBOLDT.—*Letter of Count Bresson, French Ambassador at Berlin.*—I kept it on account of the few words of Talleyrand. I had written to Mr. Bresson that the situation of France was very serious, that I still believed in peace, because, besides the wisdom of the rulers, there was an expectant treatment of want of energy and timid prudence. That these things, however, could act only for a limited time, and that those who were young, like him, would see in action what was now spreading its deep roots, as the unconscious and inarticulate desires of the nations.

79.

ARAGO TO HUMBOLDT.

PARIS, *August* 19*th*, 1834.

MY DEAR FRIEND—I cannot find words to tell you* how sorry I am at having caused you a moment's annoyance. Be persuaded, then, once for all, that whatever wrongs, real or apparent, you may have experienced at my hands, you will never suffer that of my forgetting how good you have always been to me. The friendship which makes me so happy and proud, and which I have shown to you, shall never be surpassed by yours for me. I wanted, on the occasion of your kindly dedication, to give a public evidence of my friendship, but various circumstances arising out of my position, just now so very difficult and complicated, prevented. I hope, however, that it is only delayed.

I am sorry to learn that your health is not satisfactory. Mine is very bad; but I care little about it. All that I daily see in this vile world of meanness, servility, and low passion, makes me look with indifference

---

* Arago uses *thou* and *thee* in his letter to Humboldt—the evidence of great friendship and intimacy.

on the events with which men are mostly pre-occupied. The only news that could at present cure me of my spleen, would be that you were coming to Paris. Why have I not found a single word of hope in your letter—even for a distant future?

The scientific world here is in a dead calm. Everything has a desponding look. I am going to-morrow to England with Mr. Pentland. Shall I come back with more comforting notions?

Our observatory is elegant, and very commodious. The Ministry decided that a director must be appointed, and I was chosen unanimously. I have under my orders four or five youths, who have the title of assistants, and a salary of 2,000 francs. Under this arrangement, we shall try to achieve something out of the beaten track.

Adieu, my dear and excellent friend. Mathieu, who has not yet entirely recovered from a severe disease in his eyes, charges me, as does his wife also, to recommend him to your remembrance.

Always yours through life,

ARAGO.

80.

FOUR NOTES OF FREDERICK WILLIAM THE FOURTH TO HUMBOLDT.

I.

23D DECEMBER, 1836 (*at Night*).

THE quasi nameless number* may expect the mildest of sentences. It will, doubtless, be commuted to six months, and three years' incapacity to hold office. You may therefore send some comfort, at least as a Christmas present, to the faithful Crefeld. *Perhaps* ! ! ? ! ! I shall succeed in procuring the full pardon of this list. It is, however, revolting and horrible to let the poor boy languish so long in a loathsome hole. Leaving the respectability of his parents out of the question, had they been fools or knaves, it could *scarcely* be excused. Shall we see each other to-night ?

FR. W.

II.

CHERISSIME HUMBOLDT, you are acquainted with all

---

* Humboldt had supplicated for a politically-prosecuted young man, who is alluded to under that designation.—*Tr.*

the pretenders to all the crowns. Please read the inclosed letter, and inform me who the *Seigneur Cados* may be—who were his father, mother, and ancestors, and also what are his titles to the crown of France, which I shall certainly try to procure for him?

FREDERIC GUILLAUME, Pr. Royal.

B. 21 *Feb.*, 1839.

III.

EPISODE from "The Marriage of Figaro."
Il y manque quelque chose.
Quoi?—
Le cachet.

Don't overlook the nice allusion, dearest friend! Your seal must help me out of nearly as great a difficulty as that of Countess Almaviva; otherwise the Prince would perceive that I have read all the flattering things which you have so ill-advisedly! said of me. *Pour vous divertir*, I inclose my letter. *Vale.*

FR. W.

B., 23 *March*, 1840.

(*In Humboldt's handwriting.*)—Autograph of the Prince-Royal of Prussia.—The Prince offered to Prince Metternich the chair as President of the Archæological Institute at Rome. I was called upon to write a letter to Prince Metternich, which the Prince Royal wanted to inclose in his own. As it contained some praises of the Prince, he desired to have it sealed.

HUMBOLDT.

I was honest and stupid enough not to take a copy of the letter of the King to Prince Metternich.

IV.

I COMMUNICATE you the inclosed despatch from Copenhagen, to inform you of the new "Seccatura," which will wait upon you in the shape of a sea-dog of the Sound, to ask your advice, and assistance as to a voyage around the globe. This letter having no further object, I pray God, Monsieur le Baron de Humboldt, to keep you in his holy and especial care.

Given at our Palace at Potsdam, 29th April, 1849 (1843?), near midnight.

Signed, FREDERIC GUILLAUME.

NOTE OF VARNAHGEN.—Every word exactly as above—to be understood as a joke.

81.

KING CHRISTIAN VIII. OF DENMARK TO HUMBOLDT.

COPENHAGEN, *May 3d,* 1843.

MONSIEUR LE BARON DE HUMBOLDT:

THE letter which you addressed me the day before you left Paris has called my attention to the lunar tables, for which science is indebted to the labors of Professor Hansen. I have applied to our illustrious astronomer Schumacher, in order to learn what will be still necessary to complete this important subject. By following his advice it was easy to procure everything necessary for the continuation of the labors, the comparing of the observations, and when the necessary expenses are once apportioned and allowed, Schumacher expects to be enabled to publish the lunar tables before the expiration of two years. A recompense for efforts devoted to the sciences will no doubt be found in the advancement of science itself; but the approbation of distinguished savans gives us a veritable satisfaction, and we rejoice the more in it when it comes from a man so far superior to others. Always anxious to deserve your approbation, Monsieur le Baron, I wish to be guided by your intelligence, and I shall be happy to be acquainted with the results of your scientific observations, whenever you please to address them to me.

With the highest consideration, I am, Monsieur le Baron, your well-affectionate,

CHRISTIAN R.

82.

JOHN HERSCHEL TO HUMBOLDT.

COLLINGWOOD, 21st *Dec.* 1843.
HAWKHURST, KENT.

MY DEAR BARON:

IT is now a considerable time since I received your valued and most interesting work on Central Asia, which I should have long ago acknowledged, but that I was unwilling, and indeed unable, in proper terms to thank you for so flattering and pleasing a mark of your attention, till I had made myself at least in some degree acquainted with the contents. This, however, the continued pressure of occupations which leave me little time and liberty for reading has not yet allowed me to do otherwise than partially—and, in fact, it is a work of such close research that I despair of ever being able fully to master all its details. In consequence I have hitherto limited myself chiefly to the climatological researches in the third volume, and especially to the memoir on the causes of the flexures of the isothermal lines, which I have read with the greatest interest and which appear to me to contain by far the most complete and masterly coup-d'œil of that important subject which I have ever met with. In reading this and other parts of your work on this subject, and of the "Physique du globe" in all its departments—that which strikes me with astonishment is the perfect familiarity and freshness of recollection of every detail, which seems to confer on you in some degree the attribute of ubiquity on the surface of this our planet—so vividly present does the picture of its various regions seem to be in your imagination, and so completely do you succeed in making it so to that of your readers.

The account of the auriferous and platiniferous deposits in the Ural and the zone in 56 lat. has also very much interested me, as well as the curious facts respecting the distribution of the Grecian germs in those regions. I could not forbear translating and sending to the "Athenæum" (the best of our literary and scientific periodicals) the singular account of the "monstre" of Taschkow Targanka—(citing of course your work as the source of the history)—in vol. III. p. 597.

The idea of availing ourselves of the information contained in the works of Chinese geographers, for the purpose of improving our geographical knowledge of Central Asia, appears to me as happy as it is likely to prove fertile; especially now that the literature of that singular country is becoming more accessible daily by the importation of Chinese books. What you have stated respecting the magnetic chariots and hodometers of the Emperor Tching-wang—if you can entirely rely on your authority—gives a far higher idea of the ancient civilization of China than any other fact which has yet been produced.

In a word, I must congratulate you on the appearance of this work, as on another great achievement; and if—as fame reports—it is only the forerunner of another on the early discovery of America, it is only another proof that your funds are inexhaustible! May you have many years of health and strength granted you to pour them forth; and may each succeeding contribution to our knowledge afford yourself as much delight in its production as it is sure to do your readers in its perusal.

Miss Gibson writes word that you have more than once enquired of her when my Cape observations will appear. No one can regret more than myself the delay which has taken place, but it has been unavoidable, as I have had every part of the reduction to execute myself, and the construction of the various catalogues, charts, and minute details of every kind consume a world of time, quite disproportioned to their apparent extent. However, I have great hopes of being able to get a considerable portion, in the course of the next year, into the printer's hands. Some of the nebulæ are already in course of engraving. Perhaps the subject which has given me most trouble is that of the photometric estimation of the magnitudes of Southern stars and their companions with the Northern ones. A curious fact respecting one of them—7 Argus—has been communicated to me from a correspondent in India (Mr. Mackay), viz.: that it has again made a further, great, and sudden step forward in the scale of magnitude (you may perhaps remember that in 1837–8, it suddenly increased from 2.1 m to equal α Centauri). In March, 1843, according to Mr. Mackay, it was equal to Canopus. "α Crucis," he says, "looked quite dim beside it." When I first observed it at the Cape it was very decidedly inferior to α Crucis.

Believe me, my dear Sir, ever yours, most truly,
J. F. W. HERSCHEL.

I must not forget to wish you a "merry Christmas and many happy returns of the season" in English fashion.

83.

BALZAC TO HUMBOLDT.

Berlin, Hotel de la Russie, 1843.

Monsieur Le Baron:—May I hope on my arrival in Potsdam, next Monday, by the 11 o'clock train, to have the honor of seeing you, for the purpose of presenting my respects.

I am merely passing through this city, and you will therefore excuse the liberty I take in announcing the time of my visit. May I hope that you will receive it as a proof of my ardent desire to add some new recollections to those of the "Salon de Gérard."

Should I be so unfortunate as to miss seeing you, this little note will assure you at least of my desire to recall your remembrance of me otherwise than by a card. Be kind enough, then, Monsieur le Baron, to accept the assurance of my most respectful admiration of

Your most humble and obedient Servant,

DE BALZAC.

84.

ROBERT PEEL TO HUMBOLDT.

WHITEHALL, *Sept. 4th*, 1843.

DEAR BARON DE HUMBOLDT:

I was much flattered by your kind attention in transmitting for my acceptance your most interesting work on Central Asia. It will be much prized by me, as well on account of its intrinsic value as a token of your personal regard and esteem.

There is no privilege of official power the exercise of which gives me greater satisfaction than that of occasionally bestowing a mark of Royal favor and public gratitude on men distinguished by scientific attainments and by services rendered to the cause of knowledge.

From the very limited means which Parliament has placed at the disposal of this Court, it has been my good fortune to be enabled to recognise the merit of Mr. Robert Brown. I have just conveyed to him the intimation that Her Majesty has been pleased to confer upon him for his life a pension on the Civil List of two hundred pounds per annum, in recognition of his eminent acquirements as a botanist, and of the value of his contributions to the store of botanical knowledge.

Believe me, dear Baron de Humboldt, with sincere esteem, Very faithfully yours,

ROBERT PEEL.

85.

METTERNICH TO HUMBOLDT.

VIENNA, *October,* 1843.

MY DEAR BARON :

You were kind enough to present me a copy of your "*Asie Centrale.*" I call it *your* because discoveries lawfully belong to those who make them, and because it is often better to make a discovery than to become the possessor of its results.

I have begun the perusal of the work, which is among those to which I look for mental relaxation, just as minds differently constituted from mine are apt to have recourse to light and futile productions. This is really the case. I often feel the necessity of some relief from my monotonous duties, and it is then that I seek fresh elements of life and vigor in works of profound learning. A book, therefore, like yours, is to me a source of the richest enjoyment. I learn, and I love to learn, and I feel no jealousy of your great erudition.

What I most admire in your work is "the method." You understand tracing a line without ever losing sight of it, and therefore you arrive safely at the end— which is not always the good fortune of those who start well enough upon the road. Please send me the volumes complete—I shall receive them with gratitude.

I pray you, dear Baron, accept the assurance of my highest consideration and old attachment,

METTERNICH.

86.

PRESCOTT TO HUMBOLDT.

BOSTON, Dec. 23d, 1843.

SIR—A book on which I have been engaged for some years, the History of the Conquest of Mexico, is now published in this country, as it was some few weeks since in England; and I have the pleasure to request your acceptance of a copy which sails for that purpose from New York in January. Although the main subject of the work is the conquest by the Spaniards, I have devoted half a volume to a view of the Aztec civilisation; and as in this shadowy field I have been very often guided by the light of your researches, I feel especially indebted to you, and am most desirous that the manner in which my own investigation is conducted may receive your approbation. It will indeed be one of the best and most satisfactory results of my labors.

As I have been supplied with a large body of unpublished and original documents for the Peruvian conquest, I shall occupy myself with this immediately. But I feel a great want at the outset of your friendly hand to aid me. For although your great work—the *Atlas Pittoresque*—sheds much light on scattered points, yet as your *Voyage aux régions equinoxiales* stops short of Peru, I shall have to grope my way along through the greater part without the master's hand, which, in the *Nouvelle Espagne*, led me on so securely.

The Peruvian subject will, I think, occupy less time and space than the Mexican, and when it is finished I propose to devote myself to a history of the Reign of Philip the Second. For this last I have been long amassing materials, and a learned Spaniard has explored for me the various collections, public and private, in England, Belgium, France, and is now at work for me in Spain. In Ranke's excellent history: "*Fürsten und Völker von Süd-Europa,*" I find an enumeration of several important MSS., chiefly Venetian relations, of which I am very desirous to obtain copies. They are for the most part in the Royal Library of Berlin, and some few in that of Gotha. I have written to our Minister, Mr. Wheaton, to request him to make some arrangements, if he can, for my effecting this. The liberal principles on which literary institutions are conducted in Prussia, and the facilities given to men of letters, together with the known courtesy of the German character, lead me to anticipate no obstacles to the execution of my desires. Should there be any, however, you will confer great favor on me by giving your countenance to my applications.

I trust this will not appear too presumptuous a request on my part. Although I have not the honor of being personally known to you, yet the kind messages I have received from you, and lately through Professor Tellkampf, convince me that my former publication was not unwelcome to you, and that you may feel an interest in my future historical labours.

I pray you, my dear Sir, to accept the assurance of the very high respect with which I have the honor to be

        Your very obedient servant,
                WM. H. PRESCOTT.

87.

MADAME DE RÉCAMIER TO HUMBOLDT.

PARIS, *July* 28*th*, 1843.

I FIND no words, dear Sir, to tell you how deeply your letter has affected me. You have spared me the horror of suddenly learning through the papers the painful and unexpected news. Although very much afflicted and suffering I will not lose a moment in expressing my thanks. You are aware, dear Sir, that I had not seen for many years the Prince Augustus. I received, however, continually, evidences of his remembrance. It was at the most unhappy time of his life that I made his acquaintance at Madame de Staël's, where he encountered so much generous sympathy. Alas! of that brilliant and spirited circle at the Chateau Coppet, he was the only survivor. There now remains to me no other souvenir of my youth and my past than the beautiful "tableau de Corinne," the noble and affecting sentiments of which have cheered and adorned my retirement. I have not the courage, Sir, to prolong this letter, and to answer the interesting details with which yours concludes. Allow me to speak to-day only of my sorrow, of my gratitude, and my admiration.

J. RÉCAMIER.

88.

HUMBOLDT TO VARNHAGEN.

August 31*st*, 1844.

I trust that the following autographs will prove welcome to you:—(A) Bettina under the indictment; (B) two copies of my very brief speech; (C) two letters of Spontini, with strange allusions to PrinceWittgenstein, Count Redern, full of hatred against Meyerbeer, together with my earnest reply to it; (D) a letter of Gay-Lussac, when he was so dangerously injured by an explosion; (E) a very humane letter of the Grand Duke of Tuscany.

Always respectfully yours,

A. v. Humboldt.

Saturday Night.

89.

LEOPOLD, GRAND-DUKE OF TUSCANY, TO HUMBOLDT.

Florence, *July* 20*th*, 1844.

Dearest Count :

The Professor of Botany, Philip Parlatore, is about to

leave for Berlin, and I cannot resist charging him with a letter to you, dear Count, expressive of my thanks for the recommendations whereby you have enriched Tuscany with several illustrious men.

You (the father and patron of natural science) knew Mr. Parlatore, and your good opinion was sufficient to secure him the appointment at Florence, where he is now the Botanic Director of the Museum, and President of the Botanic Central Institute, which owes its existence to him.

Another professor of physics was recommended by you, Professor Matteucci. He is a true investigator of nature. Not only leading science, he constructs instruments for its interrogation, and is on the road to important discoveries. He is now on a little excursion to recuperate his strength after his too fatiguing labors. I do not know that he will be fortunate enough to meet you, for whom he feels so much veneration and gratitude. Our University of Pisa has brought together all that is distinguished in physical science—and the fruits are maturing.

At Florence the practical studies in the grand hospital contribute greatly towards keeping medicine and surgery in the legitimate direction of natural science, supported by observation and experience. The congress of the "Amateurs of Science in Italy" will also produce desirable results. Such meetings, politically inoffensive as they always are, make science accessible to a great many persons, and establish useful connexions between men of great merit who might otherwise remain unacquainted.

We were told some time ago that you intended descending into Italy. This would have afforded us the utmost happiness, and you would have been received as the true protector of natural science.

Believe me always yours,   LEOPOLD.

90.

HUMBOLDT TO VARNHAGEN.

2d September, 1844.

IF Dr. Prutz, at Halle, in his obnoxious "Moritz," had said nothing more than what he puts in the mouth of the clown (page 40), who, speaking of the people, "One should give them two morsels, so that they may wag their tails and crawl back into their cold kennels;" and at page 53, the poetically fine lines "I conjure you, ye future monarchs," one would understand how that wonderful drama, in which Moritz contrives to plunge all his friends into the water that he may have the pleasure simply of fishing them out, dead or alive, but at any rate, cold and wet, could produce an *excitement* at the present time.* Peruse the manuscript, dear friend, and send it back to-morrow, Tuesday, before two o'clock. The steps which I intend taking will, however, be unsuccessful. The proceeds of its representation might, with propriety, be given to the inundated, and thus the police might become a hydraulic power, or even a drying machine. Yours,

MONDAY. A. HT.

91.

HUMBOLDT TO VARNHAGEN.

BERLIN, *September 6th,* 1844.

I UNDERSTAND as well as you do, my dear friend, that the speech† in question must necessarily have produced a great sensation and excitement in our "north," as well as under the sluggish Pole. *He* really excels in flowery eloquence. The figures which he presents are hardly new; but a certain delicacy of expression, and a

---

* Humboldt refers here to a patriotic drama of Robert Prutz, "Moritz von Sachsen," the representation of which was forbidden by the Berlin police.—*Tr.*

† Of the King, at the inauguration of the Provincial States.

nice perception of the "harmonious" in oratory, cannot be denied him. There is really something noble in the passion for speaking, upon every occasion, to thousands of people. His generosity in sheltering "*high officials under the veil of the royal purple*" will be but indifferently acknowledged. Does he, by this course, deliver over to our assaults those small fry who obscure the day? I am sorry that such a highly-gifted prince, acting under the most benevolent incentives, and preserving the full vigor of his mind, which constantly urges him to action, is, in spite of his good intentions, absolutely deceived as to the direction in which the state is impelled. When Parry, with a number of Esquimaux dogs, had started for the North Pole, dogs and sledge were continually driven *forward*. When, however, the sun broke through the mist, so that the latitude could be taken, it was ascertained that the expedition had unwittingly been carried *backward* several degrees. A floating field of ice, drifting in a southerly current, was the surface on which they seemed to advance. Our ministers are the drifting, icy surface. And may not the current be "the dogmatische Missions-Philosophie?" A. v. Ht.

It is now certain that the Empress (of Russia) will not come. The King will, on the 15th, be in Sans Souci.

92.

HUMBOLDT TO VARNHAGEN.

BERLIN, *Sept.* 13*th*, 1844.

I MUST be in a few moments at the Stettin depôt to meet the King, who arrives at 9 o'clock. Thence I go for a few days to Sans Souci, where I shall, unfortunately, celebrate my seventy-fifth birth-day. I say unfortunately, because in 1789 I believed that the world would have solved more problems than it has done. It is true that I have seen a great deal; but very little, indeed, in proportion to my exactions.

I have no time to-day to write you about your charming description of your sojourn in Paris in 1810. My good sense led me at once to that page, from which I could inhale the perfume of your friendship. I have learned that I have not yet grown insensible to praise. What a magnificently anti-Scythian spirit the University of Breslau has evinced! How inventive men become under political oppression! Nothing but rope-ladders, loop-holes, disguises to get out into the open air. And when once there, how really German they are in their speculations, as to whether they have improved their position. It is with them as with the Prince—"Tell me whether I am amusing myself."

Yours,
A. v. Ht.

We insert here an entry in Varnhagen's diary, dated June 26, 1844, reciting two sharp repartees of Humboldt. At the Royal table at Sans Souci, some time ago, Humboldt shot two well-directed arrows from his bow. The conversation turned on some Russian ordinance, and Humboldt, in speaking of it, mentioned repeatedly the Minister of Public Instruction. "You have mistaken, sir," said the King. "It was not the Minister of Public Instruction who acted in this matter, but the Minister of Enlightenment." Humboldt, not in the least discountenanced, hastened to reply, "Very well, Sire; then it was not the Minister of Public Instruction, but of its opposite," and continued his conversation in his usual way.

The following anecdote is still neater: General Leopold von Gerlach, who is fond of badinage, attempted an attack upon Humboldt some time ago, saying to him, "Your Excellency frequently goes to church, 'now-a-days,' do you not?" He hoped to perplex him with the question. Humboldt, however, coolly replied, "Your 'now-a-days' is very kind of you. You allude, undoubtedly, to my adopting the only road which, at present, could lead to my promotion." The bantering hypocrite was dumb.

An entry of a later date (26th December, 1848), speaks of the animosities to which Humboldt was subjected in still stronger terms. "Humboldt has called; He remained longer than an hour. He assures me that were it not for his position at Court, he would not be suffered to remain in the country, but would be expelled, so strong is the hatred of the ultras and bigots against him. It can hardly be described; however, they endeavor to discredit him with the King. In other parts of Germany they would still less endure him, were he once divested of the prestige of his position."

93.

HUMBOLDT TO VARNHAGEN.

BERLIN, *September 19th,* 1844.

CAN you command courage enough, dear friend, to devote a few moments to a conversation on the present state of French literature? I take the liberty to introduce Mr. Jousserandot of Franche Comté, a French novel-writer. He possesses much beard and much good-natured vivacity. He is the son of a wealthy physician, and was recommended me from Paris. Excuse the importunity, but you must sometimes take your share of the annoyance of being gazed at.

A. v. HUMBOLDT.
THURSDAY.

94.

HUMBOLDT TO VARNHAGEN.

BERLIN, TUESDAY, *June 3d*, 1845.
One o'clock, A. M.

ALL the mysteries were solved to-night, dearest friend. I received this afternoon from the department of Foreign Affairs, where they were stored up, fourteen parcels pell-mell, misdirected there from Paris and dating from December to May. The first thing we perceived was your handwriting; the parcel was duly directed and contained, well secured under your seal, your important political letter and a parcel for Comtesse d'Agoult, which I remit with the present. I am quite innocent of what has happened.

In the Rhine and Moselle Gazette, No. 122 of the 29th of May, I am judged guilty of Voltairianism, denial of all revelations, of conspiring with Marheineke, Bruno Bauer, Feuerbach, nay even of the expedition against

Luzerne—ipsissimis verbis—and all that on account of my Kosmos, page 381. The King had already been told that my book was the work of a demagogue and an infidel. Whereupon the King wrote me, that he could but say what Alfons said to Tasso:

> "And so I hold it in my hand at last
> And call it *mine*, if I may use that word!"

This is poetical and very civil.

With the sincerest gratitude, yours,

A. v. HUMBOLDT.

95.

HUMBOLDT TO VARNHAGEN.

BERLIN, WEDNESDAY, *June 4th*, 1845.

I RECOGNISED at once from the gracefulness of style the guardian spirit of my feeble literary efforts. I had not yet seen the precious sheet, containing, in addition, the interpretations by Neander. I avail myself of the last moment before breaking up, to write you a preliminary word of sincerest thanks for one of the most interesting life sketches—for which we are indebted to your brilliant and vivifying pen. You have represented with dignity and magnificence a subject, which popular enthusiasm out of mere perverseness has repeatedly degraded in burlesque prose. Your exquisite art of purifying is highly gratifying.

If Süssmilch will graciously permit, I shall try to accomplish my Kosmos. It is, however, true after all, that at the gates of many a temple of science (History of the World, Geology, Mechanics of the Heavens) black spectres menacingly defend the entrance.

Indeed Madame von Hormayr is a very charming lady.

With constant devotion and love, yours,

A. HUMBOLDT.

96.

BERLIN, *June 16th*, 1845.

I AVAIL myself of the few moments allotted me before going to the railroad station, dear friend, to thank you heartily for your characteristic biography of "Hans von Held." I have read but one half of it, and that immediately after having read your "Life of Bluecher." It is, therefore, but natural that I was filled with admiration. How fortunate you are in coloring all the details of military life in the one, and in describing the civil efforts of a people struggling for liberty, in the other book. The fatalistic word "fortunate," however, is out of place here, because the secret of such successes lies in the clearness of intellect and the intensity of your feelings. The whole world, as it is at present, is reflected in your "Held." Zerboni's letter on the bloody tragedy in the streets of Breslau, is as eloquently written as it is heart-rending. Such things, however, can't deter our dull, fanatical, white-livered Polignacs. They will attempt to confirm the first deed of violence and brutality by subsequent ones more systematically devised—and all this under the reign of such a King! I am very angry and deeply affected.

MONDAY MORNING.   A. v. HUMBOLDT.

As I shall have no time for reading during my hasty journey, I have left the instructive book for a few days to Buelow's, at Tegel.

97.

HUMBOLDT TO VARNHAGEN.

BERLIN, THURSDAY, *September 4th,* 1845.

I AVAIL myself of the first moments of my return from Potsdam to joyfully congratulate you on the good effect of the waters on your health. On account of the domestic misfortunes of my family, my participation in the dull and rain-spoiled Court festivities at Bruehl and Stolzenfels was a hard trial for me. I will acquaint Madame von Buelow to-morrow with your hearty sympathy. Buelow's recovery progresses rapidly. Except some weakness of memory, which, however, does not appear for whole days, no change of mind is perceptible; relaxation, however, retirement, and tranquillity of mind are still necessary. Always conscious of what he owes to his character he resigns. You know, my noble friend, that he demanded his dismissal when Itzstein was violently expelled from Prussia. Public affairs are now in a much worse condition. Buelow's retirement from office is a sad event; but the current of affairs in Northern Germany is too strong to be arrested by the effort of one individual.

Please inform Professor Fichte that although I am already an unworthy Doctor of Philosophy, I will gratefully accept anything which may be offered me from Wurtemberg's high-spirited Universities.

Yours affectionately,

A. v. HUMBOLDT.

I enclose to your safe-keeping a beautiful letter of Prince Metternich, on whom I had called on the Johannisberg; a letter from Lord Stanley, the Minister; and two letters from Jules Janin and Spontini; also a book for the Countess of Stolberg.

98.

METTERNICH TO HUMBOLDT.

VIENNA, *June* 21*st*, 1845.

MY DEAR BARON:

ENCLOSED you will find my vote for the future colleague. I expect that you will not look for my assistance beyond the sphere of my principles; but my principles are so strongly influenced by a recommendation from you, that the request and the grant are but one. I have perused your Kosmos and have treated it as is my habit with rich collections. The impression made on me by the work will be best described by the avowal that it caused in my mind two conflicting, or if you like better, two mutually neutralizing sentiments—one of satisfaction at knowing so much, and one of regret at my great ignorance. These sentiments, however, sink into nothingness when compared with the admiration of *that knowledge* which alone can have enabled you to accomplish that gigantic enterprise. Knowledge alone, however, would not suffice—and hence I am led to acknowledge the full merit of the author—his great power of representation and his method! You have applied and dignified in your work the old word *discipline*, in its relation to science. Would to God, that the true meaning of this word could, in political society, also recover its eternal rights. If my own impressions are of but little value, it is different with those of the men of science. Their judgment is overflowing with admiration, and I agree with them in the conviction, that *you alone* of all living men could achieve the task, and that the word Kosmos is the true and appropriate title of your work.

I told you, that I have *perused* the first volume of your work, I am now *studying* it, and I wish to thank you for the really delightful hours, which you have opened to me. I call all these hours delightful which I can snatch from the uninviting field of political disturbances, and devote to the natural sciences.

Accept, dear Humboldt, the renewed assurance of my sincere and well-known consideration.

METTERNICH.

99.

JULES JANIN TO HUMBOLDT.

STAR HOTEL AT BONN,
SUNDAY EVENING, *August* 10*th*, 1845.

DEAR SIR,—I beg and entreat you to do an impossible thing for me. You are the kindest friend of the literary men of my country, and you have always been the most indulgent of men to me. Please listen, therefore, to my request. I left Paris a week ago for the express purpose of transmitting to the "Journal des Débats" a faithful record of the journey of her Majesty the Queen of England along the banks of the Rhine. Before leaving, I had the honor of paying my respects to the King at Neuilly, and of securing his approval of my design. Monsieur Guizot also strongly encouraged me by saying, that hospitality required that an honest and conscientious writer should follow the royal party, and faithfully chronicle these wonderful rambles, which are now interesting and delighting the whole of Europe.

Monsieur Guizot gave me, at the same time, letters of introduction and instructions, of which I am proud. The letters are all honorable to me, and my instructions are worthy of the man who gave them.

Now, dear sir, assist me. What I wish is, not a presentation to his Majesty, your King, but an admission into the royal circle. Unobserved by all, I myself shall see everything, and thus be able to fulfil the mission with which I have been honored.

You see that it is the imperious passion, the passion of a feuilletonist, which actuates me. It is true I have no title. But, if one be necessary, you can say that I am the Lieutenant-Colonel of a Legion (militia), that I shall appear in a brilliant uniform; and further, that it is but proper that the writers whom the King invites to his table, and whom he so greatly honors on so momentous an occasion, should furnish a report of its chief features, as an authority to which future historians of the time may refer.

I am writing, dear sir, under the best auspices— under the auspices of Mr. Meyerbeer. You will make him very happy, I am sure, and with him the whole "Journal des Débats," which is so much devoted to you, and, in addition, your very humble servant, myself.

I shall await with great impatience, but with the most perfect submission, your kind reply.

I am sure that, in any event, you will have done all that you honorably could do, to secure me this favor.

Please accept, Monsieur le Baron, the humble homage of my devotion and of my profound respect.

JULES JANIN.

100.

HUMBOLDT TO VARNHAGEN.

POTSDAM, 26*th of September*, 1845.

(To his dear friend, the Privy Councillor von Varnhagen.)

KINGS AND REPUBLICS.

Por lo que desio la conversacion de los Reyes desio la conversacion de ellos dentro de los limites permitidos. Un grave consejero dixò al Rey Don Phelipe II., viendo que iva en diversas ocasiones al poder absoluto: Señor, reconoced á Dios en la tierra como en el cielo, por que ne se cause de las monarquias, suave govierno si los Reyes suavemente usan de él.—*Cartas de Antonio Perez, p.* 545.

At the time of the insurrection of the Netherlands there had already been raised the question, " Whether the Kings were going off." I translate the passage from Antonio Perez for you. He says: It is because I desire the preservation of monarchs that I advise them to remain in the limits prescribed for them. A wise Counsellor said to the King Philip II., being aware of his tendency to absolute power: " Sire, recognise the supremacy of God on earth as well as in Heaven, so that God may not become tired of monarchies—a very excellent sort of government, if it be used with moderation."

El Dios de cielo es delicado mucho en suffrir compañero en ninguna cosa y se pica del abuso del poder humano. Si Dios se causa de las monarchias, dara otra forma al mundo.

The God of Heaven is very jealous about admitting a co-partner in anything whatsoever: He is offended by every abuse of human power. Should God once be tired of monarchies, he will give another form to the political world.

A. HUMBOLDT.

101.

HUMBOLDT TO VARNHAGEN.

POTSDAM, *October 2d*, 1845.

THE curious little note containing the prophecy "that God would become tired of kings," was lying for many days on my desk, awaiting my delivering it to you, in person, my dearest friend. Whenever anything worth reading falls into my hands during the late hours of my solitary study in the chateau here, I always think of you. As I have hitherto been prevented by my efforts to arrange the manner of Buelow's discharge from calling on you, I have thought best to send you, dear friend, the little sheet, under envelope. My reason for quoting this prophecy is, the general state of public affairs, which provokes my highest indignation. Every day discloses something worse. The future looks gloomy and menacing, the greatest carelessness prevails.

I have just returned from Tegel, where the Buelows would be very happy to see you. They beg especially that you will gratify them next winter by frequent calls at their town residence.

In the " Westminster Review" a certain Dr. Cross says, the style of Kosmos is lengthened, and very indifferent; the frequent reflection on sentiment was deemed very superfluous by English savans—such a book did not contain any thing new. Then follows the denunciation of Atheism, although " creation" and the " created world" are never lost sight of in the book. And did I not, only eight months ago, in the French translation, say, in the plainest terms :—It is this necessity of things, this occult but permanent connexion, this periodical return in the progress, development of formation, phenomena, and events, which constitute *Nature* submissive to a controlling power. *Physics*, as the name itself implies, can only deduce the phenomena of the physical world from the properties of matter; the highest aim of experimental science is therefore to ascend to the existence of the laws, and progressively to generalise the same. Whatever lies beyond is no object for *physical demonstration*, it belongs to another order of *more elevated* speculations. Immanuel Kant, one of the few philosophers whom no one has yet accused of impiety, has, with rare sagacity, indicated the limits of physical explanation in his renowned *Essai sur la Théorie et la Construction des Cieux*. Koenigsberg, 1755.

The conduct of the aldermen is very praiseworthy. It is a pleasure, and a miracle at the same time, to encounter such a degree of public spirit among men differing so much in intellect and culture of mind. It is hatred concentrated against the same object, but it only appears so on the outside.

I confess that I am wrong to have not yet answered so excellent a man as the author of "The Religious Poetry of the Jews in Spain." I first wanted to read the book, and the terror of having reached the age of seventy-six years on the 14th of September, has plunged me so deeply in my "Kosmos," that duties otherwise sacred to me have been neglected. I shall call personally on Mr. Sachs, and beg you to excuse me to him in advance; as to justifying myself, that is out of the question.

Most respectfully, yours,
A. v. Humboldt.

The sketch on Hormayr, which, in a political view, stops very singularly at 1808, is very interesting. What a mass of writings! one hundred and fifty volumes.

102.

HUMBOLDT TO VARNHAGEN.

BERLIN, *October 2d,* 1845.

I would not like, my dear friend, that a friend of Thiers, whom he has warmly recommended to me, should leave Berlin without having had the pleasure of seeing you. Mr. Thomas, one of the editors of the "Revue des deux Mondes," is the author of a most remarkable work on the ancient provincial constitutions of France, compiled from archives. I recommend him to your indulgence.

Yours, in great haste, A. v. HUMBOLDT.

103.

HUMBOLDT TO VARNHAGEN.

BERLIN, *Nov. 30th,* 1845.

ALL gifts, tendered through a hand like yours, are of double value to me, my dear friend. I have immediately replied to that high-gifted lady, the Countess. You are quite right in saying that her beautiful poetry evinces an admirable familiarity of the mind with the subject.

I deem it more delicate to write to Baron Hormayr rather than to his lady. May I beg to enclose my little note, provided you approve its form? I have long had a predilection for this liberal-minded man. His literary activity is astounding. I shall have the pleasure of calling on Mr. Sachs to-day. I shall also present his book to the King myself; this is, however, a time in which no impression is permanent. All things dissolve into mere visions, which will, however, reappear, ominous and deformed, by being joined to old fancies. I am much afraid of the consequence produced by incentives, from which I had hoped to produce happier results. How has it happened that Kosmos is so popular beyond expectation? It seems to me that it must be attributed to the imagination of the reader, which invests it with additional features, or to the pliability of our (German) language which renders it so easy to describe every object intelligibly, and to picture it in words.

I will come and thank you, my generous friend, for the light you have thrown on the moral and intellectual merits of Voltaire.* Your revelations are delightful;

---

* Voltaire at Francfort-on-the-Main in 1753, by K. A. Varnhagen von Ense.

but "Duncker-Freitag," the recruiting officer, the sentinel, and the humorously excited suspicion of what was attempted at night with Madame Denis, are and will always produce an uneasiness.

With old attachment, yours,

A. v. HT.

SUNDAY.

I shall not forget Mr. Breul the merchant. Minister Buelow was very sorry that you missed him. You will be very agreeable to him and Lady Buelow any evening from half-past seven to nine o'clock.

104.

HUMBOLDT TO VARNHAGEN.

THURSDAY, *January 15th*, 1846.

MR. MILNES, and what he may have said of the King, "who showed him no personal civilities," interest me but little; but it will afford me great joy if my earnest intercession for Prutz be at last useful to him. This miserable trifle is the only thing that I can secure in my position. I shall die, however, in the conscientious belief, that to my last moment I never *abandoned* one devoted to the same principles as myself. Your approbation is *highly* valuable to me, my dear friend!

The "Quarterly Review" says I had a prolix style, and am never able to write one page of "vivid expression."

With faithful attachment, yours,
A. v. Humboldt.

Please excuse, like a philosopher, the writing on this mutilated sheet. I am in such a hurry that I have mistaken the address.

105.

HUMBOLDT TO VARNHAGEN.

Berlin, January 25th, 1846.

After an official feeding, at court, of the "knights of the peace," whose unworthy chancellor I am—after some sorrowful hours at Buelow's, whose state becomes every day more precarious—after a ball at the Chateau, from which I am just returned, I cannot seek repose without sending you my preliminary thanks for your ecclesiastical gifts. I am delighted at the review of a poetical period, the precursor of a nobler one—or, to speak more correctly, of one more pregnant with life. I will, however, turn away from the long "Ode of Grief," from "The Blue and the Black Eyes," from

"Besser's Merry Wig," and recur with new pleasure to your "Zinzendorf." This is a grand, well-executed life-sketch, a figure towering above all other things, which, in a different direction, attract the interest of our time. *Your* "Zinzendorf" was also constantly admired by my brother. How much the interest is enhanced by all that we see or rather expect to see! But where, among the intellectual "glaciers" of the present time, are those who could compare themselves with Zinzendorf, Lavater, and Stilling? . . . .

Most gratefully yours,   A. HUMBOLDT.

SATURDAY NIGHT.

I told Ranke to-day, very frankly, how much I was disgusted at what he presumptuously did at a meeting of the Academy, when I was not present, against Preuss, a much nobler character than he is. Have you not received yet the journals, in which I am immoderately praised and reproved ("North-British Review" and "Quarterly Review)? In Germany, my prose is frequently blamed as being too poetical; but the "Quarterly Review" finds it languishing, lifeless, and "not a vivid description." How differently different nations feel!

106.

HUMBOLDT TO VARNHAGEN.

Berlin, *February* 7*th*, 1846.

Yesterday afternoon poor Buelow was released from his sufferings. Thursday night, at eleven o'clock, on going to bed, he fell lifeless into the arms of his servant. An apoplexy! He closed his eyes never to open them again. In the morning a hundred and forty pulses were counted; bleeding had no effect. His end was, as lately his life was, unconscious. The family is deeply affected; the event, however, is beneficial. His excellent wife would have been sacrificed. Next Tuesday morning we will carry him, without pageantry, to Tegel, and bury him under the column of the "Statue of Hope." Under the pressure of business, caused by this event, and in the midst of letters which I have still to write to Guizot, Metternich, and Aberdeen, I can only briefly reply to the heartfelt letter of Madame von Arnim. I have but little hope, that the *old* folks now reigning at Weimar will appoint either Prutz or Fallersleben. I had formerly thought of Guhrauer, for whom you will also have some predilection to be sure. You know how happy I would have been if Prutz were appointed. I am not personally acquainted with Fallersleben. The whole passage, however, in the "*Wochenstube*,"* alluding to the King and to me, must be changed. It is based on a false rumor. I never have shown the book to the King, and I never applied to the King to quash the indictment, as he is always rather irritated against Prutz, on account of the old cousin from Kulmbach.† It was Minister Bodelschwingh who showed it to the King. On this Minister Prutz had personally made a very favorable impression, which it was easy to improve. Prutz had applied to have the indictment quashed, and besides he would hardly have been found guilty on all the counts. It was thought advisable, as he made the first advances to the Government, not to rebut him. The passage "that our King should be asked," must also be discarded, as it would give offence to the Grand Duchess, who likes to show her independence of Prussia at every opportunity. So she protected, not long ago, the Chancellor Mueller, when the Court of Weimar was diplomatically reproached for allowing a journal here prohibited to be read in a reading-room at Weimar. The Court of Weimar replied

---

* Die "Politische" Wochenstube by Robert Prutz, a satire on Schelling and his philosophy.—*Tr.*

† The cousin referred to is Margrave Albrecht, of Brandenburg, who, in Prutz's drama, "Moritz von Sachsen," is represented as a "Robber Knight."—*Tr.*

with dignity. But that Prutz or Fallersleben could be appointed seems highly improbable to me. Credat Judæus Apella. Excuse to-day my confused writing, dear friend!

Yours,

SATURDAY. A. v. HT.

107.

HUMBOLDT TO VARNHAGEN.

BERLIN, *Feb.* 20*th*, 1846.

Do you guess, my dear friend, who sent me this strange article? Do you guess anything from the seal and the name on the envelope, "M.?" Is that the author, and to what journal may the article belong? Profound, of enlarged political views, it certainly is not. The passage on p. 8 is underscored by the author himself, and it contains a contradiction! Prussia is to have unity in an American confederacy. His remarks, p. 3, on Frederick II. and on his works, and on "Kant a guillotine," p. 5, are as Minister Thiele would write them. I am indignant at both. The author knows all the news, all the names, all the gossip, of the "Eckensheher,"* and is touched by the liberalism of Bodelschwingh, p. 14, who

---

* Curbstone Guard.—*Tr.*

still defends every day the expulsion of the Baden Representatives. He does not dare to name Eichhorn with censure. The last line only is grand and fine.

With unalterable devotion,
Yours,

FRIDAY. A. v. HUMBOLDT.

108.

HUMBOLDT TO VARNHAGEN.

BERLIN, *March* 29*th*, 1846.

I have only time to tell you, that I shall certainly be in Sans Souci from June to September, and to thank you, noble friend, from my heart, for the kind manner in which you allude to the Agamemnon of my brother. To choose maliciously 16 verses out of 1700!! I once complained that they would not perform the drama in a royal palace in my brother's translation! As the *Staats Zeitung* is seen every evening by the King, they thought it well to malign the production there. The very next day I answered in the *Spenersche Zeitung* mildly, because the well-informed but unpoetical Dr. Franz is now seeking an increase of his pension. I myself took care that the King did not see my answer; at least, he did not talk to me about it. Send back the little sheet. I am at work, not without success, I believe, at the Kosmos, but in a sad mood respecting the public cause. Your news from England is very interesting.

With the most cordial friendship,
Yours,

SUNDAY.   A. v. HUMBOLDT.

109.

HUMBOLDT TO VARNHAGEN.

BERLIN, *March 30th*, 1846.

I SEND you again some autographs of little import, ten in number, of Villemain, Bessel, Victor Hugo, Rueckert (of whom you have plenty of autographs), Manzoni (full of praise for me, but in bad style), Thiers, Widow of Lucien Bonaparte, three billets de matin of the Duchesse d'Orléans. I add to these fugitive sheets a letter from me to the King, which I beseech and implore you not to show to any one, and to *send back to-morrow*, because I might have use for it. You shall have the letter afterwards. It sometimes happens that the King, instead of a billet de matin, writes his answer on my letter. This happened yesterday. The ministers who would gladly permit the "Turnen,*" throw suspicion on Prof. Massman, whom the King likes very much, and whom he wants to keep here. My letter will show you at least, that I openly say, how the tide of evil is bearing down all things before it, and how we are depriving ourselves of the means of action.

With my old attachment, yours,
A. v. HUMBOLDT.

110.

HUMBOLDT TO FRIEDRICH WILHELM IV.

As early as eight o'clock this morning I sent to the Koethener Strasse, to have an interview with Professor Massmann, after the confiding communications of your Majesty, concerning the decision of his situation. He has just gone, leaving me again with an excellent impression of his solidity, clear perceptions, and enthusiastic vigor for influencing our youth (the indelible, primæval, self-restoring institution of mankind). To be afraid of every enthusiastic energy is to take from the life of a State its nourishing, preserving power. Pro-

---

* Gymnastic Exercises.—Tr.

fessor M. did not see Minister von Bodelschwingh for two years, but the Minister then treated him very kindly, and Massmann desires very much, without intruding, to give a candid answer to every question. In view of the noble and frank character of Minister von Bodelschwingh I have great hopes of the result of such a conversation, and therefore I have to beg of your Majesty, most submissively, to communicate to me, whether, according to the orders of your Majesty, the Minister will send for Professor M., or whether he may go to the Minister on his own account, not called for, but animated by some words of your Majesty. I wonder how it could be forgotten how much Massmann has done for the poetry of the Hohenstaufen times, and how talented a lecturer he was at the University. I find praised in Gervinus Geschichte der Deutschen Litteratur: Massmann's Denkmaeler Deutscher Sprache, 1828; his Gedichte des Zwoelften Jahrhunderts, his Legenden and Ritterliche Poesie. How could a man be dangerous to youth whom the King of Bavaria appointed for the education of his princes, and by whom above all others the Crown-Prince declares himself to have been animated with the love of culture and intellectual freedom, and the true appreciation of his impending kingly duties? We live not in a sad, but in an earnest time. All action and energy are paralysed, if backbiting is permitted to deprive us of our most useful men. Enthusiastically attached to your person, to the splendor of your reign, and to the glory of our country, it makes me sad to see the most noble purposes in danger of being misunderstood. No doubt there are very honorable men who, from pure love of your Majesty, would like to see me also under the column at Tegel, or at least on the other side of the Rhine.

In grateful submission,

Your Royal Majesty's most faithful

HUMBOLDT.

BERLIN, *March* 29, 1846.

The King wrote on the fly-leaf:

My warmest thanks, dearest Humboldt. M. Bodelschwingh will send for Massmann.

In all haste, as ever.

Your faithful F. W.

ALEXANDER V. HUMBOLDT, Present.

111.

BESSEL TO HUMBOLDT.

KOENIGSBERG, *Feb.* 12*th*, 1846.

I HEAR with great regret that your Excellency has to mourn the loss of Herr von Buelow. Although I had not the pleasure of knowing the late Baron personally, I was not unacquainted with the true affection of the uncle for his nephew, and I heard frequent mention of the enthusiastic manner in which it was reciprocated. Moreover, I knew his repute as that of a noble, talented, clear-sighted man. Would that I could indite words of consolation, such as I heard them, at the time of my great loss!—but it is not given to every one to speak them. That time heals our bleeding wounds, the wounds which at first seemed mortal, I myself have experienced; that death after a *short* suffering is preferable to death after a *long* one, is a truth which impresses itself often on my mind!

The chancellor, Herr von Wegnern, communicated to me on the 27th ult. the letter which he received from your Excellency. This letter contains the first news I received since Nov. 7th, of last year, respecting the portrait by which our most gracious monarch intended to gratify a poor invalid: that your letter was extremely gratifying and consoling to me, is natural. It created the first ray of hope; it has unceasingly occupied me; it even gave rise to some kind of superstition, and I attributed my good health the whole month of December to the vivid hopes it had raised. This prospect of the restoration of my health, I thought, gave me hope of being able to indulge for a longer period in the pleasure which the dear picture of the " most highly revered one, affords me. I, however, do not indulge in the hope of this restoration," since I find my own experience as frequently opposed to as in harmony with that of others, and the result of my reflections on this obscure subject, is simply this, that it is one of the innumerable questions, which are beyond the veil that separates us both from the great secrets of our own nature, and from those which nature in general interposes between first causes and perceptible phenomena. I did, however, excuse the rising superstition by recalling the indisputable truth, that vivid agreeable effects on the mind or soul react upon the body; but why did the reaction not endure in my case? Be this as it may, it is a fact that the portrait of the King always moved before my eyes during my restless nights; I hoped every day would bring me news of it. I perfectly understand that a care for the well-being of millions of subjects, equally dear to the heart of the monarch, rules the ruler himself and compels him to abandon, under the pressure of the moment, the arrangement of a succession of innumerable interests centring in him; I also fully understand that the King, although he is no more unmindful of the honors he intends bestowing than of those he has already awarded, has not been able to fix the exact moment of conferring the intended benefit upon me. I also know beyond all doubt, that I am standing upon a mine which may at any time explode, and that to-day has no power over to-morrow. I have, therefore, thought best to conceal entirely within my own breast the hope of possessing the dearest of pictures, and to betray nothing, even to my wife and daughters, until further news of the actual approach of the hoped-for object shall render me as secure in the certainty as the case permits. I have the utmost horror against the propagation of anything the truth of which may be subjected to doubts by succeeding events; knowing from sad experience that it may not be sustained by the next moment, for which falsehood and misrepresentation are greedily lying in wait. I fear that the premature spreading of such news, moreover, may imply a sort of coercion (sit venia verbo) on the King. These reflections imposed profound silence on me. But when the letter of your Excellency to Herr von Wegnern spread the news without my co-operation, and when the realization of my hopes seemed near, this compulsory silence terminated, and I actually revelled in the idea of its possession. Next day, the 28th of January, I put down on paper the testamentary provision, which disposes of the picture after my death. I consider it the common property of our country, not only on account of its fundamental object, that of alleviating the sufferings of the sick man, but also for other reasons. I therefore do not leave it to my family; but in consequence of long and careful considerations, up to January 27th, to my native town of Minden, so that the highest military and civil functionaries of the province, together with the Mayor of the town, may decide further on the place and manner of its keeping. Moreover, on the 28th of January, I entered upon the execution of other plans relative to the fulfilment of my hopes, which entertained me in various ways during these last months. In order to receive the portrait of the "most highly revered" in a becoming manner, it is necessary to put the place where I shall keep it into the best state at my command. I have, therefore, condemned the present furniture and ornaments of my two rooms, and ordered new ones, as luxurious and tasteful (for a professor, of course) as I could decide upon. The directions for their manufacture were sent immediately, and with the opening of the navigation in spring I shall have everything I want. I shall blame no one who thinks me foolish in prosecuting plans for embellishing my residence at a moment when my leaving it for ever seems so highly probable. But if I delayed, the prospect of the arrival of the royal portrait would depress, instead of elevating me joyfully, as it does now, above much suffering. If I enjoy the sight of the picture even one day only, I shall pass through a fleeting, indeed, but beautiful "frontier scenery"—from this life into the other! One thing yet I shall add before I cease annoying your Excellency, by narrating the consequences following the invaluable expected gift of the most high Master. Mr. Chancellor von Wegnern has asked Professor Simson to express to me his wish to insert a notice of the picture in the papers. But I opposed it, partly for reasons stated above, and partly because such a notice would certainly be more appropriate after the receipt of the picture. In case I should be unable to write any more after its arrival, Simson knows what are to be the contents of the notice according to my wish.

Could I but once behold the fine appearance now presented of the comet of Biela! At our place, on the 11th of January, Wichman could observe nothing, perhaps, or probably on account of the little clearness of the sky at that time; but on the 15th he saw distinctly both heads of the comet. On the following day he described to me orally what he had seen; but I did not get a clear idea of it, and was, on the contrary, of opinion, that what he called a second head of the comet, is an accumulation of nebulæ, as other comets too had shown at a greater or smaller distance from the real head. I asked of him to make for me, when it appeared again, a diagram of it, as accurate as possible. The state of the sky and the position of the comet, which was often very low, delayed the making of a diagram and measurement till the 26th of January. Since that time the second head of the comet has been traced as faithfully as possible. Our observations are the earliest of those known; since, they have directed their attention to it everywhere, and have measured it; there will become known, in spite of the bad season, a fine series of observations, which may, as I hope, permit us to draw reliable conclusions. As now developed, forces of polarity, I believe, must be recognised in it. The further developments will, I hope, enable us to advance beyond superficial conjectures like these.

The observations of the new planet can be made here so excellently by the heliometer, which is quite invaluable for this purpose, that their accuracy far surpasses that of the best meridian observations; of course its greatest usefulness will only be attained when the stars of comparison are equally well determined in their position. To this determination, then, the power of the meridian observations is directed about the planet itself. Dr. Busch, following my counsel, does not trouble himself. I have also requested Encke and Schuhmacher to assist in determining the positions of the stars. The former has already received from here a series of excellent observations, as a foundation for his calculation of the orbit, and he will soon receive the continuation of them. It is very fortunate that I have arranged my extensive investigations on the exact reduction of observations by my heliometer, and that these are published in the first volume of my "Astronomische Untersuchungen." Without them, Wichmann would be unable to reduce them with exactness, as I can do nothing now, and the observations of the planet would thereby lose much of their interest, which exists only in the first period of observation, and therefore only when the observations are calculated immediately. I hope, that by proceeding on this basis, Encke's calculations will acquire certainty, which will prove itself up to a few seconds at the reappearance of the planet.

At last an end of this!

In accustomed reverence to the end of life,
Your Excellency's most obedient
F. W. BESSEL.

NOTE BY HUMBOLDT.—The last letter but one which I received from the great and noble man.

112.

VICTOR HUGO TO HUMBOLDT.

MARCH 20*th*, 1845.

You have been kind enough, my Lord Baron, and illustrious colleague, to promise your acceptance of a copy of "Notre Dame de Paris," and the further good office of offering it in my name to your august Sovereign, my sympathy with and admiration for whom are well known to you. To "Notre Dame de Paris" I add my solemn discourse before the Academy. It would make me happy to think that it gave you a little pleasure to receive this mark of my high and profound regard.

Yours,   VICTOR HUGO.

113.

FRIEDRICH RUECKERT TO HUMBOLDT.

BERLIN, *March*, 1846.

I HAD the misfortune of twice missing your Excellency when I called to give you my thanks for your great kindness, and at the same time to bid you a hearty farewell, as to-morrow I hasten to my rustic solitude. May God grant you many felicitous hours for the happy completion of your great work, for which I now am more heartily anxious than for any work of my own. For it is the monument of honor for Germany, her representative work before the nations of Europe; and I, as a German, feel proud that you did not write it in French. I would also ask your leave to introduce to you my eldest son, who is private tutor at the university of Jena; now, he may try his luck himself with you, as bearer of this letter. Finally, I beg of you that you will speak in my behalf with their Majesties, whom it was not my fortune to see this winter. May I yet be permitted to work something worthy of their approbation and of yours; but may you also be persuaded that it is not for me to appear in person before the public of the capital, but to shape my thoughts in the solitude and quiet of rural life, whither I am now permitted to withdraw, grateful for the highest favor of his Majesty, and with the purest reverence for you.

RUECKERT.

114.

ALEXANDER MANZONI TO HUMBOLDT.
(FROM THE FRENCH.)

MILAN, Dec. 6th, 1844.

MONSIEUR LE BARON:

I WOULD not have hesitated to express my confidence in an august and perfect goodness; but, instead of a becoming confidence, it would have been an unpardonable presumption on my part to have dared to foresee under what ingeniously amiable form this goodness would deign to manifest itself. I have thus a second time acquired the precious right (I had almost been made to forget that it is a sacred duty), to beg your

Excellency to lay at the feet of your noble sovereign the humble tribute of a gratitude which has become, if possible, more lively and more grateful. And at the risk of appearing indiscreet, I cannot refrain from availing myself of this opportunity to renew the respectful homage of the devotion which, as a dweller on this earth, and under this title, *nihil humani a me alienum putans*, I have long entertained. This homage would cease to be pure, and would thus lose its unique value if it involved the slightest sacrifice of my Catholic conscience, that is to say, of that which is the soul of my conscience. But, thank God, such is not the case; for, amid the character and the sign of the high destiny which I salute from afar, with a respectful joy, it is my privilege to admire and to love the development of the most excellent work of justice, which is the liberty of doing good.

My admiration for you, M. le Baron, if even it did not content itself with being the simple echo of so great a reputation, ought not to surprise you; for if, as I am daily told, there is not a learned man who has not something to learn from you, there are few unlearned men whom you have not taught something. In this connexion, and at the risk of abusing your indulgence, I cannot conceal from you my hope to have a memento of Humboldt—a memento less precious, no doubt, than those which I owe to his good-will, but which will also have its value. My fellow-citizen, Count Alexander Lito Modignani, in a journey made by him, entirely under your guidance, in North America, sought out, in the mountain of Quindia, the magnificent Ceroxylus at the season of the ripeness of their fruit, possessed himself of one, and was kind enough, on his return, to divide with me the seeds he gathered from it. Planted last spring, not one has yet sprung up; but on visiting them lately, I found them entirely sound, and in two of them a trace of vegetation was perceptible at the base. I should be happy, and even a little proud, to possess a memento, and that, I believe, a very rare one, of a people at once ancient and new, whom you have subjected to the victorious sway of science.

It is with the most profound respect, and, permit me to add, with that affection always so naturally entertained for a great man, and which it gives such pleasure to express, that I have the honor to be your Excellency's most humble and most obedient servant,

ALEXANDER MANZONI.

NOTE BY HUMBOLDT.—Written to A. Humboldt on the occasion of a refusal to accept the class of peace of the order *pour le merite*. I had been commissioned to write to him, that it was not to interfere with his liberty in any degree, that he was never to wear the cross, but that a name so great and so beautiful as his must needs continue to grace the list of the knights.

115.

THIERS TO HUMBOLDT.
(FROM THE FRENCH.)

PARIS, *August*, 1845.

SIR,—I take the liberty of introducing a young Frenchman, full of talents, of acquirements, and of thirst for knowledge. He desires to become acquainted with Germany, and Berlin in particular. I thought I could not direct him better than to the illustrious who does the honors of Berlin to strangers. Permit me to recommend him in a very special manner. Mr. Thomas is my particular friend, and the friend of all your friends of Paris. Be pleased to receive in advance all my thanks for the reception you will kindly accord him, and to receive the assurance of my attachment and of my high consideration.

A. THIERS.

116.

THE PRINCESS OF CANINO, LUCIEN BONAPARTE'S WIDOW, TO HUMBOLDT.

PARIS, *May*, 1845.

I SEND you, M. le Baron, a copy of my refutation of M. Thiers, in regard to the passages of that historian which assail the memory of my husband. The esteem which you bore him, as well as that of your dear brother and your estimable sister-in-law, both, to me, of sweet and noble memory, leads me to hope that you will receive with interest this token of all the sentiments I possess for you, M. le Baron, and in which I beg you to believe me. Yours affectionately,

THE PRINCESS OF CANINO,
Widow Bonaparte Lucien.

117.

DUCHESS HELENE D'ORLEANS TO HUMBOLDT.

TUILERIES, *Feb.* 12*th*, 1845.

I WILL not longer hold the treasure intrusted to my keeping, which was a source of great joy to me. Receive once more my sincerest thanks for this communication, and let me hope soon to find new material for thanks. You see, selfishness is unpardonably predominant in my character.

Your Excellency's affectionate
HELENE.

118.

DUCHESS HELENE D'ORLEANS TO HUMBOLDT.

NEUILLY, *May* 12*th*, 1845.

YOUR Excellency must suffer me often to claim your services; but to-day I come to ask something great of you. I wish for myself and for my cousin of Weimar the instructive pleasure of visiting Versailles in your society; our plan is to go there on Thursday. For the evening, the King invites you for dinner and theatre in Trianon. If you have the courage to share our altered pilgrimage, I invite your Excellency to be here in Neuilly, Thursday, half-past 11, to accompany us on our journey. But if other occupations should prevent you from going, I ask an *open confession*.

I beg your Excellency to receive the expression of my sincerest esteem,

HELENE.

119.

DUCHESS HELENE D'ORLEANS TO HUMBOLDT.

WINTER OF 1845.

I HAD not the satisfaction to bid adieu to your Excellency, and to repeat to you my thanks for your excellent work; permit me to do it now in writing, whilst I send to you the lines for my beloved cousin, and receive once more the expression of the most heartfelt wish to greet again your Excellency, after a short interval, on French soil.

With most sincere esteem, your Excellency's affectionate HELENE.

120.

HUMBOLDT TO VARNHAGEN.

POTSDAM, *April* 22*d*, 1846.

IT has afforded me a great relief being permitted to read before you, and while very much of the warm and friendly praises expressed by you are of course to be ascribed to the kindness of heart which prompts you to give pleasure to an old man, still there is a large margin for the unalloyed gratification of my love of approbation. The main object of my efforts is that of *composition* in the precise sense of the word, the command of large masses of matter compounded with care and with an accurate knowledge of details. The management of our beautiful, pliant, harmonious, and drastic tongue is but a secondary consideration. I shall certainly find an opportunity of availing myself of your excellent advice for Flemming and Mad. de Sevigné. Seneca also, though I consider him a little bombastic (Quaest. natur.) I have taken home with me for perusal.

Now for the special purpose of these lines. The King said to me on going to bed yesterday, "Let Bettina know that she may make her mind easy in regard to the leading person.* No one ever thought of giving him up to the Russians." "You should write her to that effect yourself," said I. "Yes, I hope to do so," was the answer. He spoke very kindly of Bettina.

With my old attachment, yours,

A. v. HUMBOLDT.

WEDNESDAY.

How sad is this eighth attack upon the King! Strange

* Microslawski.

that ministers and cabinet councillors are never shot at! Such events are the more unpleasant, the more the probabilities or improbabilities of their recurrence baffle all attempts at calculation.

121.

HUMBOLDT TO VARNHAGEN.

POTSDAM, *May* 18*th*, 1846.

I SEND you, dear friend, to be added to your collection, a very remarkable letter from Prince Metternich, with a semi-theological conclusion, full of mind and rhetorical fervor, with a slight dread of pantheism at the close of the letter.

With unaltered friendship, yours,

A. v. HUMBOLDT.

122.

METTERNICH TO HUMBOLDT.
(From the French.)

VIENNA, *May* 10, 1846.

MY DEAR BARON—Inclosed is my vote.* I give it in good conscience, and absolve you from the crime of that

---

* NOTE BY HUMBOLDT.—The Prince voted for Mr. Hermann, of Leipzig.

electioneering to which the world is addicted. The King and his Chancellor are the sound appreciators of scientific merit, and I know how to designate the place which belongs to me in the avenue of science, and which, to my great regret, is far from the sanctuary.

What I have just told you, my dear Baron, is neither gasconade nor an excess of modesty; it is the unvarnished history of my life. You do not know this history, and I will relate it to you in a few words.

At the age at which life takes its direction, I contracted an inclination for the exact and natural sciences which I would permit myself to describe as irresistible, and a disgust for practical life which I would call unconquerable, if I had not overcome both this disgust and this inclination. It is fate that disposes of individuals, and their qualities as well as their defects decide upon their careers. Fate has separated me from the object of my choice, and has thrust me upon the road I should not have chosen. Once started, I submitted without losing sight of the goal of my wishes, and the result was that what I should have wished to regard as the aim of my life has become only the solace of it. The King has set the mark of a learned man upon me. I know to whom this is to be attributed. If it is a question of the heart, the King is not mistaken.

What you tell me of the forthcoming second volume of Cosmos, makes me look forward to the study of it with impatience; you are not to be read, you must be studied, and the place of a pupil suits me exactly. No one is more called upon than I am to do justice to your remark relative to the influence exercised by Christianity on the natural sciences,* as upon mankind in general and hence upon all science, for that remark has long since dawned upon my mind. It is correct in all respects, and its generating cause is simple as are all other truths, those which are, as well as those which are not understood, for the latter circumstance has no effect on the substance of a truth. Error leads to error, as truth is the guide to truth. As long as the mind remained in error in the sphere of thought which is the most elevated of all those attainable by the human mind, this deplorable state of things could not fail to react upon every quarter of the moral compass upon all intellectual and social questions, and to oppose to their development in the right direction, an insurmountable obstacle. *The good news* once told, the position could not but change. It was not by bestowing divine honor on *effects* that they could be traced to the fountain head of truth; the investigation continued to be confined to the abstract speculations of the philosophers, and to the rhapsodies of poets. The *cause* once laid bare, the hearts

---

* NOTE BY HUMBOLDT.—I had spoken of the intensity of the love of nature. I had compared St. Basil with Bernardin de St. Pierre.

A. HT.

of men were comforted, and their minds opened to conviction. Nevertheless, the latter still remained for a long time shrouded in the mists of pagan scepticism, until at last scholastic philosophy was unhorsed by experimental science. Do you admit the force of my reasoning? If you do, I have no doubt you will share my fears that true scientific progress is in danger of being checked by too ambitious spirits, who desire to rise from the effects to the cause, and who finding the approach cut off by the impassable barriers which God has set upon human intelligence, and finding themselves unable to advance, roll back upon themselves, and relapse into the stupidity of paganism, in seeking the cause in the effect!

The world, my dear Baron, is in a dangerous position. The social body is in fermentation. You would do me a great favor if you could teach me the nature of this fermentation, whether it is spirituous, acid, or putrid? I greatly fear that the *verdict* will be for the last-named of these kinds, and it is not I who could teach you that these products are hardly beneficial.

Be pleased to accept the thanks of my household for your friendly memento, and the assurance of the continuance of my old attachment.

METTERNICH.

123.

HUMBOLDT TO VARNHAGEN.

BERLIN, *May* 30*th*, 1846.

PERHAPS, my dear friend, it will not be without some interest to you to possess a copy of the poem of the Crown Prince of Bavaria. The language is less crude than *that of* Walhalla; and some passages show a good deal of feeling, if but little poetical fervor.

Yours,
A. v. HUMBOLDT.

SATURDAY.

124.

HUMBOLDT TO VARNHAGEN.

POTSDAM, *November* 14*th*, 1846.

WHAT a splendid reception, my dear friend, have you given the fifth volume of my brother! Pardon me if, in the excessive bustle of the last few days upon the cold "historic hill," I have not written some commendatory remarks. I also deplore the omissions to which you are kind enough to make me attentive. Perhaps they could be supplied in the next volume. It was supposed that the letters must be printed in the form in which my brother had prepared them for publication, and in which they were offered for sale. I believe no nation on earth can produce an instance of such a life devoted exclusively to the increase of the wealth of ideas! How inexpressibly I rejoice in the mere prospect of once more beholding a master-piece of your accurate, life-like, and withal delicate representations of social and diplomatic occurrences!

With unalterable attachment,
Your grateful
A. HUMBOLDT.

While it was not entirely wise in a monarch who is great in history to have yielded, under the influence of the atmosphere of Versailles, to the temptation of offsetting the memory of the barricades with a spectacle à la Louis XIV., throwing great difficulties in the way of the successor, and attaining nothing of value, the conduct of Palmerston, and of Albert and Victoria, on the other hand, is likewise clumsily ill-mannered. Meantime, the sober Americans are establishing a universal empire in the West, which already threatens the trade of China.

My MS. "On the Textile Fabrics of the Ancients," pp. 106 and 113, appears also to have been lost among the papers of the lamented Wolf. The effect of the religious music, particularly on p. 323, contains much that is finely expressed.

In the year 1846 we find the following remark in Varnhagen's diary: "The conversation turned upon the capacity of one of the younger princes, which was declared to be inferior. Humboldt was of a different opinion. 'I do not agree with you,' he said; 'the young prince spoke to me the other day, finding me in waiting in the apartments of his mother, and asked, "Who are you?" "Humboldt is my name," said I. "And what are you?" "A chamberlain to his Majesty the King." "Is that all?" said the prince, curtly, turning on his heel. Is not that a proof of intelligence?'"

125.

HUMBOLDT TO VARNHAGEN.

BERLIN, *November 28th,* 1846.

I DO not answer to-day, my dear friend, in regard to your splendid Memoirs. How everything succeeds in your hands! .To-day I recommend you an able Frenchman, M. Galuski, who knows Germany better than we do, the author of an essay on A. W. Schlegel. He will stay but a few days. Preserve the autograph of Barante.*

A. v. HUMBOLDT.

SATURDAY.

126.

HUMBOLDT TO VARNHAGEN.

BERLIN, December 6th, 1846.

THERE will be perhaps some delay, my dear friend, in your receiving the " Cinq jours de Berlin," in which I am spoken of by the Berliners (who are introduced as speaking themselves), as a tolerably pleasant tattler, but in which I am alluded to rather unkindly, as to my moral character. If all my speeches lack consistency, I apprehend for the durability of the system of the world, the Kosmos. Mr. Barrière will probably have called on you the sixth day, and you will have suggested all that to him. The paper contains some excellent things, Cracoviana, about the vote of Prussia and Mr. de Kanitz.

---

* Barante introduced M. Galuski to Humboldt.

I send you for your autograph collection a flattering letter of Mignet, and a letter of mine, written in 1801, at Carthagena, in South America, at a turning point in my life, and addressed to "Citizen" Baudin, who, on board of the Perron, made a voyage round the world. This letter was written at a time when probably people in Europe had ceased to be addressed any more as "citizens." Baudin, instead of doubling Cape Horn, and receiving me at Lima, went round the Cape of Good Hope to Australia.

Your old friend,
A. v. HUMBOLDT.

SUNDAY.

I inclose an excellent letter of my brother to Koerner, which will be published in the sixth volume; but you must return this copy.

127.

MIGNET TO HUMBOLDT.

PARIS, July 1st, 1846.

DEAR BARON, AND MOST ILLUSTRIOUS COLLEAGUE:

You will easily understand how happy and flattered I was at hearing, that the book "Antonio Perez and

Philip II." has interested you and obtained approval so distinguished as that of your King. The applause of a Prince, of so great genius and learning, who ranks among the most acute and most infallible of literary critics, could not be otherwise than of the greatest value to me. To make the book which was honored with this august approbation worthier of it, may I ask you, my dear and most illustrious colleague, to offer the work in the new form, more complete and more elaborate, which I have just given to it, to your sovereign? This is a respectful act of homage, which the King of Prussia, by the expression of his kind satisfaction, has encouraged me to render, and for which your goodness to me will obtain, I am very sure, a gracious reception.

I take also the liberty of sending to you, for your own library, a copy of this new edition. Documents, hitherto unknown and very curious, which have enabled me to exhibit the designs of Don John of Austria, the murder of Escovedo, and the disgrace of Perez, in their true light, make the first edition imperfect.

But I must hasten to speak of the first volume of Kosmos, which you sent me, and in which you have so admirably shown, if I may use one of your beautiful sentences, "the order of the universe and the magnificence of the order." I read the book with the greatest pleasure and advantage. It is an exposition, full of the most absorbing grandeur, of the phenomena and laws of the universe, from those nebulous distances whence light comes to us only after a journey of two millions of years, to the revolutions which preceded the actual organization of our planet, and which enabled men to be born, to live, and to reign on its surface. To paint this great picture in its teeming variety and majestic harmony, one needs to be master, like yourself, of all sciences, to love nature earnestly, and to have studied her under every aspect. In addition he must unite a vivid imagination to an accurate and profound judgment. Finish quickly this charming work, for your own glory and for our instruction.

Accept, dear Baron, the assurance of my gratitude, my admiration, and my affectionate devotion.

MIGNET.

128

HUMBOLDT TO BAUDIN.

CARTHAGENA, April 12, 1801.

CITIZEN!

WHEN I embraced you for the last time in Helvetius Street, in Paris, on the eve of my departure for Africa and the East Indies, I had but a feeble hope of seeing you again, and of sailing under your orders. You have been told, no doubt, by our common friends, C. C. Jussieu, Desfontaines ... how the Barbaresques have prevented my departure for Egypt, how the King of Spain has given me permission to journey over his vast domains in America and Asia, to gather whatever may be useful to science. Independently, and always at my own expense, my friend Bonpland and I have wandered for two years through the territories lying between the coast, the Orinoco, the Casiquian, the Rio Negro, and the Amazon. Our health has resisted the frightful risks created by the rivers. In the midst of the forests we have talked of you; of our useless visits; on C. Francois, of Neufchatel; of our beguiled hopes. Just as we were starting from Havana for Mexico and the Philippines, the gratifying news reached us that your perseverance had overcome every obstacle. After making our calculations, we felt sure that you would touch at Valparaiso, at Lima, or at Guayaquil. We changed our plans at once, and in spite of the stormy gales of this shore, we started in a little pilot boat to look for you in the South Sea, to try whether by reviving up our old plans, we could join our labors with yours, and sail with you on the South Sea. A long passage of twenty-one days from the Havana to Carthagena, unfortunately hindered us from taking the route of Panama and Guayaquil. We fear that the wind has ceased blowing in the South Sea, and we have decided to continue our journey on land by the way of the River Magdalena, Santa Fe, Popajan, Quito. . . .

I hope we shall arrive in June or early in July at the city of Quito, where I will wait for the news of your arrival at Lima. Have the kindness to write me a line, directed in Spanish, " al Sr. Baron de Humboldt, Quito; casa del Sr. Governador Baron de Carondelet." In case I should hear nothing from you, my respected friend, I intend to visit Chimborasso, Losca, . . . till November, 1801, and to come down in December or January, 1802, with my instruments, to Lima. You will perceive from all this, my revered friend, that the heat of the tropics has not made me sluggish, and that I am afraid of no sacrifice where useful and bold enterprises are to be prosecuted. I have told you now frankly what I want from you. I know that I ask more from you than I can return; it may also be that particular circumstances may prevent your taking us on board of your vessel. . . . In that case, my letter may embarrass you, the more, perhaps, since you honor me with your friendship. I beg you, therefore, to write to me frankly. I shall always be glad to have seen you once more, and shall never complain of circumstances, which often govern us in spite of ourselves and our wishes. Your frankness will be the highest proof of your regard for me. I should then continue on my route from Lima to Acapulco, Mexico, the Philippines, Surato, Bassora, Palestine, Marseilles.

How much I should prefer, however, to make a voyage with you! Mr. Bonpland presents you his respects. Greetings and unchangeable friendship,

ALEXANDER HUMBOLDT.

NOTE OF HUMBOLDT, WRITTEN LONG AFTER.—This letter to Captain Baudin, written on my arrival at Carthagena (from the Havana), was returned to me, Captain Baudin not having touched at Lima.

A. HUMBOLDT.

BERLIN, *Nov.* 1846.

129.

HUMBOLDT TO VARNHAGEN.

SUNDAY, *Feb.* 21st, 1847.

I DO not recollect showing you a very beautiful letter of my brother, on the death of Schiller, dated "Rome, 1805." It was discovered but lately, and will be published in the next volume of his works. I inclose a very amiable letter from Prince Metternich, received this week, also a stiff and unmeaning one from Prince Albert. Prince Metternich has published, at his own cost, a splendid description of his mineralogical collection at Koenigswarth, having probably in view his election to the Presidency of the new Academy instead of Kolowrat. At the special request of Prince Albert I left a copy of Kosmos on his desk at Stolzenfels. He had the civility not to thank me. The "blackbird"* has improved his politeness in the present instance, and besides, he makes me talk of "roving oceans of light" and "sidereal terraces"—a Coburg version of my text, *quite English*—from Windsor, where terraces abound. In Kosmos I speak once of the "starry carpet," page 159, in explaining the open spaces between the stars. He presents me a work upon "Mexican Monuments," a copy of which I myself had purchased two years ago. A splendid edition of Lord Byron would have been in better taste. It is also strange that he does not mention "Queen Victoria." Possibly my "Book of Nature" is not sufficiently Christian for her Majesty. You see that I am a severe critic of "princely epistles."

Please return Metternich and Albert soon, as I have not yet replied to them; also Wilhelm's letter at your leisure—it is the only copy I have. I gave the original to Schlesier, who was very anxious to possess something from my brother's hand.

With old attachment, yours,
A. v. Humboldt.

---

* The Prussian order of "The Black Eagle," which had just then been conferred on Prince Albert.—Tr.

130.

METTERNICH TO HUMBOLDT.

VIENNA, *February*, 1847.

MY DEAR BARON:

I WILL begin this letter by congratulating you upon the new decoration, which the King has lately conferred upon you. The "*Eagle*," under whose wing—sub umbra alarum—you have executed so much will be a noble decoration on your breast. Suum cuique!

Now to what I wish to say further. You know, that I am no savan and that I have no pretension to be one; but notwithstanding this, you know that I am the friend of science, and in that capacity have furnished the means to some savans of publishing the little work of which I enclose the first copy to you. I hope you will approve of its execution. I think I am at the present the owner of the most complete collection of monuments* now existing of an epoch of which I cannot pretend to fix the age—and of which the "Gossau" conceals countless numbers. History written by man

---

* Petrifactions dug out in the Gossau, in Bohemia.

presents but an insignificant point when compared to that of which nature supplies the material. It was not I who christened one of the Ammonites after me—it is the doing of the editors of the opuscule.—I am, however, quite sure that neither my name nor even that of Ammon was known when my godson was alive.

Thousand sincere homages, my dear Baron,

METTERNICH.

131.

PRINCE ALBERT TO HUMBOLDT.

WINDSOR CASTLE, *February* 17th, 1847.

MY DEAR BARON:

I HAVE been constantly impressed while gradually reading the first volume of your "Kosmos" with my desire to thank you for the high intellectual enjoyment, its study has afforded me.

I am really unable to give you an authoritative judgment on this excellent work, which I received from your hands, and to atone in some measure for this defect, as well as to give some substantial character to the expression of my thanks, I present you the accompanying work (Catherwood's Views in Central America). It may serve as an appendix to your own great work on Spanish America, and thus become worthy of your attention. I do not dare to express the intense anxiety with which I look forward to the appearance of the second volume of "Kosmos." May that Heaven, whose roving oceans of light and sidereal terraces you have so ably described, be pleased to preserve you to your country, to the world, and to "Kosmos" itself, for many years, in undisturbed vigor of mind and body. This is the sincere wish of your

Very devoted,   ALBERT.

132.

HUMBOLDT TO VARNHAGEN.

BERLIN, *February 27th*, 1847.

HERE, at last, is my thankful letter to Carriere, containing three warm recommendations.

You were right in reprimanding me as to my extreme severity against the man of the "sidereal terraces." I am severe only to the mighty ones of the earth, and this man impressed me very uncomfortably at Stolzenfels: "I know you feel great compassion for the Poles under the Russian sceptre; but, I am sorry to say, the Poles are as little deserving of our sympathy as the Irish." "Mihi dixit;" and one is the handsome husband of the Queen of Great Britain!

I hasten to Potsdam to day, in order to bring all the manuscripts here, which have fortunately arrived from Erfurt. Madame von Buelow writes, that they contain a long and very beautiful passage about our Rahel, and flattering things for you.

With old attachment,

A. v. H.

SATURDAY.

133.

HUMBOLDT TO VARNHAGEN.

BERLIN, March 27th, 1847.

I AM more deserving than you would believe, dear friend! I am through with the first volume of the "Letters"* (Therese's property). I had very little to correct, and only about four pages to suppress, viz. allusions to biscuits, household details, a few sarcasms against Duke Charles of Brunswick (which he would have answered with calumnies as to the lady's virtue), and more such things. The letters are excellent both in thought and expression. They furnish a picture of a most remarkable life. Their contempt of all worldly

---

* Wilhelm von Humboldt's "Letters to a Lady Friend" (Charlotte Diede), bequeathed to Therese von Bacheracht.

happiness or unhappiness beyond the narrow circle of one's own feelings, this mixture of scriptural and Christian dogmas, of stoical indifference to the affairs of the world, together with so much delicacy and gentleness in a correspondence, continued to the four last days of a life, and written by a trembling hand on ruled paper. The torments of love-sickness, *qui n'impatientent*, are left untouched, in order not to lessen the impression of that powerful individuality. I repeat, all that I struck out amounts to only five or six lines—all that I suppressed as dull or trivial, would not fill two printed pages. You will, however, see much, very much, in the manuscript stricken out, thus ⁓⁓⁓⁓⁓, sometimes half pages; this is, however, not mine but the old lady's doing. This "Daughter of the Pastor of Taubenheim"* had, perhaps, hysterical fits of prudery now and then. The different ink shows that I am a stranger to these obliterations.

The first volume has a beautiful passage on Therese, and says much in praise of the King of Bavaria. In the second volume a description of Rahel will please you. Of Bettina she speaks less approvingly, as Madame von Buelow told me. I shall try to modify it in this respect. I think the first volume will be ready for delivery next Tuesday, and the second will soon follow. I shall bring

---

* A most sentimental and tragically-ending German love story made popular by Bürger's ballad.—Tr.

it myself, together with notes and facsimiles, all locked in a tin box, which must be shortened. Then you will be in possession of the whole treasure, and I "salvavi animam meam." The thing will create much provoking but salutary scandal, and will elicit much conflicting criticism.

With sincerest friendship, yours,
A. v. H<small>T</small>.

Please don't let the book be printed at Berlin, and have it (if possible) advertised before it is in the trade. My letters to Carriere will have duly reached you, I hope?

On the 30th March, 1847, Varnhagen wrote in his diary:—"Just when I returned home, Humboldt came in and brought a pack of manuscripts—the letters of his brother to Mrs. Diede. Humboldt regards affairs here as desperate, as I do myself. He consoles himself with the belief that the constitution presented, though good for nothing at first, may result beneficially. He expects violence of every description—atrocities committed by the police, popular rage, and military strokes. The King, however, Humboldt thinks, has no misgivings. He is in high spirits, having prepared his opening speech, and no longer minds the 11th of April, and its consequences. He never yet talked with Humboldt on constitutional affairs. As to Michelet, Eichhorn has instigated the King very much; but after all they will not find a reason to dismiss him, although the King would like very much to do it, and the Minister urges him on to it."

On the 31st March Varnhagen adds: "Humboldt told me but yesterday that the King was firmly believing the restoration of Don Miguel, Don Carlos, the overthrow of the July dynasty, and that he would yet go to Paris, to salute the legitimate king. Also, that he, Humboldt, was deemed a Jacobin, who carried the tri-colored standard in his breeches pocket. As for myself, I was considered a royalist, but the King had prejudices against me. They think it strange that my old friend Canitz should not have enlightened the King on my behalf; that they did not ask my advice, and avail themselves of my services in the present situation. Wittgenstein also has talked in this manner with Humboldt. They forget only one thing: that I neither can nor will —the one and the other, with equal determination.

The nobility is terribly excited; the change is remarkable; self-esteem is mightily roused. The devil himself could not have invented more efficacious ways of provoking the hostility of this whole class than this monstrous "Herrenstand."

A Dream.—I saw the King weeping bitterly, and crying: so far it has come. Well, I will resign! May my brother take charge of the whole, and be happier than I was!

March 27th, 1847, Varnhagen wrote the following repartee of Humboldt in his diary: "Humboldt recited, good-humoredly, that a certain Mr. Massow, in the Assembly, had characterized liberalism as a felony. He, Humboldt, was therefore a twofold felon, as Minister Bodelschwingh considered literary men felonious."

On the 11th July, 1847, Varnhagen observes: "This morning Humboldt came in quite unexpectedly. He is in good health and spirits, and denies having been really sick. He says that the King lives in a whirlpool of pleasure, that he is often extravagantly gay; thinks no longer of the Chamber, except when reminded of it, when he becomes immediately grave and sullen. The ministers, however, are full of anger—Savigny and Eichhorn particularly so. Foremost, however, is Bodelschwingh, who is always exciting the King to strong measures. Canitz acts this time in a conciliatory and compromising spirit. Bodelschwingh cannot bear being deprived of the imaginary triumph of his visionary premiership by the Chambers. Humboldt is engaged on the final sheets of his second volume. He is going to Paris next September.

134.

BERLIN, *Jan.* 18*th*, 1849.

IF I appear slow, my dear Varnhagen, and rather laconic to-day in offering you my thanks for your friendly presents and your letter, and your congratulations, you will not ascribe it to a diminution of my true esteem and friendship. I have had but now the enjoyment of what you alone are entitled to call "A Plain Discourse."*

How much more fearful, and at the same time hopeful, a turn events have taken. They only know how to oppose brute force to the impending danger, and are afraid themselves to pluck the proffered fruit.

Romuald's "Vocation"† deserves, no doubt, the severest censure. What an abuse of his most eminent talents! We will talk about it as soon as I shall have done with the "Ordenstag‡" and the annoyances of the

---

* A pamphlet under that title, written by Varnhagen, in commendation of the King.—*Tr.*

† Romuald ou la Vocation, par Mr. de Custine. Paris, 1848. 4 vols.

‡ The day on which the Prussian government yearly distributes orders and decorations.—*Tr.*

Academy elections of my order. *La petite piece* side by side with the great world's drama.

<blockquote>With the old attachment,
Yours, A. v. Ht.</blockquote>

There never was nobler praise bestowed on the King than in "The Plain Discourse."

The little work, "Plain Discourse to the Germans on the Duties of the Day. Berlin, 1848," is from the pen of Varnhagen. A few months later, on the 10th of May, 1849, the author himself thus speaks of it in his diary: "I have been re-reading what I wrote in August last on Frederick William IV., and what I wrote in 1840, the day after he received the homage of his subjects. What strange sensations it provokes! Do what I will, awake or asleep, I cannot for a moment shake off the nightmare of consciousness of our political condition, although I know full well how ephemeral it is, how certain the retribution, and how bright the ultimate future. Arouse then, my country, arouse! Civil war is thy fate, but it is not thy choice. Go on thy way undaunted, and be the blood on the head of those who willed it not otherwise. At a time like this it is not the successes but the failures of the moment that are of profit to the people."

This is the place to interpose another visit from Humboldt to Varnhagen. On the 12th of February, 1849, the latter wrote in his diary: "Humboldt called. He thinks it absurd in the ministers to talk of meeting the Chambers, when they cannot find men to make up their own number. Even Kuehlwetter disdains to join them. My opinion that the constitution imposed by the government is merely a husk concealing the germ of a new revolution, which will shortly burst forth, startled him a little; but he was much pleased with the notion that the King has been embroiled with the canon of logic for the last eight years past. He says the King was disposed to return to Canitz as Minister of Foreign Affairs! Eichhorn also vouchsafes his advice, and, like the lady of Privy Counsellor ———, talks of the Pietists as if he had never belonged to them.

"The 'Staats Anzeiger' publishes the Austrian note in regard to the German question. Austria will not withdraw, but will have a voice in the counsels of the empire, and will not tolerate a variety of things, such as popular sovereignty, or any leadership except its own. A fling at Prussia, a fling at Frankfort, and particularly at Gagern. There it is! Everything plays into the hands of the revolution!"

135.

HUMBOLDT TO VARNHAGEN.

POTSDAM, *August* 16*th*, 1849.

WHENEVER I enjoy the fancy of having written a few lines grateful to my ears, I always ask myself whether they would also please you, my valued friend. You know, or rather you do not know, that the Princess of Prussia has deposited a splendid album, with numerous autographs and painted initials, in those halls of the Chateau at Weimar which have been dedicated to Goethe, Schiller, and to Herder and Wieland, maligned by Schiller in his letters to Koerner. I have been compelled to write a preface, which Galuski has translated quite happily. The Grand-Duchess desired a French version for the benefit of foreign travellers who might open the album. Look upon this little memento of your friend with indulgence. There is blood on the horizon, and it makes me sad. I need not remind you of the friendship and esteem of

Yours,   A. v. HUMBOLDT.

SUNDAY.

136.

HUMBOLDT TO VARNHAGEN.

Potsdam, *October* 15*th,* 1849.

I HOPE, my dear friend, that my "Views of Nature," enlarged, and, for two-thirds of it, almost re-written, are at last in your hands! It was owing to an unfortunate confusion, occasioned by my long absence from Berlin, that this my favorite work was so long in reaching my favorite reader. Perhaps you will derive a brief pleasure from contrasting the picture of the nocturnal din of the woods with that of the stillness of high noon —vol. i., pp. 333 and 337; or from glancing at the golden visions of young Astorpileo, vol. ii., 352.

In love and friendship, yours,

In haste.   A. v. HUMBOLDT.

Increase your collection of autographs by a very agreeable letter from the man who now lives in Brussels. The phrase "votre fortune morale" is used with great freedom. But the newspaper, all disfigured with bloodstains! What a year, in which all the feelings of the heart run wild!

137.

METTERNICH TO HUMBOLDT.
(FROM THE FRENCH.)

RICHMOND, *Sep.* 17*th*, 1849.

MY DEAR BARON:

I SEE by to-day's papers that the 9th of September, 1769, gave you to the world, and that thus you have just celebrated your eightieth birth-day. Had I been near you I would have joined your friends in offering my good wishes; at the distance which separates us, I approach you alone. Let me say in a few words that I render thanks to the giver of the faculties which have rendered your name imperishable. To be born is of little account; to make life valuable is excellent. You are numbered among the richest, and you have made a noble use of your moral fortune. May God preserve you in safety and in health!

Receive, my dear Baron, with the expression of a congratulation of which you do not doubt the sincerity, that of my sentiments of devotion and friendship, of a date as ancient as all that has a place between us!

METTERNICH.

138.

HUMBOLDT TO VARNHAGEN.

Potsdam, *October 29th*, 1849.

My dear Friend:

A German letter of the Duchess of Orleans, to whom I have sent all my writings for many years, and who is very fond of them. She writes a hand so cabalistic to my eyes, that I beg to avail myself of your diplomatic experience in decyphering, and to be favored with a legible copy. The purport appears to be of a political nature. It will not be without interest for you, and on this account I appeal all the more confidently to your good-nature.

Your faithful friend, A. Humboldt.

139.

HELEN, DUCHESS OF ORLEANS, TO HUMBOLDT.

Your Excellency will accept my most heartfelt thanks for the token of the remembrance, so valued by me, which you devote to the hours we passed in times but recently gone by, which the course of events, however, seems already to have thrust back into antediluvian periods.

I see with joyous gratitude that the conversations in my red saloon in the Tuileries and in St. Cloud, ever present to myself, still live in your recollection also, and thank your Excellency for this constancy of sentiments, doubly precious at a time like this.

The kindness of my beloved cousin had already enabled me to refresh myself by the perusal of your latest work, which is hailed as a fountain of health by so many hearts smitten by the rude hand of fate, and minds stunned by the wild confusion of public events; and my son has also found nourishment in it to assuage his thirst of knowledge. Nevertheless, I thank you most cordially for the jewel you have sent, which receives additional value from being accompanied by your letter.

As you say, in words so mild and yet so truly appropriate, "Men are at present laboring at a *fable convenue;* they strive in part after what is unattainable, and in which they themselves do not believe!" But where will the light appear that is to lead them to the truth, and what events will yet be required to convince them of the impracticability of the most contradictory demands? I agree with your Excellency in thinking that the present tranquillity is destined to be of brief duration. I also do not see in it any real pacification, but only the apathy and indifference which enervates without convincing. Who can fathom the future? The riddle of the coming day remains concealed—how much more must we await in patience the developments of coming years? But courage and resignation must not be impaired by this uncertainty; on the contrary, our hearts should be steeled by it.

During my visit in England, the King asked many questions in regard to the health of your Excellency; the Queen also received with great interest such reports as I could give her. They hold in grateful remembrance your frequent visits in Paris. My children ask to be commended to your recollection, and I also hope to revive in it from time to time.

With heartfelt reverence and gratitude, your Excellency's friend and admirer,

HELEN.

EISENACH, *Oct.* 23, 1849.

140.

HUMBOLDT TO VARNHAGEN.

POTSDAM, *October* 31*st*, 1849.

A THOUSAND, thousand thanks for the interpretation, my dear friend. How the political tempests have ravaged even this handwriting, once so fine, or, at least, so distinct. The "beloved courier" I read "beloved cousin," the Princess of Prussia, who first showed the Duchess the latest "Views."

A little address delivered by me before the delegates from this city, in which I referred to the views of my brother, a Potsdamer by birth, on a political life which develops itself freely from within, has been printed by the "Spikersche Zeitung," with numerous typographical errors. Inclosed is my own report, written immediately after delivery. I would have been pleased if the answer had been correctly given in the Constitutional and other truly liberal papers. With my old devotion and friendship,

Yours,
A. Ht.

Wednesday Night.

(INCLOSURE.)

I cannot, fellow-citizens, more vividly express the profound gratitude I entertain, than by saying, that you have given me as great a pleasure as you have bestowed an unexpected honor. A pleasure such as this shall not be dashed by the question how I can possibly deserve this distinction at the hands of your beautiful city. You have worthily shown, not only that you value her material prosperity, but that you are alive to higher interests, and accord sympathy and respect to efforts directed to the advancement of knowledge, the education of the people, and the general culture of mankind. As a reward for a portion of these efforts, to which my long and chequered life has been devoted, I accept with pride your flattering gift. By the favor of two illustrious monarchs it has been my privilege, for twenty-two years, with but little interruption, to live as your townsman, and to find, in scenery beautiful by nature and art, those inspirations indispensable to a life-like portraiture of nature, which aims to display the workings of the powers of the universe. Grateful for this good fortune, I have adorned almost all my later writings with the historic name which has become dear to me, and in the walls of which the year 1767 witnessed the birth of my brother, whose memory lives in the hearts of those who have preserved a sense of the enlarged proportions of a political life which progresses in obedience to laws inherent in the constitution of society.

A. v. Humboldt.

On receipt of the Honorary Citizenship of Potsdam.

141.

HUMBOLDT TO VARNHAGEN.

POTSDAM, *November 4th,* 1849.

WHAT pleasure you have given me, dear friend, by so agreeable a communication from England! But on account of my brother's memory, and in order to reply to those who calumniate me for remaining at this court, I am very anxious to see my response to the deputies of Potsdam correctly printed in a liberal journal. I would like to send it to the "Constitutionelle Zeitung," which has not yet mentioned the subject. I have no copy, however—nothing but the bit of paper I sent you. Have the goodness to send it back to me soon.

How important is the news from Paris! The forward one may attain the consulate for life (to which the words *durée et stabilité* seem to refer); but he will fall, nevertheless, and awake the sleeping lion. Liberty will lose nothing by it, and the German statesmen (are there any such besides Herr von Gagern?) will then understand, that in the centre of Europe is the France of 1789, the same, about the nullity of which so many sarcasms have been uttered. The centres of gravity change.

With cordial friendship, yours,   A. HT.

SUNDAY.

142.

HUMBOLDT TO VARNHAGEN.

BERLIN, *March* 19*th*, 1850.

ACCEPT, my dear friend, my heartfelt thanks for the lines you gave M. Rio, whose praises had already been sung to me by Cornelius, Olfers, Radowitz, and the King himself, on account of the book, "De l'Art Chretien." The new incarnation of a deputy to the Erfurt Parliament, and his supervision in the interest of the Prince President, was unexpected; but Rafael himself was a good deal of a mannerist.

Very truly, and in some suspense,

Yours, A. v. HUMBOLDT.

TUESDAY.

143.

HUMBOLDT TO VARNHAGEN.

POTSDAM, *July* 2*d*, 1850.

IN the gloomy period of reaction, I am delighted to receive so pleasing a memento at your hand, my dear friend. I am also glad of your journey to Kiel, to the little region where German spirit finds an expression free and consistent. The state of public affairs is like the water-bottle shaken by D'Alembert, in order to produce a mixture of bubbles of different shapes. "Calculez moi cela," he said, in irony of hydraulic science, of which he was himself so great a professor. Many a bubble will burst before the diplomatists find time to calculate its evanescent figure.

I shall render my heartfelt thanks to Herr von Froloff. I made a futile effort to dissuade him from inserting a mass of explanations and metaphors, intended to facilitate comprehension. He wished to accomplish what is absolutely impossible, and seemed to have but little understanding of the form of composition. I shall say nothing more to him about all that. Hybrids are never successful in literature.

I was extremely unwell, confined to my bed even; but now, in spite of the dispersion of all matters of interest, I am well, industrious, and not cheerful.

In friendship as of old, yours,

A. v. HUMBOLDT.

144.

HUMBOLDT TO BETTINA VON ARNIM.

(Copy in Varnhagen's Handwriting.)

BERLIN, *June 7th,* 1851.

You could not doubt, dear lady Baroness, that I would respond with the greatest warmth to your wishes for a composer of such sterling merit as * * * * In consequence of malignant prejudices against music, originated by my brother, and transmitted through the King to me, my voice upon a subject which no one ever mentions to me, is somewhat lacking in tone, particularly when church music is in question. What with Warsaw, Olmuetz, Russian Grand Dukes, and, to name something of a higher order, Rauch's inspiring master-piece, it was impossible hitherto to obtain a hearing. Warsaw is now succeeded by Hanover, by the visit to your royal friend and mine. I have not yet seen our monarch at Potsdam again, and surrounded by all the horrors of a cosmic transmigration, shall wait for the returning tide from Warsaw (the alluvium of Batavian and Mecklenburgh highnesses), and when the rock-bound seas are calm again, I shall go to work systematically, as your cheerful and genial letter inspires me. But at this gloomy period everything oral is unheard, and what is written is scarcely noticed. The latter, however, is an insuperable necessity. In order, then, to accomplish so attainable a purpose, a very brief writing addressed immediately to the King, will be required, to be delivered by me with a warm recommendation. Our excellent friend asks the King for a trifling assistance in point of funds, to enable him to travel to Munich. The statement of a specific amount is not necessary, but it will simplify the matter. The man's delicate sense of honor will not be offended by my suggestion, as the request is made not for himself, but for a noble service to the cause of art.

With all devotion and grateful reverence, your most faithful and obedient

A. v. HUMBOLDT.

145.

HUMBOLDT TO VARNHAGEN.

POTTSDAM, *November 1st,* 1851.

You have given me an inexpressible pleasure, my dear, my noble friend, by your kind letter. I am heavily in your debt, and my long silence and apparent neglect might have provoked some suspicions of coolness or diversity on matters of opinion. With a man of your mind and goodness of heart I ought to have entertained no such apprehensions. Before I received your dear letter with Baader's portrait, it was my intention to bring you personally the third volume of Kosmos (two parts in one), now finished with great difficulty, and which unfortunately is exclusively astronomical. I was certain of a kind reception, and your letter of the 24th of October, which had been left behind in my house at Berlin, confirmed my purpose. Ottilie von Goethe gives me cheering news in regard to your health. As usual you will combat her opinion. But what astonished me was, that the president of the council, usually cold as a glacier, was delighted with Ottilie, and is entirely disposed to gratify her wish for the appointment of Wolfgang, at the Prussian embassy at Rome. Was it necessary, however, for Wolfgang, after publishing a very able little work on Nature and Legislation, to go to press with a collection of poems, containing but rare gleams of imagination?

Written with the devotion of better days, in a time of gloom and feebleness, by

A. v. Humboldt.

On the 24th of November, 1851, Varnhagen wrote

in his diary: "Backbiters are busy with Humboldt. Littleness and mediocrity, conscious of their nothingness beside him, combine their envy and spite, and thereby hope to be something. The one comes to the other with smiles, and makes him the confidant of the dislike he entertains, and of the foibles and defects he claims to have detected. The other welcomes the suggestion, responds with similar remarks, they clasp each other's hands, and are fast friends in enmity of the hero. Those who pretend to be the most faithful lend themselves to such intrigues. Singly they amount to nothing, but when lumped together they constitute a stumbling-block, which obstructs the light of day, interferes with what is good, and destroys life and spirits: such vermin tormented Goethe, and now they torment Humboldt. I know these fellows by experience; in Rahel's time I have seen my fill of it! The brothers, the nieces, how glad they would be to make common cause with the most inferior beings, to place their united mediocrity above the genial power of heart and mind, by which even they were yet constantly lighted and warmed! Humboldt's weak points are well known, he does nothing in secret, men see him as he is; but his greatness is unimpaired, the greatness of his mind and the equal greatness of his heart. And eighty years—what a bulwark! Who will dare assail it?

146.

HUMBOLDT TO VARNHAGEN.

BERLIN, *January* 28*th,* 1852.

HERE is my Cosmic present, my dear friend! I choose not to bring it myself lest it should seem that I dare not come without it. Cast a look at p. 1—25, Mars p. 511, and the concluding passage p. 625—631.

I may call to-morrow, Thursday, at one o'clock, may I not? I shall be sure to come.

With the old attachment, which will never grow cold,

A. v. HUMBOLDT.

WEDNESDAY.

With two yellow pamphlets, to his friend of many years, Varnhagen von Ense, with old admiration and attachment. The author.

On the 29th January, 1852, Varnhagen's journal reads as follows: "Humboldt came at one o'clock, wonderfully robust for his time of life! Speaks with indignant scorn of the *coup d'état* in France, the undisguised outrage, the arbitrary banishments, and particularly the robbery of the estates of the Orleans family. The King was at first full of rejoicing, he and the court saw nothing offensive in the crime committed against the people, the legislature, the law, and the sanctity of oaths, but that the adventurer preserves universal suffrage, rests upon the people, practises socialism, and even wants to be emperor; this is what makes him detested! Humboldt is of opinion that in the revolution of February the establishment of the Provisional Government, which was immediately obeyed throughout France, was a piece of even greater audacity than the present usurpation of the one man who has already been president, and worn the name of government for three years. I reminded him of the parliament, and the committee of fifty at Frankfort-on-the-Main. In the disposition to acquiesce, he sees that national feeling of unity and cohesion which, among Frenchmen, suppresses all party feeling. Humboldt says there is no doubt that Louis Bonaparte is a son of Admiral Verhuel, and his brother, Morny, a son of General Flahault, who, he says, lived with both the sisters, the Queen of Holland and the Queen of Naples. Of Persigny—Fialin de Persigny—he speaks with the utmost contempt, calling him a raw, unkempt non-commissioned officer, who still arrogates to himself discoveries about the pyramids. Passing on to our own affairs, he deplored the narrowness, the pitiful character of our ministry; he considers Raumer the most stupid of them all, stupid and unmannerly both; the King is cross and peevish, capricious, and prone to excuse himself by saying that he is powerless, and must be governed by his ministers.

On the 30th of January, 1852, Varnhagen adds: "Humboldt takes a lively interest in the widow of the philologist F.; her husband has done much work for him. At Humboldt's urgent advice, she has petitioned the King for a pension, and Humboldt and Boekh were to support the petition by their signatures. But F. was a democrat, not an active, but an avowed one, and the King might have heard of it. To neutralize this, Humboldt proposed to request Stahl to join in countersigning the petition. His own name can now accomplish nothing with the King! On what days have we fallen, when Humboldt asks Stahl to give him countenance!"

147.

HUMBOLDT TO VARNHAGEN.

BERLIN, *Feb. 5th*, 1852.

I BELIEVE, my dear friend, that the letter I have just received, will greatly confirm your ideas about Paris. Galuski, the translator of the second volume of Kosmos, is a man of noble instincts, great talents, and much philological learning, but very moderate in his love of liberty. What he says of his first impression, is a pretty impudent expression of this moderation. He also was seized with a marvellous dread of coming events. My opinion has always been that the wildest republic cannot do so much and such enduring harm to the intellectual progress of mankind, and to their consciousness of right and honor, as *le régime de mon oncle, le despotisme éclairé, dogmatique, milleux*, which applies all the arts of civilization to subject a people to the caprices of an individual. Read, to increase your abhorrence of such degradation, which threatens to spread like a pestilence, in the " Journal des Debats" of this morning (February 3d), the reasons for drawing up a list of recommendations of those who might be elected (according to the " Constitutionnel)." The " Spenersche Zeitung" of yesterday did not fail to follow suit with a communication in favor of a similar set of proposals for our second chamber!

I hope soon to procure for you the Histoire de l'Academie (by Bartholmess). I have made many vain efforts to advance the interests of Professor F.'s widow.

Your most attached,
A. HUMBOLDT.

SUPPLEMENT.

"Spenersche Zeitung," of 1852, Feb. 4, No. 29.—The transactions in reference to the formation of the second Chamber have repeatedly been the subject of our communications. It is perhaps not equally well known, that at this moment the attention of higher circles is also directed to the formation of the Second Chamber. The present electoral law presents the right of suffrage as one to be exercised or not at the option of the voter, without a corresponding obligation on his part. A law compelling men to vote would seem to be equally inexpedient and impracticable. But by refraining from voting in any number, the voters repose the decision of the question in the hands of an unknown minority, who, by exercising their privilege, frequently bring about a state of things by which representation is given, not to the political views of the constituency, but to their very opposite. The principles had in view in fixing the reconstruction of the First Chamber, have, by force of logical inference, led to the proposals to alter the electoral law for the Second Chamber in this manner, *that His Majesty, the King, shall appoint in each district, long before the election, a government candidate, who shall be the representative, unless the majority of the voters should at the election record their preference for another.* The specific arguments in support of such a plan will appear to-morrow in connexion with its details.

148.

HUMBOLDT TO VARNHAGEN.

BERLIN, *February* 12th, 1852.

It may interest you, dear friend, to see collected on one sheet all the efforts making by the Orleans dynasty to counteract the robbery. The Duchess of Orleans sends the paper by the Princess of Prussia.

Are you acquainted with a candidate for theological honors, named William S., of Dresden, disguised under the name of Wilfried von der Neun, who torments me by sending aphorisms in manuscript?

Yours,   A. v. Ht.

Be kind enough to return the enclosed at your early convenience.

149.

HUMBOLDT TO VARNHAGEN.

BERLIN, *March* 23d, 1852.

One of the many inconveniences of old age is that of liability to attempts at conversion. Do you care to deposit this curious, good-natured letter among your psychological curiosities? (The man who is entirely convinced of Bernadotte's salvation, circuitously informs me that Satan wields the baton of command in my heart, as in that of Goethe, that of the pious Kant, and that of Wieland.) And our parliament!! If necessary the cities must be expunged from the face of the earth—such is the desire of our diplomatist at the Diet.

With heartfelt attachment,
Yours,
A. Ht.

TUESDAY, late at night.

The enclosed letter from August. Grau, of Montgomery County, Ohio, dated February 6, 1852, contains the following: "A gentleman who has travelled over a large portion of the earth, who, by the publication of so many excellent writings, has erected for himself so durable and so resplendent a monument on the field of literature and science, is not to be named by any German without the greatest esteem. When the names of great warriors who have spilt the blood of their fellow-men upon the battle-field shall be forgotten, your name will blaze for hundreds and thousands of years in the annals of history. But it is singular, at the same time, that the greatest naturalists, philosophers, and astronomers who have occupied the principal portion of their lives with new inventions, and with investigations into the elementary powers of nature, are often totally indifferent to their salvation or perdition in the world to come. Goethe, Schiller, Wieland, and Kant, were all distinguished characters and brilliant ideals, and in their walk and conversation were more or less observant of what are called the laws of morality, so as probably to abstain from cards, nine-pins, playhouses, and dancing, but their sphere of operations did not reach into eternity, and the fate of their fellow-men in the other world—their salvation—was of little interest to them." After launching into further sanctified regrets at the scarcity of true godliness, and its absence even in princes and royal chaplains, the writer continues: "The last King of Prussia, and his truly royal Louise, had some knowledge of a state of regeneration, as well as the last King of Sweden, the former French Marshal Bernadotte, Prince of Ponte Corvo. A poor peasant was better able to enlighten him on the means of salvation than one of the first bishops of the Lutheran church. O, Sir Privy Councillor, while I do full justice to your unblemished life, your high character as a statesman, and your acquirements as a man of science; and while I rejoice that Berlin—ay, that Prussia may boast of such a man as your Excellency, yet my joy would turn into holy exultation if I should have the honor of seeing you a warm disciple of Him who died upon Golgotha. Without Him, Lord Chamberlain, with all our acquirements, with all our boasted knowledge, we are singularly unhappy." Further on, the letter reads: "Goethe says, on a certain occasion, that during the whole course of his long life he had not spent four happy weeks. These are the words of a great man of science. If Christ has not taken up his residence in our hearts, who else can be there but Satan? One of them, surely, must be there—one must wield the baton of command. It is manifestly impossible at one and the same time to serve two masters! Worthy sir, my gracious Lord Chamberlain, I am penetrated with great esteem for you and your lofty merits; I love and revere you. I am not worthy to unlace your shoes. This is the unconstrained language of my heart; although I have occupied myself with acquiring the elements of seventeen different languages, and can even at this day read the writings of the New Testament in seven different tongues. But I have not only been firmly convinced of the truth of the Christian religion for thirty-one years, but experience the influence of the Holy Ghost from day to day, and almost from hour to hour." The letter is subscribed, "Your Grace's most devoted servant and brother in Christ, Augustus Grau." Humboldt adds the remark: "An attempt at conversion, from the State of Ohio."

150.

HUMBOLDT TO VARNHAGEN.

BERLIN, *March* 13*th*, 1853.

THE confusion of my lonely life, my dear friend of many years, at a time of such profound moral degradation, leaves me in a harassing uncertainty as to whether I have or have not sent you the seventh volume of my brother's complete works. I am greatly ashamed, but I know that you have not yet learned to be angry with me. The article against Capodistrias, the demand for the surrender of Strasburg, sounds like the irony of fate upon our present humility. . . . . .

With ancient love and reverence, yours,

A. v. HUMBOLDT.

The death of Leopold von Buch bows me deeply. A happy blending of the most noble, philanthropic sentiments, momentary impulses, and a little despotism of opinion; one of the few men who have a physiognomy. He has given a new form to his science; he was one of the greatest illustrations of our times; our friendship has endured sixty-three years, unruffled, although we often tilled the same field. I found him, in Freiberg, in 1791, where he had come to the Mining Academy before myself, although five years younger. His funeral appeared like a prelude to my own, C'est comme cela que je serai dimanche. And in what a condition do I leave the world—I who lived in 1789? But centuries are as seconds in the mighty development of advancing humanity. The swelling curve, however, has its little indentations, and it is irksome to be found in such an interval of decadence.

151.

HUMBOLDT TO VARNHAGEN.

BERLIN, *March* 14*th*, 1853.

HEARTY thanks for the comfort derived from the characteristic word of Fontenelle's, hitherto unknown to me—but twenty years are too short to see anything better! Your Buelow von Dennewitz is great and good news to me! The treasure of the warm-blooded Leopold von Buch I return inclosed. May not Friedrich Schlegel's astronomical vision be connected with conversations I had with him at Vienna on the certainty that we shall see the southern cross rise again in Germany, where it has already shone in *historic* ages? Let me remind you of a passage in my Kosmos (II. p. 333), which derives some interest for you from its reliable chronological date. "It was not more than 2900 years before our era that the cross became invisible in Northern Germany. The constellation had ascended as far as the tenth degree above the horizon. When it disappeared from the Baltic skies, the pyramid of Cheops had already stood five hundred years. The shepherd nation of the Hyksos invaded Egypt seven hundred years later. The past becomes apparently less remote when we can measure it by reference to memorable events."

Persevere in your diligence upon Buelow von Dennewitz, who became very dear to me in Paris. Fond of music, he was very affable in the family of Lafayette, in the little chateau of Lagrange, at Paris—Lafayette's country-seat, where Buelow was quartered.

Yours,   A. v. HUMBOLDT.

I shall bring volume VI. myself.

NOTE BY VARNHAGEN.—As a comfort for his eighty years, I had written to Humboldt that even these could be transformed into a comparative youth, as appeared by Fontenelle's example, who, at the age of a hundred years, attempted to pick up a fan dropped by a lady, and, unable to do it as quickly as he wished, exclaimed, " *Que n'ai je plus mes quatre vingt ans !*" Of Friedrich Schlegel I had told him, that shortly before his death, he prophesied to Tieck, at Dresden, that, at no very remote period, though he could not exactly define it, a mighty change would take place in the heavens, the great constellations would leave their places, and combine to form an immense cross.

152.

HUMBOLDT TO VARNHAGEN.

Berlin, *August* 15th, 1853.

Separated from you, my dear intellectual friend, by the prolongation of my dreary sojourn at Potsdam, my first approach to you is to petition. You, you alone are my literary adviser, you who combine such depths of feeling with so wonderful a command of the harmonies of language. In my extreme old age, timidity in regard to my own powers increases in an almost morbid degree. A separate volume is to contain a selection of the sonnets of my brother, in which there is not always a perfect consonance between form and substance. I crave your permission to come to you to-morrow, Tuesday, at one o'clock, to read you a preface I have been compelled to write! By all means send a verbal assent by the bearer.

With indestructible friendship, yours,

A. v. Humboldt.

153.

HUMBOLDT TO VARNHAGEN.

BERLIN, *August* 31st, 1853.

For once in this gloomy time, when a fell simoom blows from the Pruth to the Tajo, I have had a real and a keen delight—your return, your encouraging message, and even the assistance I implored. Your superb letter finds me at the *bon à tirer* of a little, I hope unpretending, preface to the sonnets. As it will be unfortunately impossible to-morrow (on Friday the King arrives at Potsdam, when I must hand him a good many things, according to promise), I take the liberty of sending you my proof sheets this evening.

I beseech you to be severe in your treatment of these sheets, with which I have incorporated a remarkable fragment (in illustration of the ideas and frames of mind manifested in the " Letters to a Lady Friend") and to note on a separate piece of paper what I ought to *alter*, and especially what I ought to *substitute*. I follow *you* implicitly.

I dislike the phrase on page 4, " *Schoen* errun gene Himmelsgabe."*

---

* Beautifully extorted gift of heaven.

The pious fragment is an autograph, nearly illegible, and requiring some emendation in the construction of the sentences; thus on page 11 : Perhaps you prefer the phrase " *bei* Annerkenung." The phrase is heavy, even now.

On p. 14 you will not disapprove of " eben nicht," in place of " haben nie gerade," which is still more vernacular. The four lines stand there like a fallen aerolith. They must be preserved at all hazards, if only on account of their *freedom*.

Could not you help out page 13 below somewhat? Is the close of the phrase " voice of conscience—has laid" clear to you? It is not so to me. Perhaps a few words would make the sense clear.

Roma, the verses to me from Albano, and all the choruses and Pindarus will form another volume.

With old affection and profound esteem,

Yours,

A. v. HUMBOLDT.

The saddest news of Arago's family; swollen hands and feet, diabetes, and almost blindness! Forty years of life go with him!!

154.

HUMBOLDT TO VARNHAGEN.

BERLIN, *September 2d*, 1853.

A THOUSAND pardons for troubling you in suffering! I have adopted every suggestion, taken every hint. But I should like also to insert the reflection you made in regard to p. 6. Would you approve of the following interpolation: "A long sojourn at Rome, and perhaps a lively interest in certain epochs of Italian poetry, appear to have imbued my brother with a particular preference for a little lyric form, which, if melody is not to be sacrificed, closely fetters the thought, but which he handled with a freedom, the result of intention and confidence." Or would you have it, "which he freely handled with the confidence of a clear intention," or, "which he handled with a freedom of which he was perfectly conscious?" "When the poet, urged by his realistic and individual peculiarity, felt most keenly the desire of welding ideas into the flood of sentiment."

Be good enough to return me your MS., which is a treasure of critical research.

Very thankfully, yours, HUMBOLDT.

NOTE BY VARNHAGEN.—I selected "which he handled with a freedom of which he was perfectly conscious," as most in accordance with the metaphor of the fetters, and as otherwise clearly indicative of the idea intended to be conveyed.

Varnhagen reports under date of September 9th, 1853, in his diary: "Humboldt had advised me of his coming; he came about half-past one o'clock, and remained till half-past two o'clock, a mere visit, nothing of business; he felt the necessity of unburdening himself of many things. First he vented his bitter and indignant scorn on the speeches of the King in Elbing and Hirschberg, and on the utter absence of vigor, which makes itself known in such disconnected ebullitions. Then he spoke with the utmost contempt of von Raumer, the Minister of Public Worship and Instruction, of his brutality and insolence, his hatred of all science, his pernicious activity. 'The King,' Humboldt said, 'hates and despises all his ministers, but this one particularly, and speaks of him as of an ass; what particularly nettles him is, that Raumer opposes all the King's wishes, and he keeps him in office nevertheless, as he keeps all of them, because he has them, and every change is a troublesome affair.' The case of the brothers Schlagintweit was cited as an instance. The King wished to aid them in their voyage to the Himalaya Mountains; the minister refused; the King ordered him to hear the opinion of Humboldt, which was a most favorable one, but Raumer insisted upon his opinion, which, he said, was not changed by Humboldt. Then the King, who confessed himself to be powerless against his minister, wrote to Bunsen, who took the matter in hand, and the brothers Schlagintweit now receive English aid. And the very same King, who pretends to be so jealous of his prerogatives, permits them to be thus encroached upon? 'Yes, sometimes he delights in playing the part of a constitutional monarch, absolves himself from all responsibility when the matter is a delicate one, answers demands made upon him by adverting to the difficulty of obtaining the signatures of his ministers, and even pretends to regard that "baggage, the state" as something with which he had little concern, accuses the ministers of forgetting him in their devotion to that "baggage, the state," &c., &c.

"'In the asking of small sums the King often experiences the greatest resistance, large ones he gets; he is refused three hundred thalers for a poor scientific man or artist, forty thousand thalers for buying something, they dare not refuse. What a mess of confusion and disaster! The King is quite satisfied that he is permitted to cook up church matters to his heart's content, for these are considered separate from the state, no minister has a word in them.' That I do not understand and it cannot be so, the ministers I believe have their hands in it too. 'The meanest fellow of the whole concern is privy counsellor Niebuhr, a low, canting parasite, full of spite and venom.

"'Garcia cannot sing here, he said some time ago, she is too red;* all representations, that her singing would not be red, were in vain. At last I told him to send to Bethania† for deaconesses to sing. He will be happy to see me under the sod.'"

On the 25th of September, Varnhagen narrates in his diary: "They say, on the presence of Humboldt in the High Ecclesiastical Council, that the priests had had in their midst their greatest adversary, who puts all of them to rout—the man of natural science, before whom all their mist and deceits flow into nothingness. 'Abaellino is among you!' one might have cried out."

155.

HUMBOLDT TO VARNHAGEN.

BERLIN, *Dec.* 12*th*, 1853.

AGAIN, my noble friend, you have shown your skill in giving me pleasure. After our departure from Pots-

---

* *I.e.* too much of a Red Republican.

† A Hospital near Berlin, administered by Protestant Sisters of Mercy.

dam, which transformed itself entirely into a Buddhistic "cold hell," was prevented for a long time by the delicate health of the Queen, I at last moved over here on Saturday. You have shed renown upon the Prussian arms, and, what touches me in a more human manner, on the warrior of many-sided culture.* The gallery of your biographies stands in singular grandeur in our German literature. I am enraged by the treatment of my friend Arago in the last number of the "Quarterly Review" (September)—an ebullition of political party spirit, exactly as I was treated by the same journal from 1810–1818. A note at the end of the number for September says, with rare *delicacy*, that the article was written before his death was known; but it was known generally in London that he had become blind, and that he suffered infinitely from dropsy, one of the symptoms of which is to fill the mind with apprehensions.

With ancient gratitude and devotion, and admiration of your talents, your faithful

A. v. HUMBOLDT.

MONDAY.

* Leben des Generals Buelow von Dennewitz. Von K. A. Varnhagen von Ense. Berlin, 1853.

156.

HUMBOLDT TO VARNHAGEN.

Berlin, Thursday Night—from the 13th to the 14th of April, 1854.

Receive, noble friend, my most heartfelt thanks, you and the amiable confidant of the "demons."* The King is now invisible to me, on account of the spiritual preparations, and on Monday he goes to Potsdam for five or six days, on account of military affairs; but a very warm letter, written by me, will be in his hands to-morrow, at eight o'clock, in Charlottenburg.† Thus we have at least done our duty faithfully. I am fast becoming the responsible minister of the *Conservatives;* for three days ago I asked the fourth minimum of the red bird‡ for a man who has *conserved* his real estate for one hundred and fifty years, for Bouché, a gardener, an adopted son§ from the Champagne. It is a great joy to me that my introduction, which has only

---

* Bettina.

† Informing that on the 17th is the golden wedding of Savigny.

‡ The Prussian order of the Red Eagle.

§ Ludwig von Gerlach, in the Second Chamber, had called the representative Bethmann-Hollweg an adopted son of Prussia.

the merit of liberal sentiment and faithfulness, has also pleased you in regard to form. As a sign of gratitude, I send you for your collection of autographs a document not unimportant on account of the political situation—June, 1848. The other papers, which contain the sublunar miserabilities of the disagreement,* which, alas! has become public, I beg you to return hereafter.

Everything noble is drawn down in the mud. I was compelled to write a few lines in answer. I live in a monotonous and sad mood—*et mourant, avant le principe.*

With old fidelity, yours,   A. v. HUMBOLDT.

I shall certainly make my appearance on Monday in a wedding garment.

157.

ARAGO TO HUMBOLDT.

PARIS, *June 3d,* 1848.

MY DEAR AND ILLUSTRIOUS FRIEND:

My son has left for Berlin a few days ago, in the capacity of Minister Plenipotentiary. He quitted me animated with the best of sentiments, with the most

---

* Mons. Mathieu had protested against the statement on the title-page, that Mons. Barral was appointed editor by the author.

decided ideas of peace and conciliation! And yet this day your Chargé d'Affaires waited upon our Minister of Foreign Affairs to represent to him the apprehensions which the mission of my son has excited in your cabinet and among the population of Berlin. This is my recompense for the efforts made since my arrival at power to maintain the accord of the two governments, in order to remove every pretext for war! Who can be made to believe that, animated with the sentiments which I publicly profess, I would have consented to entrust Emanuel with an important diplomatic mission, if he had been in discord with me, if he belonged to a hideous socialist sect, to *communism*, for, I am ashamed to say it, the accusations made have not stopped short of that? As to the rest, I appeal to the future; all such apprehensions will disappear as soon as Emanuel shall have entered upon his functions. Your Chargé d'Affaires will then regret the untimely protest addressed to M. Bastide.

I am very happy, my dear friend, to receive your welcome letter. Nothing in the world could be more agreeable than to hear of the continuance of your friendship. I am worthy of it, because of the price I set upon it. I have an abiding faith that my conduct, during the last three months (I had about said the last three centuries), has not caused me to lose in your esteem.

Ever yours, with heart and soul,   F. ARAGO.

158.

HUMBOLDT TO VARNHAGEN.

BERLIN, FRIDAY, *April* 14*th*, 1854.

As the King held his churching on Thursday, I dined in Charlottenburg to-day, and can give you news agreeable to us, that the King, as he told me, had known of the day of honor* (not by Uhden!!)† and had prepared everything for it long ago. The ingredients of the spiritual or material feeding are buried in Cimmerian darkness. Your faithful
HUMBOLDT.

The Prince of Prussia knows nothing of the invitation for noce et festin.

159.

HUMBOLDT TO VARNHAGEN.

MY American connexions having entailed upon me the predilection of the Peace Society, I am molested

---

* Savigny's golden wedding. † Minister.

by them with many of their writings and tracts. But the last number of the "Herald of Peace" is so remarkable on account of the political movement of the pietistic peace Quakers, that perhaps it will amuse you for one moment, my dear friend, to read for yourself the testimonies. Destroy the sheet!

The missive, at the same time, is intended for a sign of *life*, that is, of most intimate and faithful friendship for you in these sad times of weakness and folly. I have disentangled myself from the new "Stahl-Ranke" council, for reasons which are not those of old age; I resigned. I add an unkempt letter of poor Bunsen, which you must keep quite secret, and send it to me, if there is an opportunity, to my Berlin residence. First Heidelberg and afterwards Bonn, constantly vibrating between the perturbating recollections of two archbishops. With the dangerous tendency of the noble man for theological dispute, and for his newly-invented apostolic church, under the firm of Hippolytus, a residence in England, that is to say, in the country between London and Oxford (on account of the books), would be more favorable than Bonn. The Anglican High Church, intolerant though it be, is less inconvenient in a *free* country, than a ministerial church diet in Prussia. Moreover, in the interest of Bunsen's scientific reputation, I look forward with dread to the impending productions, full of hypotheses on aboriginal nations,

Egyptian, Indian, and excavated Assyrian Semitic, as also on the situation of Paradise, for which *a map has been ordered* at Kiepert's. Maps on the creeds of nations can ascend from the ship-fastening myth at the ocean and the Himalaya mountains to the Ararat and to Aramea Kymbotas, even to the Mexican Coxcox, vagaries, not unknown to the Mormon bible. (See Supplement.)

The Weimar fancies are of a more exhilarating kind; controlling the climates by means of crystal palaces, which, at the same time, are taverns, and make superfluous Nicos and Madeira, and demand only a capital of one and a half millions of thalers, an undertaking in the deserted Potsdam town of barracks. And such a device, hatched in the brains of a well-informed man like Froriep.

In faithful friendship, yours,   A. HUMBOLDT.

POTSDAM, *July 4th,* 1854. In the age of crystal palaces.

It was but the other day, in glancing at a letter of Gneisenau's, of 1818 (in the pointless biography of Stein,[*] p. 262) that I stumbled upon a passage, doubtless long familiar to you: "H. strives again for the centre, but there are wanting to him confidence, *esteem, character*, and courage." Sheer personal hatred alone can have moved the vain Gneisenau to speak thus disreputably of

[*] By Pertz.

my brother. I recollect, indeed, to have heard of him, that Gneisenau was hostile to him when he was dismissed. By-the-by, what was said by all parties in those times on political institutions looks to me now, and did so already in the years 1815–1818, as if I was reading a book of the thirteenth century on physical science; fear of provincial estates was alone praiseworthy— c'est de la bouillie pour les chats.

On this letter Varnhagen remarks in his diary, July 5th, 1854:—"I found a long letter from Humboldt, who communicated to me, accompanied by fine remarks, the latest number of the Herald of Peace, a letter of Bunsen—four closely-written quarto pages—and another by Robert Froriep, of Weimar. 'The missive at the same time is intended for a sign of *life*, that is, of most intimate and faithful friendship for you in these sad times of weakness and folly.' Farther: 'I disengaged myself from the new "Stahl-Ranke" council, for reasons, which are not those of old age; I resigned.' Then he speaks of Froriep's plays of imagination, who wishes to build a crystal palace to control the climate in the 'deserted town of barracks,' Potsdam, with a loan of one and a half million of thalers! Finally, he blames Gneisenau's misjudgment on Wilhelm von Humboldt, pronounced in a letter of 1818, which Pertz communicates in his 'pointless Biography of Stein;' and Humboldt rightly condemns the mean misjudgment of his brother.

"The letter of Bunsen is written in a very unconnected manner—Humboldt calls it an 'unkempt' one, which characterizes it admirably. Bunsen intends to live for the future in Bonn, but he complains that the university has deteriorated so much, particularly the theological faculty. Dorner and Rothe have been jostled out, and their places are held by the most mediocre and narrow-minded people to be found in all Germany, such as Lange and Steinmeyer; from Hengstenberg's study, through Gerlach, all bends, he says, to ignorance and darkness, the present gloomy period of the most intellectual king of the century will come to be deplored even more grievously than the age of Woellner; every thing is imbued with the reactionary political character of the squirearchy; hypocrisy and *real* infidelity can grow out of this unholy system, and a most violent reaction must ensue; body-guards and policemen can enforce any political programme as long as it lasts; but the German never submits to the enthralment of the mind, and his curse will pursue through all the centuries those who have attempted it. Thus writes Bunsen! But he writes thus now as a deposed favorite! How was he, and for what did he work before? For the same ignorance and darkness. Quite like Radowitz, who also played the liberal at last!"

160.

VARNHAGEN TO HUMBOLDT.

BERLIN, *July* 8*th*, 1854.

WITH emotions of gratitude I received the dear letter of your Excellency. Yet a sign of life, indeed, a sign of the most vigorous life! Whenever the question could arise how you felt and thought in this gloomy time, such a sheet would be the most decided answer, the most brilliant testimony, to a sentiment and activity which always kept on in the same direction, and never proved false. The letter from London—the epithet "unkempt" is singularly happy. I send back dutifully, as directed; how I should have liked to incorporate it with my collections! It is a remarkable sign of the present situation; many expressions in it strikingly significant. Had the writer but expressed himself thus before his last personal experience! The scientific renown which you believe in danger from the threatening deluge of writings seems to me to have stood from the first upon unsafe ground, upheld by external props, with which it must fall inevitably. Perhaps a political career will be open to him again, but certainly not through literary aid, for which, in part, this sudden literary taste seems intended. Silent rest would be far more useful. But this can hardly be expected in the place selected, where Catholic hatred is already alive, and nourishes and strengthens that political rancor which will continue in vigor, fed with fuel from here.

The late Prince Wittgenstein once congratulated me that I had not to sit in the Council of State, and that was the old Council, of which your Excellency also was a member! How much more must I congratulate you on your escape from the new one, of which Stahl and Ranke are members! To the latter, no one will dispute the part of the clown; to the first, every one will accord that of the sophist.

The words of Gneisenau, which Pertz alludes to in Stein's Leben (v. 262), are so entirely inapplicable to William von Humboldt that one would be tempted to interpret the H. differently, if an acceptable conjecture could be found. I have myself, indeed, heard from Gneisenau's lips expressions of dissatisfaction, but never such extravagant ones, which might be contradicted so easily and perfectly. What Gneisenau blamed chiefly in your brother was that he never tried, by the respect which he commanded and by the superiority of his mind, to unite all those of equal sentiment into a communion, by which much might have been undertaken and effected. But this reproach, if it be one, Gneisenau himself deserved as well, and received from his adherents! The book of Pertz is full of aspersions and incongruities, which, indeed, in most cases originate in Stein himself, but are confirmed by Pertz in blind partiality; he, while communicating everything, even in many cases things which do not belong to the subject, leaves out important documents without hesitation as soon as he finds them not entirely for the benefit of his hero. The same will take place when he writes the biography of Gneisenau, for which the hand of a tactician would seem to be the first desideratum.

The pious quaker-sheet was already known to me; one could hardly have thought such monstrosities practicable in the English language! But our time abounds in such. The psychographer takes the place of the moving table; they try to enforce my faith in the absurdity; I excuse myself, that at my time of life a man is a little backward, and that I have just arrived at table moving, but of that they do not want to hear any more. This reminds me of something, I will not suppress! It of course happens often, that remarks of your Excellency, in particular such made at the royal table, come to the ears of the public, and are repeated with zeal, and by this assume widely different forms; thus, quite recently, a reply to Herr Senfft von Pilsach, in which the original form seemed lost to a great extent, it would certainly be desirable if the latter were always authentically preserved.

With my repeated most heartfelt thanks, in most faithful reverence and submission, I remain immutably, your Excellency's most obedient,

VARNHAGEN VON ENSE.

Some strong expressions in the London letter, as welcome to me as they were unexpected, remind me that Herr von Radowitz indulged in similar ones, and even had them printed (Gesammelte Schriften IV., 210, 256, 281); in the second passage he even goes so far as to reverse the motto, "Against democrats soldiers alone avail!"

161.

HUMBOLDT TO VARNHAGEN.

BERLIN, July 9th, 1854.

RETURNING from the Russian Saint's day celebrated in Sans Souci, I found your amiable letter. As I cannot refuse you anything, I add Hippolytus! Satisfy in return my curiosity. I believe that I never in my life spoke to Herr Senfft von Pilsach; I might meet him in the street or in society without knowing him. Notwithstanding all this I may have dined with him at the King's. After what I heard of him I do not feel well affected towards him. Since I always sit opposite the

King, I talk aloud only to him, but very freely, because I know that it will be reported, colored certainly according to the color of the reporter, and this the more especially in a country where anything like a gentle allusion by way of criticism is lost on account of the complete want of development of conversational language.

The judgment of Gneisenau is certainly on my brother. These often are ebullitions of the moment. Schiller writes to Koerner, when I arrived in Jena, "that I was by far more ingenious and gifted than my brother;" afterwards, in a time when he saw me daily and overwhelmed me with tenderness, he wrote to Koerner that "I was a man of narrow understanding," without poetry or soul, who, in spite of all my restless activity in my walk of study, never would accomplish anything great; that Herder's works were diseases, discharged by his mental constitution." (One thinks it is a passage of Zelter's letters!) In an autograph of a collection at Augsburg, which they wanted to give to me, but which I sent back, my friend Prince S. writes to Koreff: "Alexander H. again accompanies the King to the Congress at Aachen only as a pointer!" Thus they play on the boards of the world for credulous posterity.

The Emperor Alexander had told the late King that my brother was doubtless bribed by the Jews to be of service to them in the Congress of Vienna, as Baron von Buelow was bribed in the Belgian affair by the French, according to the King of Hanover. In Schoening's very interesting War of the Bavarian Succession, interesting by the correspondence with Prince Heinrich and the reflection cast on the present disputable state of things, there is mentioned on p. 294, a political project, which was unknown to me, the Austrian proposition to give Burgundy as a kingdom to the Bavarian dynasty in return for a cession of Bavaria. This title of King of Burgundy was the object of the ambition of the Duke of M. in 1815, though he would have contented himself with Lorraine and Alsatia. Napoleon also once had a momentary intention to make the Principe de la Paz, King of Baetica (Andalusia and Grenada) from recollections of "Télémaque," and the King of Sardinia, Roi de Numidie, although the donor had not a foot of land in Africa to dispose of.

With warm friendship, always equally incorrect and illegible, your most faithful,

A. v. HUMBOLDT.

SATURDAY NIGHT.

NOTE BY VARNHAGEN.—As early as the year 1743, Austria offered to the Emperor Charles VII. a kingdom not yet conquered, to be composed of Alsace, Lorraine, and Franche Comté, in return for Bavaria. See "Mem. de Noailles," Tome vi.

162.

HUMBOLDT TO BETTINA VON ARNIM.

(Copied by Varnhagen.)

BERLIN, *July 8th*, 1854.

To what purpose, most gracious baroness, did the Eternal shower down upon you, from the horn of plenty that he so sparingly opens upon this miserable, sinful earth, the bountiful gift of genius and the more precious adornment of a noble heart, if you believe the absurd gossip uttered "about those from whom I am separating myself!" What you call your prophetic vision could not alarm me, because the same double sight has fallen to my lot! Not a syllable of your book has the King read or desired to have read to him, as I hear from others; I rarely attend in the evening, and have not read to him for years. But how, my honored friend, am I to gain his ear in this matter, when I never pronounce the words Cathedral, Orchestra, Theatre, or Concert Room, and never have heard of the existence of a Central University Cathedral Building Association at Bonn, or of a Board of Managers of the Berlin Association? Such things are undoubtedly desirable; but even if those who are now called influential would advocate them by word of mouth, their intercession would not even receive attention; success is only to be hoped for from an official exposé of the project, addressed immediately to the King himself, with the autograph signature of the managers, with specific and distinct requests. The decision rests exclusively with the cabinet, and to be discussed there, a full and explicit petition to the King is necessary. This is doubly important at a time so eventful as the present, when the King never remains longer than a few weeks at Sans Souci. Painter Rattis' Titian, political insinuations, and great unknown personages, are all subjects of which I receive the first intimation from your kind letter. It will be my study to repel the insinuations, although, on account of my well-known opinions, these "*essais de blanchir*" will be but a feeble support. Among the many painful impressions you so sedulously cultivate in the midst of your glowing love of the true, the free, the noble, and the good, it gives me great delight to direct your attention to two special matters of gratification—your Goethe monument is a fixed fact, and the great man's grandson, whom I regard and esteem, has succeeded in obtaining a recognition of the value of his services, and a less constrained position in the Roman embassy.

With unalterable devotion and friendship,
I remain your Old Man of the Hills,
A. v. Ht.

163.

HUMBOLDT TO VARNHAGEN.

BERLIN, *July* 10*th*, 1854.

SUCH a rough "Hind Pomeranian!"* direct answer, dear friend, you could certainly not expect from me! I have no idea of the question about the animation of pinewood at the King's table, where everybody believes in it as in the Persian host seen in the air at the Eichsfeld. The "drama" of the "Kreuz Zeitung," like everything emanating from this bad party, sick with mental poverty, bears the stamp of cowardly malice! You are not to be pitied, for you possess a treasure in the power of animating recollections of the great period of 1813. I have always kept at a respectful distance from the *Revue des Deux Mondes*, which is edited with spirit and address. Two parties may hate the same thing without hating it from the same motives. The present Liberals there think themselves justified in *barking*, but not *biting*, after the fashion of the Berlin

---

* The province of Pomerania is divided into "Vorpommern"— *Fore Pomerania*, and "Hinterpommern"— *Hind Pomerania; i. e.* Pomerania before and behind the Oder.—*Tr.*

muzzles, "because, without the rescuer* they would all have been drenched in blood." *Credat Judæus Apella!*

Your faithful, A. V. HUMBOLDT.

Monday.—At another funeral!†
A workman, unknown to me, addressed me at the funeral of Benjamin Constant: "N'est-ce pas, mon bon Monsieur, vous n'avez rien de si beau en Prusse, mais ce sera bien plus beau quand nous enterrerons M. de la Fayette."

164.

HUMBOLDT TO VARNHAGEN.

BERLIN, *July 29th*, 1854.

IN Spain, the virtuous rebels, like the virtuous order of St. John on the Wilhelmsplatz, have raised the cry of "Long live chastity!"—"Viva el pudor" (Isabella)! "Viva la moralidad" (disinterested Christina)! But, will you, dear friend, think it possible (July, 1854!) that the Minister of Public Worship and Instruction,

---

* Louis Napoleon.—*Tr.*

† Of M. Borsig, a machinist, a few days after that of Mad. Amalia Beer. The old man of eighty-five attended both of them.

though hitherto without success, is also shouting "Viva el pudor!" He has quite officially demanded a royal order for the imprisonment in the arsenal of the wanton group* which so wantonly disport themselves on the bridge; all this without fear from the press, since the new press law, promulgated by the Diet at Frankfort, only resembles the ingenious Berlin muzzles, not yet exhibited in the Muenchen Crystal Palace, which prevent authors from biting only, but not from barking.

The third cry, "Viva la libertad!" has succeeded in the Peninsula, after all, in spite of the disavowals of good society.

Your faithful   A. v. HUMBOLDT.

AT NIGHT.

165.

HUMBOLDT TO VARNHAGEN.

BERLIN, July 31st, 1854.

ALAS! no! I was in error thinking that the monument for Weimar was definitely bought, only that the enlargement of it, desired by our excellent lady friend, was given up. In the circles with which I am acquainted

---

* In marble.—*Tr.*

we cannot hope for an active participation. The expression, "Is not art itself a vestment?" is fine and felicitous.

Most gratefully yours,   A. v. HUMBOLDT.

Monday, waiting for the train to leave.

In the United States there has, it is true, arisen a great love for me, but the whole there presents to my mind the sad spectacle of liberty reduced to a mere mechanism in the element of utility, exercising little ennobling or elevating influence upon mind and soul, which, after all, should be the aim of political liberty. Hence indifference on the subject of slavery. But the United States are a Cartesian vortex, carrying everything with them, grading everything to the level of monotony.

166.

VARNHAGEN TO HUMBOLDT.

BERLIN, *January 8th*, 1855.

I HAVE to thank your Excellency most heartily that, in dispensing bounties, you always think with favor also of me! No one shall surpass me in anxiety to receive, in estimation of the gift, and in gratitude for the noble donor! This preface, at once temperate in form, rich in substance, and elegiac in tone, is the worthiest and most lasting monument of the prince,* of whom I hear on every side accounts which make one mourn his loss in the prime of life. I shall try to procure his work which is so highly recommended by your Excellency.

The gloomy cover of mist which veils the light of day, corresponds with the sentiments by which I at least feel myself weighed down. I have not succeeded in becoming cheerful for some days.

With the warmest wishes for you, in faithful reverence and most grateful submission, immutably

Your Excellency's most obedient,

VARNHAGEN VON ENSE.

167.

HUMBOLDT TO VARNHAGEN.

BERLIN, *April* 26*th*, 1855.

REVERED FRIEND—A strange missionary experiment, enveloped in a somewhat idyllic ghost story, political and religious, in a style of singular "finish" and bombast, which I cannot refrain from showing to you. I take it to be the work of a male author.

The saturnalia of despotism and of flatteries, the wan-

---

* Waldemar of Prussia, the traveller in India and Brazil.—*Tr.*

ton festival of *oblivion* (as if there was no history of 1813 and '14), is now played out among the free insular people, a kind of monkey comedy. There is only this consolation which uplifts my spirit, that out of all this something will arise, which both parties do not at all intend. That is, *le principe*, which outlives us all. I am so cruel as to include you too. To my brother, Wilhelm, the Kassel book seems to have done good up there. In old attachment and reverence,

Your faithful   A. HUMBOLDT.
WEDNESDAY.

Be good enough to return the ghost story, by all means.

NOTE BY VARNHAGEN TO HUMBOLDT'S LETTER OF APRIL 26TH, 1855.—A "stranger is emboldened to transmit words of power to the spirit." "They are given to her with the order to repeat them." In case Humboldt should answer, he is requested to send the letter with the chiffre A. W., to the store on the left of the house, at No. 120 Linden Street, and receive further details. A wanderer is described as sitting down to rest. Brother Wilhelm appears to brother Alexander and exhorts him to think of the kingdom of heaven, and how splendid it is up there, how misty on earth. As a token of identity, he reminds him of the eighteenth warm birthday, "where they swore to love each other," an oath which reaches beyond the portals of death, and which he now fulfils. It is a bombastic farrago, frequently repeating the word "finish," which strikes the reader as eminently inappropriate.

Of the above-named direction Humboldt observes: "That it is the boarding-school of Frau von Wenkstern and Widow Poppe."

168.

HUMBOLDT TO VARNHAGEN.

BERLIN, *August 9th*, 1855.

I HAD already heard with sorrow from the gifted Princess von Wittgenstein, that you, noble friend, suffered more than usually. Receive me with indulgence on Saturday, about 10 o'clock, in spite of my long absence, and of my inconvenient trilogy, Berlin, Tegel, and Potsdam. I shall then also bring you a few lines of thanks to your cousin, the Imperial Brazilian Chargé d'Affaires in Madrid. His history, founded upon archival monuments, seems to become of great importance; but what a strange missive without adding the first pages, and notes also without a beginning.* I doubt of my ever catching those commencements in my cosmic disorder. As I spent almost an hour alone with the Prince of Prussia yesterday, I shall be able to tell you something not uninteresting, although not at all decisive. The Prince, whom I take to be veracious,

---

* Historia general de Brazil, tomo primeiro. The pieces wanting here he had already sent as specimens.

assures me of having always asserted, faithful to his principles, that war would probably have been avoided, if Prussia and Austria had from the first co-operated actively with the Western powers against Russia. They answered in St. Petersburg that the Emperor would not have yielded, but this the Prince doubted. . . . .

   With old attachment, yours,

        A. v. HUMBOLDT.

THURSDAY.

You will explain to me orally the mythological name of Sorocaba.*

Varnhagen narrates in his diary, under date of August 11th, 1855 :—" About 1 o'clock Humboldt came, looking well, quite vigorous, in fresh and lively spirits; when he make a worse impression a short time ago, as Dirichlet thought, it was the effect of sickness, and is passed now. First, he spoke of the book of my cousin, which he praised, for which he thanks him (in a letter). The expression Sorocaba I cannot explain to him. Humboldt was but recently made a knight of the great Brazilian order, on account of an arbitration between Brazil and Venezuela, respecting a large tract

---

* Francisco Adolfo de Varnhagen's dedication of his book to the Emperor over his own signature. The title-page contains the words : " Por um socio do Instituto Historico do Brazil, Natural de Sorocaba' (the native place of the author, west of Rio Janeiro).

of land. 'Formerly they intended, in Rio de Janeiro, to arrest me as a dangerous spy, and to send me back to Europe, the order drawn up for the purpose is still shown there as a curiosity; now they make me an arbitrator! I, of course, decided for Brazil, because I wanted the large order; the Republic of Venezuela has none to confer!' These words, spoken in the gayest irony, I interrupted with the exclamation, 'How times change!' 'Yes; the order of arrest, and then the insignia of the great order!' 'Oh, no,' I replied, 'I did not think of this personal affair, but of the historical; formerly the pope was the general arbitrator!' Humboldt saw the last volumes of the life of Stein on my table, and expressed his displeasure on the external arrangement, the meagreness of the text, and the unsifted character of this book; he thought that the gold snuff-box, with brilliants, which the King had already sent to Pertz for these volumes, was entirely too much. Injustice, crying and mean, perpetrated by Stein against old Prince Wittgenstein. Pertz, too, he said, was unjust to Wittgenstein. Stein had not at all been a firm character, no one had changed views and judgments more easily. (Beyme said the same thing, and adduced instances of it.) His early liberal ideas on national economy, civil institutions, commerce, and trades, were a product of the times, which he afterwards entirely renounced and disputed when the current of opinion set in that direction. He surrendered his former sentiments so shamefully that his former friend, Kunth, who remained faithful to them, but also wished to avoid committing Stein, burned more than three hundred of Stein's letters, because, as he thought, they would bring nothing but disgrace on the revered man, and would show him in the greatest contradiction with himself. Of the Prince of Prussia, Humboldt said that he had told every one in St. Petersburg, as well as here, that the war would have been avoided if Prussia had from the first acted resolutely. The Emperor Nicholas would have yielded. The imperial family he represented as harmonious, including the Grand Duke Constantine, who did not seem so dangerous to him as usually described. The Emperor's mother used to say they were all mere children, and that she must remain with them in order to keep them together. The war was severely felt, business at a standstill, the country drained of men, the armies not very numerous; Poland, the Baltic countries, and Finland but weakly garrisoned; the greater part of their forces was in the Crimea; the losses immense and irreparable. Gortschakoff reports that the daily combats cost him 180–200 men—a frightful number for a month; that Nesselrode contemplates a renewal of negotiations, but before that heavy blows would first be dealt on one side or on the other. Sebastopol itself was by no means considered out of danger. The Prince has gone from here to Erdmannsdorf to the King; thence he hastens on to Baden. The King has Lieutenant-General von Gerlach, with him in Erdmannsdorf, among others, also Radowitz, in case he is not 'already tired of him, as happens so easily.' Humboldt talks of Radowitz decidedly as of a Jesuit, calls him Ignatius, mocks him, and jests on him a long time. 'The great destinies of Italy' leave the King very indifferent; but a colored pane of glass, a quaint device on an old monument, a family name, enlist his greatest interest, occupy, and amuse him; and for such trifles Radowitz was the right man! The same is the case with Bunsen, with whom the King corresponds on theological and patristic curiosities. He has asked him to write articles in the papers against the Bishop of Mainz; but Bunsen makes the condition to be allowed to refer in his articles to the command of the King, since otherwise they would possess neither influence nor effect. Humboldt thinks Bunsen would not resist a call hither, even if it was not official, but only a personal one by the King. The Duke of Coburg-Gotha desires an enlargement of his territory and a higher title—that of a 'King of Ostphalia' is already proposed. The King jestingly calls him by that title already. He counts upon England and France, and willingly flatters and accommodates Bonaparte, who would meet with little difficulty in being the recognised Protector of a new Rhenish Confederation. So much for Germany and Teutonism. It is betrayed most assiduously by its sworn defenders. Finally, Humboldt added: 'When a man has the misfortune to be compelled to live among such wretches as this Gerlach, Raumer, and the rest who have crept into this Court.' .... He went from me to the Koethener Strasse to look at a picture, and left me much excited. I could not keep in mind and write down one-tenth of all he said."

Varnhagen adds, on the 12th of August, Humboldt said of the situation of Prussia, it reminded him of a trial he once heard in Paris; the lawyer had to ask damages for a box on the car, and had exclaimed triumphantly at the close: "Au fond nous n'avons pas reçu le soufflet, nous n'avons eu que le geste!"

169.

HUMBOLDT TO VARNHAGEN.

BERLIN, *January* 13*th*, 1856.

SMILE, dear friend (you are fully justified!) at the strange lines of Princess Lieven, and at my troublesome inquiry. Madame de Quitzow, who has not written to me for twenty-five years, wants to know, whether the

Emperor Paul, in the epoch of his political insanity, had made the proposition through Kotzebue, that the ministers for foreign affairs should measure swords personally instead of the armies. I was at that time (1799 and 1800) in the deltas of South America, and was entirely ignorant of the anecdote which the Russian Princess now, as it appears to me, so occidental in her predilections, desires to corroborate. The obscure researches I have made would seem to lead to the result that the duel was to be waged not by the ministers but by the monarchs themselves. I pray you, noble friend, to write me a few lines on what your excellent memory supplies, and still more I pray you to tell me consoling words about your health at the return of the injurious cold weather. Bunsen writes me that he expects a fourth edition of his letters. Does the great reading demand for this excellent or rather useful book indicate that the German public is less chloroformed against action than we had supposed? *Dubito.* The German landlord of a (dicunt) very dirty hotel, which glories in my name in California for many years—beside a more cleanly one of "Jenny Lind,"—sends me German California papers from time to time. In a discourse on the moral and intellectual state of the English, the French, and the Germans, the editor recently said: " We Germans are a nation of thinkers, deeply occupied with the world of ideas, we also have the *great advan-*

tage before the members of other nations who live here, that we care little or not at all about civil or political affairs." Thus we boast on the shores of the Pacific, buy the "Zeichen der Zeit," but hardly 5 per cent of us go to the primary elections. It is inconvenient, we think. With old love and reverence,

   Yours,   A. v. HUMBOLDT.

Was not the young Tyrolese very amiable poet Adolf Pichler (properly speaking a geologist by trade) with you? I do not believe in peace during this quite . . . . or at least uncomfortable humiliating . . . . *
year, though certainly in useless diplomatic transactions.

NOTE BY VARNHAGEN.—In the third line stands "Madame de Quitzow," clearly a mistake instead of "Madame de Lieven." What may have been the reason that that name, here entirely without meaning, should have protruded itself, cannot be guessed.

LATER NOTE BY VARNHAGEN.—The Princess Lieven is closely connected with the late Minister Guizot, they even say secretly married to him. Guizot, pronounced German easily sounds Quitzow, a well-known name in the Mark. Humboldt, always inclined to jesting, and particularly here, may have given her this surname—perhaps current already at the court—with full intention. [This is quite right.]

   * These two words are illegible.

170.

THE PRINCESS LIEVEN TO HUMBOLDT.

PARIS, *January 8th*, 1856.

You have not forgotten me, my dear Baron. I know that by two kind messages which Baron Brockhausen brought me from you. I have charged him to testify my lively gratitude; but I now prefer to express it myself. On this occasion, it serves me as the passport to a question which I take the liberty of addressing you.

Can you, who know everything, remember the following fact? In 1799 or 1800, the Emperor Paul took it into his head to propose a combat on a tilted field, where England, Russia, Austria, and I know not what other power, should adjust their differences by the persons of their Prime Ministers, Pitt, Thugut, etc. The task of drawing up this invitation was assigned to Kotzebue, and the article inserted in the "Hamburg Gazette." This is my very distinct recollection. I have not dreamed any part of it. Could you complete the tradition? I can meet with no one who remembers it. I have thought you might be able to sustain my memory, and I hope so still, for I am suspected of having lost my wits.

Paul I. was not such a fool, after all. Do you not consider the follies of our time much greater? What a chaos? And for what? ....

My dear Baron, I live here in a little intimate circle of old friends, who are your friends also, and who hold you in affectionate remembrance. What a pleasure we should have in seeing you here, and together forgetting the troubles of the hour! O that men and things were worth more at this day! Is this an old woman's commission with which I trouble you?

Adieu, my dear Baron. I ask your recollection and regard, and promise a bountiful return.

   Ever yours, THE PRINCESS LIEVEN.

171.

VARNHAGEN TO HUMBOLDT.

BERLIN, *January* 27*th*, 1856.

WITH joyful thanks I profit by your Excellency's goodness in sending me the copy of your beautiful response to the deputies of the city of Berlin. Were it not presumption to praise, where praise has already become a habit and a superfluity, I should say that the speech is as full of sterling merit as of noble intention. The brightest passage, to my mind, is the (I hesitate whether to call it felicitous or masterly) allusion to the King, in terms so dignified and delicate, so warm and graceful; and every pure heart must at once acknowledge, that in this connexion the remark was singularly appropriate and beautiful. In your Excellency's last favor, the expression, "Madame de Quitzow," at first puzzled me a good deal. But I may boast of having solved the riddle by the power of the head—as the Jews say, where we speak of cudgelling our brains—and am constrained to acknowledge that the little sally is not only a good joke, but proportionably a mild measure of punishment. The Grand Duke of Saxe Weimar desired to see me; but I found myself chained down to my rheumatic complaint.

With faithful reverence and most grateful devotion, unalterably your Excellency's most obedient,

VARNHAGEN VON ENSE.

172.

HUMBOLDT TO VARNHAGEN.

BERLIN, January 28th, 1856.

My far from dormant ambition has been abundantly gratified by the grateful praise bestowed by the great master of our language (to avoid the expression rhetorician), upon my manner of speaking of the King, and my relations with him. In praising that with which the party praised is but scantily supplied, we point him to the honorable road, and justify ourselves before the people. A man of the woods, who is supposed to have been tamed at court, is in need of such justification. Madame Quitzow, whom I could not sooner obtain from the King, I now repose in your hands, as your own. Our former minister, General Thiele, was firmly persuaded that the Guizots of the neighborhood of Montpellier were disguised remnants, softened in pronunciation, Frenchified and Protestantized, of the emigrated Quitzows* from Langkloder. And your poor excellent Dora, who pities all your friends for the sufferings she knows so well how to alleviate! Give her my kindest regards.

Your faithful
A. Humboldt.

At Night.

The Grand Duke, whom you escaped, sends much love. He has curious theories, probably imbibed somewhere or other (Bœotia was near to ancient Attica),

---

* A Brandenburg family of the Middle Ages, who came near hanging one of the Electors of Brandenburg, predecessor of the Kings of Prussia. They were representatives of those "Robber Knights" who long successfully resisted the introduction of regular government by the Electors.—*Tr.*

and misunderstood. There are two classes of sculptors, the one inferior, to which Rauch inclines, and which works *inward from without*, while the better (represented by Rietschel) works *outward from within*. But what an exposure. Philarète Chasles in the "Journal des Debats!" I wrote to Paris: "Vulgaire dans les idées comme dans les formes des langage, indigne d'un littérateur du Collége de France."

173.

HUMBOLDT TO VARNHAGEN.

BERLIN, THURSDAY, *Feb. 7th*, 1856.

As it would be impossible that you, dear friend, should not have seen the new book by Montalembert (the friend and companion of the Abbé Lammenais on his journey to Rome), I hope to give you a little pleasure by offering you the King's copy for a few days (five or six). The only thing racy in it is the conclusion, levelled at the present state of affairs in France, p. 284 to 298. I wish it were possible to have the whole of it translated and published in Germany.

Most gratefully yours,   A. v. HUMBOLDT.

How is our excellent Dora doing? I had a patriarchal time yesterday until seven o'clock, at Potsdam, at a christening of a child of a very handsome and accomplished daughter of my Siberian waiting-man's, Seifert, who,* a traveller named Moellhausen, who, at Baron Gerolt's and my recommendation, accompanied the great exploring expedition of Captain Whipple, of San Luis, San Francisco, and Panama, in the capacity of topographer and draughtsman for the American Government. It is about a year since the King appointed young Moellhausen custodian of the palace library at Potsdam.

An excellent article by Laboulaye, on the domestic Institution, and the flagitious Pierce's extension of the outrage upon territory, hitherto free, met my eye yesterday in the "Journal des Débats," of the 5th of February, I believe!

Keep the very commonplace verses "Oh, Gentle Jlm."

174.

VARNHAGEN TO HUMBOLDT.

BERLIN, *March* 14*th*, 1856.

YOUR Excellency's kind and precious gift come into the seclusion forced upon me by the rude relapse of

---

* "is married to," evidently omitted in the original. Humboldt took a great interest in Moellhausen, and wrote a preface to his book on the above journey.—*Tr.*

winter, brighter and more enlivening than the sunbeams which accompany them! Receive my repeated thanks and the assurance that I know how to appreciate every one of them, and most of all the beneficent intention, which remember me so well, and gladden my heart so cheerily! The pencil lines of the dying Heine are a valued keepsake, and shall be continued to be devoutly treasured in the envelope superscribed by your Excellency. The boon of to-day, the significant combination of Archimedes and Franklin in reference to their tombstones, I have also read with the warmest appreciation.

I see that you do not dread the wind or the weather, and that, fortunately, you need not dread them, when a duty of honor is to be performed. The present time imposes curious tasks upon us! The death of a chief of police in a duel is probably unprecedented in the communities of modern Europe. The summoning of a Minister of Foreign Affairs to Paris, to attend at the close of important negotiations, with a box of writing sand from the Mark,* has also a fabulous aspect. However, Allah is great!

In the most faithful reverence and most grateful devotion, I remain immutably

Your Excellency's most obedient,

VARNHAGEN VON ENSE.

---

* The Mark Brandenburg, a very sandy province, sometimes facetiously called the sand-box of the Holy Roman Empire.—*Tr.*

175.

HUMBOLDT TO VARNHAGEN.

BERLIN, *April 14th*, 1856.

I COULD not but speak, being the Nestor of Prussian mining officials, and prone to boast of my calling. My reliance upon your *indulgence*, dear and worthy friend, is so great, that I am emboldened to send even *you* a copy of these unimportant lines. Count B. deserved this praise. Free from opinion of any kind, he is useful to the art of mining, and still occupies himself with scientific pursuits since he has resigned the direction.

With unshaken constancy, yours,

A. v. HUMBOLDT.

NOTE BY VARNHAGEN.—Enclosed was the address delivered at the fiftieth anniversary of the entrance into the royal miners of his Excellency the Actual Privy Councillor and Captain of Miners, Count Beust. April 9th, 1856.

178.

HUMBOLDT TO VARNHAGEN.

BERLIN, *September* 11*th*, 1856.

KNOWING the warm interest you take, my dear friend, in the slavery question, and in what concerns myself, I send you the last letter of Gerolt, which was very long in coming, but which will certainly command your attention. Most unfortunately Buchanan will be the next President, and not Fremont, the traveller of great acquirements, who has four times travelled the land route to San Francisco, surveying the country over which he passed, to whom it is owing that California did become a free State. Do *not* return the letter, nor the enclosure. On the heels of this African absurdity comes another folly, of a more serious cast, though richly fraught with ridicule, not royalistic so much as aristocratically Bernese, and spiced with a little railroad speculation as to whether the route by the way of Neufchatel or that by way of Chaux de Fonds is to be preferred! And the heroic Count,* who executes the coup d'état à la Napoleon, whence did he derive his

---

* Pourtalès, conspicuous in the Neufchatel embroglio.—*Tr.*

inspiration? From Berlin, while we have a minister at the Diet, whom at this day we pretend never to have recognised. How are these things to be reconciled? We shall have a similar fate with our three ultramarine possessions, the Jade, the Zollern, discovered by Columbus Stillfried, and Neufchatel. I feel for the Constantinopolitan Pourtalès, who finds himself involved in an awkward conflict between his dynasty (the Prussian earldom) and his official liberalism. It is fortunate that the mouth of the English Parliament is still closed.

Your faithful A. v. HUMBOLDT.

177.

THE PRUSSIAN MINISTER RESIDENT, VON GEROLT, TO HUMBOLDT.

NEW YORK, *August 25th*, 1856.

MY MOST DEAR AND HONORED PATRON!

Since my last letter to your Excellency, of the 8th inst., I was made happy by your favor of the 27th of July, from which I learn, with the most sincere regret, of your temporary indisposition. For the information it contains I return your Excellency my most hearty thanks, and hasten to comply with your wish by sending two extracts from papers published here (the "New

York Herald" and the " Courrier des Etats Unis"), containing your publication on the subject of slavery in Cuba, as well as the excuse published by Mr. Thrasher, which is, it must be confessed, exceedingly lame.

The affair has excited great attention here, and could not but be welcome to the opponents of slavery, who have made Fremont their candidate.

Some days ago, his German supporters, many thousands in number, held a mass meeting in his support, and honored him with a splendid torch-light procession in the evening.

The slavery question is becoming more alarming from day to day. While the House of Representatives refuse to appropriate moneys for the support of the army, news is daily coming in from Kansas of bloody conflicts between the free-soilers and the slaveholders. It is hoped, however, that after the presidential election (in November), domestic peace will be restored.

The unwholesome climate in Washington has driven me out for a few days, as the heat was intolerable last month, and now the fever and ague begins.

I am going to Albany to-day, to attend the meeting of naturalists to which I have been invited. I expect to meet a number of savans of distinction there, and to report the details to your Excellency hereafter.

Mr. Heine is very much delighted with the expression of your Excellency in his favor.

Mr. C—— and the *beau monde* have retreated to the mountains and the sea-baths long ago, and I shall not see him for three or four weeks to come.

Mr. Fillmore would be the best President; but he appears to have little hope of succeeding against Fremont and Buchanan; and the Knownothings have lost all credit.

My poor wife and children are counting the hours which must elapse before my return, and I am not less anxious to find all that is dear to me again in the country of my home, next year, at the close of the Congress.

The approaching departure of the mail for England compels me to close this letter, which I do with the most heartfelt wishes for your Excellency's continued well-being.

With immutable reverence and affection, I remain your Excellency's most devoted GEROLT.

178.

VARNHAGEN TO HUMBOLDT.

BERLIN, *September 13th,* 1856.

THE great influence of the name of your Excellency in the United States, as in America in general, is a gratifying sign of the improvement of those countries in civilization, and a sure pledge of the ultimate triumph of the philanthropic principles which you have consistently advocated through the course of a long and eventful life. I thank you heartily for the letter of M. v. Gerolt, and its printed inclosure, which will be a valuable addition to my collections. At this moment, it is true, the chances of Fremont are a little doubtful; nevertheless the latest accounts represent the zeal of his supporters as very great and by no means hopeless.

Our domestic events—domestic in their origin though the scene be laid abroad—it would be more agreeable to pass in silence, as it is difficult to find the proper expression with which to characterize them, and impracticable to make use of those expressions when found. The most consoling observation to be made is that of unanimous condemnation on all hands, where there are no private ends to gain. For the veritable Prussian of the good old school such things as Jade, Neufchatel, and even Zollern, are at all times nothing but distractions, having no legitimate concern with the core of the Prussian state. In regard to Neufchatel, I fear that a momentary favorable nod of France is over valued, and will lead to inextricable entanglements; Reynard* is apt to incite his friends to dangerous adventures; the escape from them is their affair, and he takes a malicious pleasure in looking on.

* The Fox, i. e. Louis Napoleon.—*Tr*

The other day Lady Bettina von Arnim contributed to my collections near a thousand autographs. One of the most valuable is a letter from your Excellency to Ludwig Achim von Arnim, on petrifactions; it is not dated, but I refer it to the third decade of the present century.

I well know on what day I write these lines. It precedes the day more widely and more enthusiastically celebrated than any other. May it please your Excellency to accept the modest tribute of my warm good wishes with kind favor! In faithful reverence and grateful devotion,

Your Excellency's most obedient,

VARNHAGEN VON ENSE.

179.

HUMBOLDT TO VARNHAGEN.

BERLIN, *September* 22d, 1856.

THE Grand Duke of Weimar, who has just left, commissions me to beg of you as a particular favor, the permission for him to visit you to-morrow (on Tuesday) between nine and eleven o'clock. He is determined to see you in person.

A. v. HUMBOLDT.

MONDAY.

180.

HUMBOLDT TO VARNHAGEN.

BERLIN, *Sept. 23d,* 1856.

CHER ET *introuvable* AMI!

How the improbable can become real! How royal huntsmen and royal coachmen cannot find you, cannot look for your direction in the prosaic directory. I send this direction at this moment to the Grand Duke, who has the anguish of having detained my revered friend. May he be more fortunate in a new attempt. The enclosed sheet is a Berlin curiosity for your archives.

  Faithfully yours,   A. V. HUMBOLDT.
TUESDAY, 2 O'CLOCK.

181.

(ENCLOSED.)

GRAND DUKE CHARLES ALEXANDER OF SAXE WEIMAR TO HUMBOLDT.

AT THE CHATEAU OF BERLIN,
Tuesday Morning.

HAD I had the skill of the Marquis of St. Germain, of whom, if I am not mistaken, it is told that one fine morning he departed through four gates at one and the same time, I could not have been more desirous to find M. von Varnhagen than I was. Nevertheless, it was all in vain. No one could tell me where he lived, and it was of no use to take the measure of the "*Maurenstrasse*." Nature having made me the most obstinate of all Grand Dukes, I still persist in my intention to see the invisible, and hasten to attain that consummation by requesting your Excellency to tell me where M. de Varnhagen actually *does* live. Pardon my repeated importunities; but in conscience I know of no route which could be shorter or more direct. I remain, with the inextinguishable attachment of the most devoted admiration and veneration for your Excellency,

CHARLES ALEXANDER.

182.

VARNHAGEN TO HUMBOLDT.

BERLIN, *September 24th*, 1856.

YOUR EXCELLENCY:

You have had not a little trouble on my account lately, which I lament with shame. Most of all I regret having missed your kind visit, which is always an honor as well as a good fortune. That the Grand Duke could not find me yesterday, although he drove up and down the Maurenstrasse, and made several inquiries, would be incomprehensible if the servants of a Court were not a very peculiar fraternity. It is nearly thirty years that I have resided in the largest house in the street, which the Grand Duke himself has entered in visiting Prince Wilhelm of Baden. To-day, however, he arrived punctually at eight o'clock, was very pleasant and affable, spoke with a good deal of frankness and much cordiality, and mentioned your Excellency with great esteem and gratitude. His real errand did not appear until his visit came to a close; in referring him to me, your Excellency has done me great honor, but you have also involved me in no inconsiderable perplexity. The affair is of great importance, and may lay the foundation for the happiness of a worthy man; the wish itself is creditable to the Grand Duke, and it will give me great pleasure in any way to subserve his noble purpose. I shall take it into consideration, and, if a result is attainable, shall respectfully submit it to your Excellency. At the first blush, I named young H., which, however, led to nothing, the Grand Duke doubting the extent of his acquaintance with the French language. The visit lasted nearly an hour, and much that was said was remarkable; my share in the conversation must have been unpleasant, at least the physical part of it, which is entirely ruined and quite unintelligible from coughing, influenza, and rheumatic compression of the chest.

With the best wishes for your Excellency's welfare, I remain in profound reverence and gratitude,
Your obedient   VARNHAGEN VON ENSE.

183.

HUMBOLDT TO VARNHAGEN.

BERLIN, *Sep.* 24*th*, 1856.

BEFORE I bury myself again for some days in Potsdam, a sacrifice to the Queen and to her solitude, I shall, dear friend, justify the Grand Duke and myself. The Grand Duke visited you, which honors him, not to consult you, but out of respect for your fine talents and your character, because he had, as he said, inherited the idea from his house, that one must see two men in Berlin, you and me. That we must both accept with gratitude as an inheritance from the *old gentleman* and the Imperial Highness, who is a worthy lady. He had not at all the idea to speak with you of what he seeks and never will find (equal inclination for science and poetry, history of geographical discoveries, art, painting, gems and sculpture, refined social manners, fluent French speaking and writing, also reading aloud). That bantling is yet unborn. I said, *j'aviserai,* and quite casually I added, that I would ask your opinion. Only when taking leave, which he introduced officially by very far-fetched phrases on the "noble grey-haired youth," he asked me whether it would be contrary to my wishes to submit the problem to you also. The visit had for its motive the manifestation of inherited reverence, and a desire to produce an effect, which must be connected with some self-denial at eight o'clock in the morning, on the day of departure. To vaccinate him with our excellent H., we might send the latter for four months to Paris and London; but would a mind like H.'s put up with it? *J'en doubte.*

  Most cordially, your   A. v. HUMBOLDT.
WEDNESDAY.

Gerlach intends to separate himself from the King, and to oust Reyher, whereby he would still remain quite near the King, ay, even nearer than at present, for the cause of little animosities (electricity from contact) would then disappear.

184.

HUMBOLDT TO VARNHAGEN.

POTSDAM, *November 9th*, 1856.

I FORGOT to inform you, my revered friend, that I fulfilled punctually your wish to send to Weimar the letter you addressed me, and to recommend urgently the proposed "Private Secretary," and all this a few days after I knew your intention.

A German letter from Prince Metternich, expressing sentiments full of graceful language, will interest you. I present you the letter for your archival collection The occasion was a moulding in plaster and copy, partly by the Prince's own hand, of an old Egyptian column of granite, which he had received twenty-five years ago from Mehemed Ali. The old Prince gave me this copy, three-fourths of a foot in height, to decipher the long inscription in Demotic writing. This has been done by Dr. Brugsch, the talented young Egyptologist, author of a Demotic Grammar, universally admired in other countries. Dr. Brugsch, who had the first edition of his Grammar printed in Latin, when he was still in the first class of August's Gymnasium* (the second edition is written in French), has found a good deal of very remarkable astronomy in the inscription; and in order to give pleasure to the old Prince, Brugsch has published the whole under the name of "Stele. Metternich," in the "Journal for the Orient," and in the "Athenée." Brugsch was in Egypt for two years, at the expense of the King; he is the son of a poor sergeant, and is familiar with Greek, Arabic, Hebrew, Coptic, and Persian.

* The Koelnische Gymnasium, Berlin, of which August was director.

Pardon my horrid writing, illegible, and in wild, incorrect style.

The letter of the maccaroni King* to Louis Philippe, in the "Spenersche Zeitung," will not have escaped you, I hope. *Non v'a bisogno*—entirely as Rochow-Seiffart (in his first manner) to the Elbingers:—"It is not at all necessary that my people think; I think for them; the people, who have betrayed me so often, submit to my power."

Your faithful   A. HUMBOLDT.

185.

METTERNICH TO HUMBOLDT.

KOENIGSWART, *October 14th,* 1856.

MY OLD FRIEND!—I received gratefully the information on the stele which Herr Brugsch calls by my name, and I beg of you to hand over to the learned investigator the words you find inclosed. After my return to Vienna, I shall avail myself of the interpretation, already so instructive, of the monument, to point out the way

---

* The King of Naples, known in this country as King Bomba. In Naples the best maccaroni is manufactured. Was this letter really directed to Louis Philippe, or was there not a mistake in the name? Was not Louis Philippe dead before that time?—*Translator.*

to archæologists in which they may obtain copies, by an advertisement. I did not doubt that I could not do better than to address you for light on the scientific value of the present of Mehemed Ali, which for many years slept in my multifarious collections, and of which I was quite ignorant. May you and Herr Brugsch receive my most sincere thanks.

I have had the good fortune to find the King in excellent health, and in the usual kind disposition towards myself. Great recollections in long lives are a fine bond between man and man, the power of which is well tried when it has resisted the storms of time. It is more than half a century since my first intercourse with the young heir-apparent. What vicissitudes have occupied this long interval is matter of history. That they have never deprived me of the confidence of the two kings, father and son, is with me a source of pride —that is to say, of a sensation which the term peace of mind and heart would better characterize than the unsafe word that has escaped my pen.

You, three years my senior, have just celebrated your eighty-seventh birthday. That you and I have understood "the art of living," we may confess. That we shall do well to cultivate it still longer, is not to be denied.

With sincere friendship and esteem,

METTERNICH.

186.

HUMBOLDT TO VARNHAGEN.

BERLIN, *November 20th,* 1856.

I WANT your literary aid, my noble friend. Our great landscape painter, Hildebrandt, who was in Brazil, Canada, Egypt, Palestine, Greece, and recently at the North Cape, has executed an admirable aquarelle picture of my "Interior Household," in order to replace a smaller one sold in many hundreds of copies in America. "La renommée, fruit d'une longue patience de vivre, augmente avec l'imbécilité." I am compelled to make an inscription to this picture of mine, with my own hand. This is no easy task. I pray that you will visit me on Saturday, at one o'clock, if it is possible to you. You shall guide me.

Your most grateful

THURSDAY.   A. v. HUMBOLDT.

187.

HUMBOLDT TO VARNHAGEN.

BERLIN, *November 21st,* 1856.

I YESTERDAY prayed, dear friend, that you should make me the pleasure of your visit on Saturday. I pray to-day that you will not come; I hear with sorrow that you suffer much. The great picture of Hildebrandt remains yet a long time in my house. Every later day will also be useful to me. I only beg of you that you will kindly announce to me the day, beforehand, on which I may expect you. Choose the twelfth hour, under any circumstances, because I am sure to be free then. I also am in a condition in which I desire to *run out of my skin.** As an old man, I suffer as from musquito bites; and moreover, a hyper-christian, Mr. Foster (living at Brussels), consults me from time to time, whether I believe that the souls of the lower animals, such as bed-bugs and musquitoes, are included in the scheme of salvation, and destined to go to heaven. So they threaten me up there too, where I shall find the animal souls, well known to me from the Orinoco, chanting a hymn of praise.

In old friendship, yours,
A. v. HUMBOLDT.

FRIDAY.

And the disgraceful party which sells negro children, and distributes canes of honor, as the Russian Emperor does swords of honor, and Graefe's noses of honor,—who prove that all white workmen should rather be slaves than free—have succeeded. What a crime!

---

* A German proverbial expression for feeling very uncomfortable.—*Tr.*

Nov. 22d, 1856.—Varnhagen writes in his diary:— "I started at half-past 12 o'clock, and drove to Humboldt in the pouring rain. He was rejoiced at my coming, and soon led me to an adjoining room, where hung Hildebrandt's great aquarelle picture, in a frame; an excellent picture, indeed, in the rich variety of which the sitting figure of Humboldt predominates. Now came the question about the inscription to be chosen for it. I had rightly expected that he did not so much expect propositions from me, as my approval of those chosen by him already. Contrary to my expectation, no short sentence, but a longer speech, a rhetorical composition, which happily compares the searching traveller with the returned man of science. Some alterations were approved in the beginning, but disapproved again in the end. Hildebrandt gave the picture not to Herr von Humboldt, but to his valet Seiffert. It is to be engraved. We looked at the rooms, in three of them; his apparatus of study is strewn about; all three warmed to 19 degrees Réaumur, an intolerable temperature for me. A library hall not warmed. Pictures painted by Madame Gaggiotti, whose talents he praised highly; he wondered and rejoiced that I knew her too. He complained of itching; I said it was a well-known complaint, pruritus. "Senilis," he immediately added. In a box he had a living chameleon, which he showed me, and of which he said, that it was the only animal which was able to direct one of its eyes upwards, and at the same time the other downwards; that our parsons only were able to do the same, with one eye directed to heaven and the other to the good things of this world. We talked of Neufchatel too; he said that the King was full of good hopes, and counted upon Louis Bonaparte; that Manteuffel did not see things in such a favorable light, but made merry of them. The Russian Chancellor, Graf von Nesselrode, said to Humboldt on his last visit, that the present constitution and position of Switzerland made the best impression on him, and were such as to win esteem and favor for the republic.

188.

HUMBOLDT TO VARNHAGEN.

BERLIN, *November 30th*, 1856.

ESTEEMED FRIEND:

At this moment I receive a letter from a *pupil*, deserving of moderate praise for clearness of thought and diction. I shall not write before having first come to see you, my dear friend. The last fifteen lines of the letter are utterly illegible and unintelligible to me. I had written to him about the laying of the telegraph cable between Ireland and Newfoundland, but had not made him any offer. I cannot read what is underscored!

Keep my pupil's letter by all means, including the information that I am the subject of discussion in the Belgian Chambers, as a materialist and republican, who ought to be discharged! Where the dinner of the Baron d'Arhim (Arnim) took place, I cannot guess. I may have said, that I was as liberal as Arago, but certainly not that I was a Republican. Deposit M. Jobard in your archives, my friend,

Your faithful,   A. v. HUMBOLDT.
SUNDAY.

What men believe and disbelieve does not generally become a subject of contention until after they have been officially buried and bepreached by Sydow.*

The "Spenersche Zeitung," besides discussing Neufchatel and the evacuation of the Danubian principalities, contains a daily health return about five little silkworms of Fintelmann, the court gardener. How all things diminish in importance! I have often written letters dated from the hill of Sans Souci, which formerly was historical. Now the Peacock's Island becomes historical by the still life of two caterpillars. Thus the world moves. It must be remembered that when the Angora goats made illustrious the administration of Richelieu in France, the *Moniteur* contained the announcement: " Le moral des chèvres s'améliore de jour en jour."

* A fashionable preacher in Berlin.—*Tr.*

189.

CHARLES ALEXANDER, GRAND DUKE OF SAXE-WEIMAR, TO HUMBOLDT.

WEIMAR, *November 29th,* 1856.

As I fortunately have the honor to be known, truly known to your Excellency, I may flatter myself that you will not estimate my gratitude for your services and those of M. de Varnhagen, by the length of time which has elapsed since the day I received your letter of the 31st, and the present time. My sincere thanks shall here receive a place. They have been delayed by the very nature of the transaction. Such could not but be the effect, for in an affair of that kind it is impossible to form a sudden resolution, and accordingly I now write for the sole purpose of not appearing ungrateful, and because, on the other hand, it is necessary to secure the possibility of forming a fixed resolve. To do this I must have time and freedom of election. Both are secured by the kindness of yourself and M. Varnhagen, for you join in proposing to send the young man so as to enable me in the first place to make his acquaintance. The question arises, when can this be done? for I do not care to begin by calling * * * here with the trombone of an appointment. Nothing remains, therefore, but to beg your Excellency to make inquiries at what time the gentleman would be at leisure and inclined to undertake a journey to the bank of the Jlm. Having asked this question, I would pause above all things, in order to proceed to the expression of my thanks for the important news you have the goodness to communicate. If I add the question, whether your Excellency will kindly send me the map for an admiring inspection, and if you should possibly find this question wonderfully troublesome, I take refuge under the shelter of your goodness to me, which has often made me proud, and to-day, perhaps, indiscreet. Yet I am proud of your goodness, which is ever coupled with truth, and in the latter I put my trust, that you will decisively reject my petition, if it troubles you, to whom, in reverence, I remain the most grateful scholar,

CHARLES ALEXANDER.

190.

JOBARD TO HUMBOLDT.

BRUSSELS, *November 26th*, 1856.

MONSIEUR LE BARON:

PERHAPS you will not be displeased to learn the rôle

you have been made to play in the unfortunate debate of our religious politics.

The old Minister Dechamps, who sat on your right at the dinner of the Baron of Arhim, and who was so much astonished at hearing you say that you were as much of a Republican as your friend Arago, having associated your name with those of the illustrious believers who profess the Catholic faith, a liberal journal this morning answered him as follows:—

"M. Dechamps, in the last homily delivered by him in the Chamber, cited the name of M. de Humboldt to prove that science could well be made subservient to the creed. It must be admitted, as Mr. Devaux showed, that the example could not have been worse chosen. M. de Humboldt is one of those rationalists, pure and simple, against whom M. Dechamps has already written so many letters. If M. Humboldt had taught in Belgium he would most certainly have been pursued in pastoral letters, and discharged by M. Dechamps, if M. Dechamps had been the Minister. Nevertheless, it is thus that history is written, and thus that the most important questions of our intellectual and moral future are appreciated!"

Here is another unmixed and undisguised political opinion:—

"As often and so sure as you base your church upon human obtuseness, the gates of the mind will not prevail against it, because there will always be consummate fools, old fools, and little fools, to uphold and repair it. Pure reason has not the same chance."

Yours, ever devotedly,

JOBARD.

191.

LINES BY VARNHAGEN ON HILDEBRANDT'S PAINTING OF HUMBOLDT'S APARTMENTS, AND THE MOTTO ATTACHED.

(TRANSLATED BY CHARLES GOEPP, ESQ., AT EASTON, PA.)

This was the latest, the peaceful home, where the mighty explorer,
Early ascender of summits, reposed on the heights of his glory.
Hall of the Castle of Knowledge, the limner has deftly restored thee!
Lofty and light, rich hung with trophies of noble endeavor;
Treasures of nature and art, and of love, and the weapons of science.
While in the midst sits, earnestly glad, thoughtfully commanding
All the profusion around, himself thy sovereign, breathing
Speech and significant life into every shape of the picture;
Plying the wonderful shuttle of thought, until it produces,
Painting and painted at once, fresh images, brighter and brighter.*

VARNHAGEN VON ENSE.

BERLIN, *December 1st,* 1856.

* Spaetes Daheim des einst in ruestig kaempfender Jugend
 Weitgewanderten Forschers, der, gleichwie Hoehen der Erde,
 Hoehen des Ruhmes erstieg, hat dargestellt uns der Maler,
 Schoen, reich ausgestattet mit herrlichen Schoetzen des Wissens:

192.

HUMBOLDT TO VARNHAGEN.

BERLIN, *December 3d,* 1856.

So my pedestrian prose has led you back, my friend, to the regions of the noblest of rhythms! It would make me proud, if the universe were not entitled to your favor. With even more modesty than the poor, for whose benefit the old man with the moss-grown beard* exhibits himself for the small compensation of five silver groschen. With what excellent taste you have transferred the English "*home*" into "*Daheim.*" Indescribably beautiful is your poetry, full of grace

> Werke der Kunst, der Natur, und Schrift und Geraeth des Gelehrten.
> Aber ihn selbst inmitten des neidenswerthen Besitzthums
> Sehen wir froh sein Reich mit sinnigem Blicke beherrschen,
> Deutende Sprache verleihen dem wundervollen Gemaelde,
> Durch lichtvoller Gedanken beredsam glückliche Fügung
> Schaffend ein neues Bild, ein geistiges, staunendem Anschaun!

* *Bemoostes Haupt* is an expression often applied to a student who has grown grey without passing an examination, and which, in this connexion, has an effect at once humorous and pathetic, which is inimitable.—*Tr.*

and delicacy, and of a solemn monition of what should have been extracted from nature and art, and the weapon of science. If my brother William, who, in his correspondence with Wolf, discoursed so largely on lax and severe hexameters, could but have lived to witness this family honor!

Your advice, even when not clothed in verse, is law to me. I shall follow it at once; and you have made matters a great deal easier than they were. *Alea jacta sit!* Could you, perhaps, dear friend, transfer the last ten syllables (or lines) of the Grand Ducal letter into your classic chirography, so as possibly to enable me to guess what it is that I am understood to have promised.

Fremont's portrait reminds one vividly of Chateaubriand. A biography of the former has just appeared in New York, dedicated to me—" Memoirs of the Life and Public Services of John Charles Fremont, by John Bigelow (?)." The dedication says: " To Alexander von Humboldt this memoir of one whose genius he was among the first to discover and acknowledge, is respectfully inscribed by the author." Delicate words, a little artificially combined. There is a copy of the letter written to him from Sans Souci, in the King's name, in 1850, accompanying the great prize medal for science and art, upon his having projected the most extensive barometrical level ever executed, from Missouri to the South Sea. It closes with the words of which Sans

Souci has no reason to be ashamed: "*La Californie, qui a* NOBLEMENT *résisté à l'introduction de l'esclavage, sera dignement représentée par un ami de la liberté et des progrès de l'intelligence.*"* The biography has passages of a strange romantic interest. At one time cold and hunger have driven a party to fury and almost phrensy, when they all pray and sing, and then an oath from Fremont that there shall not in any case be a resort to cannibalism. As soon as my own curiosity is satisfied I shall send you the book. For the present, you may occupy yourself with the miracle performed by the chaplain of an army division in Magdeburg, on a Mr. Assemann, in Quedlinburg. I have lighted upon it in my capacity of naturalist. It is to be found on p. 34.

Gratefully yours,   A. v. HUMBOLDT.

NOTE BY VARNHAGEN.—The water color paintings by Hildebrandt, that of Humboldt among them, were exhibited in the hall of the Art Union, for the benefit of the poor. Price of admission, five silbergroschen.†

Suicide a Folly and a Crime; Two Sermons by Dr. Crusius, Chaplain of a Division of the Army: Magdeburg, 1855. 8vo. The miracle consists in this, that one, who under the qualms of a guilty conscience, was long occupied with thoughts of suicide, was suddenly cured of them, permanently, by an invocation of the name of Jesus. The

---

* California, which has nobly resisted the introduction of slavery, will be worthily represented by a friend of liberty and of the progress of intelligence.

† About eleven cents.

production is also remarkable as containing, on p. 34, the following allusion to Schleiermacher: "It is said of a distinguished divine, that he was once sorely tempted to commit suicide. Such is the influence which suffering of body and mind may exercise even upon good and godly men."

193.

HUMBOLDT TO VARNHAGEN.

BERLIN, *December* 17*th*, 1856.

ANOTHER grateful, unconstrained, and amiable letter from the Grand Duke. He fixes February for the visit, and desires the drama to open with a request to search the archives. The permission being given, the material part is to follow, as he says, symbolically. You will arrange that with care, my dear friend. We are approaching the goal of our wishes.

I have another funeral to-morrow at the column in Tegel, which, under the hand of Thorwalsden, promises *Hope*. The oldest niece (daughter) of my brother, the wife of General Hedemann, born in Paris in 1800, a few days after Madame von Humboldt's return from Spain, has departed after much suffering (liver complaint connected with dropsy), an amiable, cheerful housewife, who enjoyed good health for forty years in a very happy marriage. I live to bury all my kith and kin.

               Yours,   A. v. H.

WEDNESDAY EVENING.

194.

CHARLES ALEXANDER, GRAND DUKE OF SAXE-WEIMAR, TO HUMBOLDT.

WEIMAR, *December 16th*, 1856.

LIKE unto Nature, eternally invoked, eternally giving, because eternally bountiful, you respond with ever returning goodness to every repeated solicitation. The proposal of your Excellency in regard to the young man of science, as suggested by the plan of M. de Varnhagen, is so excellent, that I can only beg for its speedy execution. For that purpose, it would seem desirable that M. de Varnhagen should instil the idea into the young men that our plentiful archives would repay a thorough search, if I could be induced to sanction it. I would do so at once, permitting the material part to follow hereafter. The period beginning with February of next year would seem to me best adapted for the literary investigation. The real object of the journey should remain a secret, so that I shall be entirely at liberty to see him, to appoint him, or not to appoint him.

I thank you with all my heart for that printed inclosure. This task also, by no means an easy one, you have performed with a master hand, and could do so better than any one else, because you, more than most men, have spoken to the world by noble actions.

I shall appropriate the Journal of Petermann. My veneration for you is the pledge of the effective truth of my aspirations. I beg you to preserve your interest in it, and your goodness also, being your most grateful admirer and servant,

CHARLES ALEXANDER.

195.

HUMBOLDT TO VARNHAGEN.

BERLIN, *Feb. 7th*, 1857.

WHEN I read anything in Berlin that enlists my political or literary attention, my first thought is of you. Lasaulx of Munich, of Baader's tribe, was only known to me as a man of the "Kreuz Zeitung" and of Schubert's World of Darkness, and the new historical work he sends me contains little originality of views, but it manifests, by way of allusion, a wealth of positive knowledge, which I had not expected of the man. Numerous citations indicate a great preference for the views of my brother. The Slavonic passage in regard to the Messiah is also remarkable, and the notes present a rich collection of antiquities. I should not look for anything of the sort from President Gerlach and his brother, to whom Professor Gelzer of Basle, and others, of opinions opposite to his, have been officially referred in the Neufchatel negotiations. If Lasaulx is not agreeable to you on account of his wishes for the restoration of the ancient German empire, you may find it interesting to skim over the work, and glance at the notes.

My cutaneous disease is much better, as also my nocturnal diligence. The fourth and last volume of Kosmos will consist of two parts, *i. e.*, of two volumes, each of thirty-five sheets, the first of which has already left the press. Both the parts, however, are to appear *together*, to avoid spoiling the effect of a continuous description, beginning with the internal warmth of the earth, and ending with the different races of man.

The presumptuous want of caution with which the pitiful Neufchatel affair is carried on here, exposes Prussia to great humiliation at Paris. Waterloo will be avenged on Prussia as it has been on Russia.

Yours most truly,
A. v. HT.

196.

VARNHAGEN TO HUMBOLDT.

Berlin, *Feb.* 9*th*, 1857.

Your Excellency will receive, accompanying this, with my most hearty thanks, the book so kindly lent me. I have read it with varied emotions, I might say with painful interest. True, the author makes concessions, and opens up points of view, which I should not have expected any more than the luxurious learning of his manifold citations. But the pretty collection of notes fails to mantle the kernel of the text, which is extremely bitter; the apology of negro slavery, the brutal praise of warfare and of standing armies, and the beneficence of *aristocratic* revolutions, in spite of his far-fetched compliments, which look like invitations to be converted, the author really offers nothing but the fare of the " Kreuz Zeitung," in a preparation somewhat more delicate than that of Professor Leo, whose "mire of cultivation" and "scrofulous rabble" are here cooked up with spices. *Latet anguis in herba!* I must say that I always take the alarm when philosophers undertake to measure the course and the stage of human development, and to combine the meagre dates of our puny history, of at most a few thousand years, with laws for the possibilities of millions of years. Neither Fichte, nor Schelling, nor Steffens, nor Hegel, were particularly fortunate in their essays; the assignment of the ages is best left to the poets. What is especially singular in our author is that he confesses to a strong doubt of his own doctrine, for he "cannot practically renounce the national Ideal of a restored emperor and empire, although his theoretical faith in their realization is slight" (p. 157). One who writes thus has written his own sentence. A friendly answer at the hands of your Excellency the author may hope to receive, an approving one you will not be able to give him.

To hear that your welfare, your activity, your energy, continue unaltered and progressive, is refreshing and encouraging to us authors, who stand in need of great example to protect us from flagging in our daily work, ὀλίγον τε φίλον τε. The views of the new volume of Kosmos give me great delight, and, as Schiller said when Goethe produced one of his masterpieces, "I thank the gods that they have suffered me to live to see it."

The Neufchatel affair, even in its present stage, has in it much that is disheartening, and I was from the first opposed to our negotiations at Paris, which had all the appearance of snares, in which much may yet be entangled. The zeal displayed by many is not at all sincere, but seems an excellent means for the attainment of other ends, and will probably be successful. Nevertheless, I am without anxiety for the future, the light cannot be extinguished and must triumph; it is only the moment of darkness that is hard to bear.

With the best wishes, in the greatest veneration and devotion,

I remain your Excellency's most obedient,

VARNHAGEN VON ENSE.

197.

VARNHAGEN TO HUMBOLDT.

BERLIN, *February* 20*th*, 1857.

WILL your Excellency pardon me for trespassing on your valuable time a moment? Not for myself, but for a literary project from which I cannot withhold my personal interest, if only on the score of old acquaintance! Professor Francis Hoffmann, of Wuerzburg, is engaged upon the publication of the works of Francis von Baader, which he pursues with self-sacrificing perseverance. I may say against wind and tide. He is about closing the enterprise with a sketch of the life of his author, and is anxious not to pass over unmentioned the fact, that Baader attended the Mining Academy at Freiberg, at the same time with your Excellency. It would be invaluable to him to obtain a word of reference to the matter from yourself, a bare hint as to whether any relation of moment took place between you, or whether he made any impression upon you? I would not presume to trouble your Excellency, if I did not take for granted that either a memento, or the contents of a single line, would dispose of the matter!

The crowd and your Excellency's early departure prevented me from making my salutation at the Artists' Festival. It is more than twenty years since I have ventured into such deep waters.

Strange reports are in circulation. I hope it is only a jest that presents M. Niebuhr as the Future Minister of finance, and M. Wagener as Privy Councillor, with a seat in the cabinet.

With a repeated request of your indulgence, I remain, with the most profound esteem, and in the most sincere devotion,

  Your Excellency's most obedient,
    VARNHAGEN VON ENSE.

On Humboldt's attack of sickness, Varnhagen's diary of February 27, 1857, contains the following: "M. Hermann Grimm called, coming from Humboldt's apartments, where he had conversed with Seiffert, the valet. It is not a cold that has befallen Humboldt, but a far more serious attack, a paralytic stroke. After the court ball on Tuesday evening he felt unwell, in the night he left his bed to drink some water—wished to avoid disturbing the servant—and fell upon the floor. Seiffert awoke with the noise, and found his master speechless and unconscious; it was some time before he revived. Privy Councillor Schoenlein is not sanguine; he had not a very good night.

Humboldt's loss would be irreparable. He is a counterpoise to so much that is mean and contemptible, which, after his death, would boldly seek the light and glory in its own depravity. The honor and influence of science are embodied in him, and both would sink if he were taken away. There is not now a name in Germany, or in Europe, like his, not an influence in Berlin more extensive or more generally recognised than his. And how painful would his loss be to me! His name and his intercourse is attached to fifty years of my life, he has known those who were near and dear to us of old!

Under March 14th, Varnhagen narrates in his diary: "When the King was with Humboldt, Schoenlein said to the latter, that he would not be able for some time to stand firmly on his left side, to which Humboldt rejoined: 'For all that, it will not be necessary for me to sit on the right with Gerlach.' "*

---

* Leader of the most reactionary party.—*Tr.*

198.

VARNHAGEN TO HUMBOLDT.

BERLIN, *March* 17*th*, 1857.

I CANNOT deny myself the pleasure to offer to your Excellency my most heartfelt congratulations for your happy and perfect recovery! The finest and most powerful testimony of it is the letter to Privy Councillor Boeckh, which appeared in the papers this morning, and which no epithet of praise will suffice to describe. Such an invocation has never yet fallen to the lot of any man, and the receiver will not fail to honor and appreciate it as the most precious of all the gifts bestowed upon him. How fresh must have been the mind, and how warm the heart, from which it emanates, and how sterling and graceful at once is its expression! Even its narrative form—its Herodotic narrative, I might call it—is of inestimable value, and shows us a beautiful combination of youth preserved and old age achieved.

May your Excellency pardon this overflow of sentiment! You have no need of my words, but to me it is not possible to suppress them, and I therefore will give free vent to my most fervent desire, that the radiating star, covered for a moment by a cloud, may still shine upon us for a long time in accustomed splendor, and may forebode, as heretofore, health and wealth at home and abroad.

With profound veneration and gratitude,
>> Ever faithfully your most devoted
>>> VARNHAGEN VON ENSE.

These lines are not so presumptuous as to expect an answer.

199.

HUMBOLDT TO VARNHAGEN.

BERLIN, March 19th, 1857—at Night.

How should I deny myself the pleasure to thank you, the dearest, ablest, and most attached of my friends. Not indulgence—no, praising expressions on my address to Boeckh—a praise of form, of the vesture of thought—has been my lot from the lips of the master of language, and of the delicate turns of good-will. You caused me great joy, more than you anticipated. What my nervous affection was, which produced a paralysis of such short duration, with the functions of the brain remaining entirely free, with pulse unchanged, with preservation of sight, and of all motion of the extremities subject to will, I cannot divine. There are magnetic storms (the polar light), electric storms in the clouds, nervous storms in man, heavy and light ones—perhaps, also, sheet lightning, *foreboding* the others. I had serious thoughts of death, *comme un homme qui part, ayant encore beaucoup de lettres à écrire.* Other interests, which for ever remain alive in me, bind me to the memories of yesterday!! I believe myself in full convalescence; but as I had to rest much on the bed without occupation, sadness and displeasure of the world have increased in me. This I say to you alone. I shall soon come to you, and thank you orally from the depths of my soul. All around us puts us to shame.

In most intimate friendship, your most faithful

A. v. HUMBOLDT.

Varnhagen writes in his diary, March 19th, 1857: "Unexpectedly a letter from Humboldt! I had written under my congratulation, that these lines were not so immodest as to expect an answer. But he, nevertheless answers, and in the most obliging, most heart-gladdening manner. He gives a remarkable report of his sickness. The bad reports were all untrue, at least exaggerated; he never lost consciousness or language, his pulse remained as usual. Yet he did not conceal from himself, that it might be the end. "I had serious thoughts of death, comme un homme qui part, ayant encore beaucoup de lettres à écrire!" Grand and fine is what he adds: "Other interests, which remain for ever alive in me, bind me to the memories of yesterday!! (of the 18th of March!)* I believe myself in full convalescence, but as I had to rest much on the bed without occupation, sadness and displeasure with the world have increased in me. This I say to you alone."

200.

HUMBOLDT TO VARNHAGEN.

BERLIN, *April 6th*, 1857.

IF you, dear friend, understand the letter of the Grand Duke as I do, ——— must go. I had proposed that he should come to Weimar, under the pretext of studying the archives; he would bring a letter of introduction from you or me; should be invited to court and if he did not please, should simply be asked whether he meant to return to ———. That this should be a shibboleth as a bad end of the drama, quod Deus avertat. I also proposed to advance the stipulated sum of money. On this head the tyrant does not answer distinctly. ——— goes, I think, by way of Berlin. Shall

* Day of the Prussian Revolution of 1848.

we then give him the letter of recommendation with the galvanic stimulants? I do as you wish.

Your faithful
A. v. HUMBOLDT.

MONDAY.

Keep the letter of the Grand Duke, which ends nicely, and in good taste.

201.

KARL ALEXANDER, GRAND DUKE OF SAXE-WEIMAR, TO HUMBOLDT.

WEIMAR, *April* 3d, 1857.

A MISUNDERSTANDING is the key to my behavior towards ———. I believed and expected that he, after he had, in January, I believe, asked the permission to search our archives, would immediately come hither. Then only of course I would have paid his expenses. Just in these last days I wondered neither to hear nor to see anything of ———.

Then arrived the second letter of your Excellency, which, asking explanation of me, gives explanation; and I hasten to answer it by saying that ——— may come in about ten days, and I would be prepared in any case to make the payment, the amount of which your Excellency yourself named. According to understanding, both of us, I and the traveller, would consider ourselves entirely free yet, and therefore observe due discretion on the proper cause of this journey.

Dante would have spoken still more truly if he had said: "Viver ch' è un correr a l'eterna gioventù." You prove it, for eternally your immortal spirit rejuvenates. its excellence is also a proof of this.

In grateful reverence and love, your faithfully most submissive

KARL ALEXANDER.

202.

VARNHAGEN TO HUMBOLDT.

BERLIN, *April 7th*, 1857.

YOUR Excellency's kind and very much desired communications I forwarded in haste to ——— that is to say, the substance of it. It is to be hoped that ——— will start immediately, but I expect first to receive an answer from him, and as I do not believe that in the short time the Grand Duke has left him, he can make the détour by way of Berlin, it will be best for him to receive the letter of introduction in Weimar.

The Grand Duke insists upon discretion, and justly so!

It is convenient for him, and delicate and sparing for the other party. ———— has acted correctly in this respect up to the present time. I am very anxious to see the end of the matter; taking for granted that there was a good relation present in the germ. Success would give me extraordinary satisfaction.

The present you make me of the letter of the Grand Duke delights me very much. Not only the end is in good taste and fine, but the whole style has agreeable turns; and above all, the reverence for your Excellency expresses itself in a manner, the heartfelt sincerity of which cannot be misunderstood.

For some days I have been living entirely in recollections of past times and relations. The correspondence between Gentz and Adam Mueller, just now published by Cotta, keeps me spellbound, and I must contemplate the whole series of those experiences in my reviving recollection.

I have known both men early and intimately, and have had much intercourse with them, personally, of a friendly character, in measures generally an adversary. The superiority of Gentz over the younger friend, whom he greatly overvalued, never was doubtful to me, and is here confirmed anew; only at last when the murder of Kotzebue deranges and stupifies the mind, the force of terror drives the statesman, who formerly was fond of clearness, into the gloomy nebulous strata, to which the frightened friend had retreated long before. This correspondence is certainly unique in its kind. The transactions, disquisitions, mutual influences, inclinations, and feuds are invested with dramatic interest. In Adam Mueller, by-the-by, is contained the complete germ of the " Kreutz Zeitungs" party, though in ideal elevation, still without contact with the real world, and therefore without offensive vulgarities.

Your Excellency kindly promised me a few lines on Franz Baader; may I remind you of them in the most modest manner, and with the remark, that really a few lines only would suffice for the purpose?

In most faithful reverence and most grateful submission, immutably your Excellency's most obedient

VARNHAGEN VON ENSE.

203.

VARNHAGEN TO HUMBOLDT.

BERLIN, *April* 10*th*, 1857.

I HAVE the pleasure to announce to your Excellency that Herr——— will start from ——— to Weimar on the 14th. Much as he would have wished to make the détour by way of Berlin, if only to lay at the feet of your Excellency the most cordial expression of his boundless gratitude for so much friendly intercession, he is compelled by the brief period fixed by the Grand Duke to renounce the realization of that wish for the present. I therefore venture to solicit the favor of the introduction to the Grand Duke you were good enough to promise; a single line would suffice. I would immediately despatch it to Weimar, so that Mr. ——— will find it there on his arrival. The young man is well aware that the journey concludes nothing, and that he must be prepared for a denial; but he is much pleased to see that the long delay in the progress of affairs is ended, and he is at last in motion. By your kind inquiry your Excellency has produced this result, and dispelled the clouds of misconception; the most grateful heart will acknowledge this with heartfelt devotion! His sentiments are warmly shared by myself, in this case, as in so many earlier cases!

With the best wishes for your welfare; with profound veneration and attachment I remain unalterably,

Your Excellency's most obedient
VARNHAGEN VON ENSE.

204.

HUMBOLDT TO VARNHAGEN.

BERLIN, *April* 13*th*, 1857.

HERE, my valued friend, is the archivary recommendation for ———, just as prescribed. May the matter be successful. With heartfelt attachment,

Yours, A. v. HUMBOLDT.

205.

HUMBOLDT TO VARNHAGEN.

BERLIN, *April* 21*st*, 1857.

To my great regret, dear friend, I cannot accept the kind invitation of yourself and your amiable niece to a cup of coffee on Thursday, as I shall return late and much fatigued from Charlottenburg. During my illness, a number of unimportant matters have accumulated, which must be disposed of after dinner, because they are trumpery affairs of *orders* and dedications, a presentation of Betel in preference to gifts of money. The fourth class* operates like Betel chewing, it occupies

---

* i.e., of the order of the Prussian eagle.

the time, but affords no nourishment. On Thursday the King hopes to close and settle with me. Be pleased to write Professor Hoffmann, of Wuerzburg, that I am grateful for his torso, but no assistance is to be expected from the King, not only (what you must *not* write), because something like a holy horror of the Catholic zeal of Baader is rooted in the King's mind, but also because all literary assistance dwindles down in *the cabinet* to a present of forty or forty-five thalers. In preference to the publication in the preface of a miserable letter of introduction, which may have been written in a moment of ill-humor, I enclose a memorandum as requested.

With the same friendship as of old,

A. v. HUMBOLDT.

(INCLOSURE IN A LETTER FROM HUMBOLDT TO VARNHAGEN.)

You ask me, dear friend, what were the earliest impressions produced upon me by Franz Baader! I first saw him in June, 1791, while studying the art of mining in Freiberg, after the journey with George Forster to England, and after my sojourn in the Hamburg Commercial Academy of Buesching and Ebeling. For eight months I enjoyed the daily intercourse of this amiable and gifted man. Franz Baader had then published his work on caloric, and his inclinations were all of a chemico-physical nature, with a slight infusion of ideas on the philosophy of physical science. He was active underground, more occupied with practical mining and furnace operations than with geognostic researches; thorough in the observation of fact, cheerful, and satirical, but always with good taste, and not intolerant of those who differed from him. His imagination was not then specially directed to religious subjects. He was generally popular, and a little feared at the same time, as is so common where there is a consciousness of mental superiority. His political opinions were liberal. It was the period of the Congress of Pillnitz in our neighborhood—a time and a neighborhood which gave occasion to political utterances.

206.

HUMBOLDT TO VARNHAGEN.

BERLIN, *April 25th*, 1857.

"THE gate of the oracle, the abyss of the archives of state, analogies leading down to the depths of the sea." This is inferior to the last letter. Rafael's manner is not always the same. I am surprised to find that curiosity appears to have led him to avoid seeing ——— before the journey to Hanover! Preserve the vapid letter, my dear friend! The bottom of the sea refers to a map of the sea from Newfoundland to Ireland, which I recommended to the Grand Duke, but which is not to be procured because it was published in *Carthage* by Perthes! The Times flatter themselves, in all seriousness, that the French race is on the point of extinction; well, the pugs are extinct also.

Yours,

A. v. HUMBOLDT.

I have disagreeable *rudera* of the correspondence with a certain Dr. Gross Hoffinger, in Vienna, who accuses himself of having written against Prussia in 1848, and now asks Prussia to recommend him to the Austrian government. Have you any recollection of him?

NOTE BY VARNHAGEN.—" Carthage" means Gotha, a town not far from Weimar, but under the sovereignty of the Duke of Saxe-Coburg, between whom and his cousin there is a constant rivalry, such as of old existed between Rome and Carthage.

207.

CHARLES ALEXANDER, GRAND DUKE OF SAXE-WEIMAR, TO HUMBOLDT.

YOUR Excellency's letter was duly received by the hands of Mr. ——. Accept my thanks for these lines, for this new token of your constant kindness to me.

The bearer is for the present immersed in the abyss of my archives. As soon as I shall return from Hanover, where an invitation will detain me a few days,* to seek him out, awaiting further developments at the hand of time, like the people at the gate of the oracle.

Analogies lead me from deep to lower deep, and then I descend from the archives to the bottom of the sea. How am I to obtain the map of which you wrote? When I inquired for it in Gotha, some time ago, the inquiry was futile. So I return to the source, ever rich and bounteous, of whom I subscribe myself the most grateful and obedient

CHARLES ALEXANDER.

VIENNA, *April* 22*d*, 1857.

208.

HUMBOLDT TO VARNHAGEN.

BERLIN, May 28th, 1857.

I AM uneasy, my dear friend, about Weimar. The Grand Duke is everywhere, except in Weimar "Athens." What will become of our warmly recommended? Has he been spoken to by the eloquent Prince? You have not wished me joy to the order bestowed upon me by

---

* An ellipse, probably of Grand Ducal origin.—*Tr.*

the "Hamburg Moniteur" as Grand Officier, which Guizot gave me fifteen years ago. • Raumer's conversation is very interesting; he was at Pesth, at Milan, dined with the Archduke, and called on Cavour. He has again returned with something of a hankering after the Austrian régime in Lombardy, like the Republicans when they visit the United States, where arsenic, the torture, or Fremont-worshipping negroes, cause a criminal colic to Cuba-mad Buchanan. *Multa sunt eadem sed aliter.* The Russian Minister of Enlightenment, Noroff, who had a leg shot off by the thigh at Borodino, and who has carried his wooden leg to Jerusalem and Egypt, and even to the top of the Pyramids, is here, and attends as a guest, sitting among the students, the lectures of Johannes Mueller and Diderici. His companion, the young Count Ouwaroff, the author of a great work on Hellenic antiquities in the Chersonese, attends the lectures of Michelet and Boeckh. Both are very agreeable men. The former is accused of being over spiritual, but not intolerant; both are much pleased with the freedom of our student life, and with the absence of policemen from our university building. I did not care to disabuse the mind of the one-legged Raumer, as they will leave soon. *Decipitur mundus.*

  With old affection, your tiresome
A. v. HUMBOLDT.

NOTE BY VARNHAGEN.—"The United States, where arsenic, the torture, or Fremont-worshipping negroes, cause a criminal colic to Cuba-mad Buchanan." This passage alludes to the circumstance, that at a hotel in Washington, the President, and many others with him, were seized with a violent colic after dinner, so that suspicions of poison were entertained; and it was only after a legal investigation that the whole was found to have been caused by impure water.

BY THE TRANSLATOR.—" Fremont-worshipping negroes" must refer to the slaves who were reported to be in insurrection soon after the accession of President Buchanan, in Tennessee or Kentucky, and of whom it was said, that they believed Fremont and all his men to be encamped at the bottom of the Cumberland river, ready to emerge for their delivery.

209.

HUMBOLDT TO VARNHAGEN.

POTSDAM, THURSDAY. *In haste,*
June 4th, 1857.

A TRULY grand ducal letter, indelicate without excuse, cutting off every prospect, as he said "Au revoir" on going away, after the preconcerted shibboleth. Silence as to the costs, which are unnecessarily heavy. You and I shall cease "steering in the ocean of investigation," as acquaintance with the party proposed does not suffice to determine him. I have a mind to answer somewhat mockingly. It may be agreeable to you, my

esteemed friend, to enrich your archives with an autography of Thiers, who is now an Orleanist. Duvergier de Hauranne also came here after a pilgrimage to Eisenach. The Duchess is going to England. Preserve both letters, the bad one and that which is simply good.
　　　　　Yours,
　　　　　　　　　　　A. v. HT.

On Saturday I expect to come to Berlin with the King. The Queen is coming on Monday.

210.

CHARLES ALEXANDER, GRAND DUKE OF SAXE-WEIMAR, TO HUMBOLDT.

ETTERSBURG, *June* 1, 1857.

YOUR Excellency has probably learned already, that I have seen, repeatedly conversed with, but finally refrained from appointing ——. He interested me, I may say he pleased me, but I thought I could not recognise in him the secretary who could not only keep me informed of everything of moment in the spheres of science, art, and literature, but should attend to my correspondence, my intercourse, verbal and social, in various languages; and to appoint him at hazard I feared to venture. To retreat was, then, the only resource. I did so in order to steer further in the ocean of investigation. Whether you will continue, even in this matter, to cast upon me, as a star of good omen, the light of the goodness ever extended to me—is what I may be permitted to wish, but can hardly be permitted to hope — although we agreed that the acquaintance of the party was not to include his selection.

I shall now retire into various forest solitudes of Thuringia with a number of books, among which I anticipate particular pleasure from the perusal of Barth's itinerary. I bow in reverence before such endurance in the love of science, before such indomitable energy; how much the more must I do so before his prototype, before you? Remaining your most devoted, most grateful servant,

CHARLES ALEXANDER.

211.

THIERS TO HUMBOLDT.
(FROM THE FRENCH.)

PARIS, *May 14th*, 1857.

MY DEAR M. DE HUMBOLDT—I take the liberty of commending to your goodness shown so often to myself and to Frenchmen generally, M. Duvergier de Hauranne, who goes to Germany to show it to his young son.

You know our country too well for me to tell you what important and always honorable part has been sustained by M. Duvergier de Hauranne in our assemblies, where he has ever been faithful to the cause of rational liberty; and not faithful alone, but eminently useful. Having returned to private life and devoted himself to study, he goes to see your excellent country, and I thought I could not do better than to recommend him to your kindness. To his young son it will be an imperishable recollection to have seen the illustrious savan who does the greatest honor to the century, and whom we Frenchmen have the vanity to consider as French, and belonging to us no less than to Germany.

I do not write on current affairs here, for M. Duvergier de Hauranne knows them, and can make you acquainted with them better than any other man.

Accept the renewed homage of my respectful attachment.
A. THIERS.

212.

HUMBOLDT TO VARNHAGEN.

BERLIN, *June* 19*th*, 1857.

To my greatest joy, a beautiful portrait of yourself was brought me by Mr. Richard Zeune, during an excursion to Tegel. I know not which most to admire, the fresh, vivid, characteristic likeness of features so dear to me (the talent of the skilful Miss Ludmilla Assing), or the writing of your hand, so pregnant in thought and expression. The latter I have copied myself and shown it to my friends, because it is to be ranked with the best of what our language contains in the sententious compression of ideas. The unexpected arrival of the brothers Schlagintweit from Cashmere, Thibet, and the Kuen Luen mountains, which bound Thibet on the north, as the Himalaya on the south, has unreasonably delayed my acknowledgment of your kindness, as they are going to the King at Marienbad, without, it is to be hoped, the three hundred and forty boxes they have brought with them. All the *passes*, even those most convenient for travel, are 18,000 feet high. From the liberal grand ducal power (not liberal in the prosaic sense of filthy lucre), not a syllable, probably because he is expecting us to send him fresh proposals, fresh victims. No one but the honorary Hungarian monk* and the princess is now a riddle to me. Yours most faithfully,

A. v. Humboldt.

The Emperor Napoleon has adroitly mended what before was dubious, by means of very amiable letters, rich in delicate turns of language, addressed to me by

* Liszt.

Prince Napoleon (plon plon), and Walewski. As Niebuhr, the Prussian Cabinet Councillor, is publishing a book on Noric Antiquities, nothing remains to cause surprise, not even the FREE canvass for the *free* election in *free* France. I believe a few weeks in Branitz will be of benefit to you.

213.

HUMBOLDT TO VARNHAGEN.

BERLIN, *June* 30*th*, 1857.

I AM at a loss for words to express to you, my honored friend, and to the amiable and brilliant artist and authoress, Ludmilla Assing, what pleasure you have provided for my solitude, by "Elisa von Ahlefeldt," a pleasure still to be enjoyed by all who will deprive me of it for a few days. Who can read without emotion a fate so tender, so simple, told in such glowing language, by Miss Ludmilla; who can escape the most anxious reflections about the tortures of sentiment which the most noble and cultivated of mankind are skilled in inflicting on themselves about passion half-dogmatic in character, for the gratification of which the difficult institution of official marriage is inadequate. Elisa von Ahlefeldt loved Adolph von Luetzow, but only as the vigorous representative of a noble political sentiment. The motive for the disruption of the fetters, indelicate on his part, has something depressing. Immerman wishes to be loved, dreads the constraint of marriage, as Elisa does, but marries nevertheless!! The man who most occupies my thoughts in all these matters is Friesen, who worked so hard with me at the Mexican atlas in 1807, who was so dear to me, and to whom I was so much. I have mentioned him with tenderness in the Essai Politique sur la Nouvelle Espagne. Had I known the beautiful work of Miss Ludmilla, I would gladly have offered her a few lines. Her book, however, will go through many editions. As I am unfortunately compelled to go to Tegel for a night, I inquire, my dear friend, whether I may call upon you at three o'clock on Friday, and whether I may hope then to find Miss Ludmilla with you. So much skill in art and literary genius united in one and the same person is a rare luxury. It might lead to misfortunes. The course of the world refuses to admit of great exceptions to its compensatory system of pleasure and sadness.

Your   A. v. HUMBOLDT.

TUESDAY.

In great haste, and incorrect.

(Inclosed, a Letter from Friesen, of the year 1807, with this Superscription by Humboldt.)

A little gift for Miss Ludmilla Assing, the brilliant authoress of Elisa von Ahlefeldt, an autograph of my dear young friend Friesen, with sentiments of sincere thankfulness.

A. v. HUMBOLDT.

JUNE 30*th,* 1857.

Varnhagen's diary of July 4, 1857, contains the following: "Yesterday Humboldt spoke of the time when he lived in a house at the side of George's Garden, and was so assiduous in his magnetic observations that he once stinted himself of sleep for seven successive days and nights in order to examine the state of things every half hour; after that he changed the watch with substitutes. This was in 1807, just fifty years ago. I often saw the little house in which the experiments were made, when I visited Johannes von Mueller, who also lived in a house at the side of the same garden; or Fichte who lived in a garden house in the middle of the garden. When old George, a wealthy distiller, showed the garden to his friends, Humboldt went on to say, he never failed to boast of 'his learned men.' 'Here I have the famous Mueller; there is Humboldt, and there is Fichte, but he is only a philosopher, I believe.'"

214.

HUMBOLDT TO VARNHAGEN.

BERLIN, *July 6th*, 1857.

So ignorant of German poetry as to know nothing of the fame of Mr. —— of what he calls the dreary Mecklenburg, I must ask you, my dear friend, to specify the degree of politeness with which the man ought to be answered. Eight volumes, a compensation of forty louis d'or, four for myself, four, as usual, for the King, and a nonsensical letter, are before me. The man appears to have sung of the great Napoleon and Ney, but to have vainly knocked at the door of Napoleon III., Stephanie, Walewski, and Edgar Ney. It is made my duty forthwith to read a Trajan, a Bianca, and a Henry IV. Neither does he seem to have an extravagant idea of what is to be obtained from the King, a circumstance which discourages me from delivering the treasure. Elisa von Ahlefeldt has given great pleasure in Tegel, where I went with Kaulbach yesterday, as delicate and pure in taste. Not in Tegel but in Berlin, some court chaplains or officers, anxious to acquire the title of consistorial councillors, may have mooted the ecclesiastical question, whether a husband

and a friend are both allowable? The Berliners manage to talk about and to soil whatever comes into their fingers.

Most gratefully fully yours,
A. v. HUMBOLDT.

MONDAY NIGHT.

I shall send for the two volumes again in a day or two.

My best and most grateful compliments to Miss Ludmilla, the poetic artist, who combines the poet and the painter.

215.

VARNHAGEN TO HUMBOLDT.

BERLIN, July 8th, 1857.

THE two volumes of poetry kindly sent by your Excellency, no doubt manifest considerable literary culture, and a skilful management of language and of metre; but this would seem to exhaust the truthful measure of their praise. The number of men of this order of talent is very large, and where there are not further excellences they can hardly be called otherwise than ordinary. The claims advanced on the basis of such performances are frequently exorbitant, and such is the case in the present instance, where not appreciation merely, but actual remuneration is demanded. The author is not known to me, and his reputation certainly far from extensive. That his youth has been hard, and that his present condition is far from pleasant, is much to be deplored, but the manner in which he seeks to better himself, by supplication to the powerful—bestowing praise upon men of all parties and all shades of party, without a conviction of his own,—is none the less disreputable, as well as his letter to your Excellency, which has received the proper epithet at your hands. In the answer with which you will honor him, the severe expressions I have used are sure of being softened to the full extent of what is desirable by your inexhaustible and unchangeable humanity and goodness.

My niece, Ludmilla, thanks you from the fulness of her heart for the friendly interests your Excellency has so kindly manifested, and which she will never cease to count among the greatest treasures of which she could possibly become possessed!

Yesterday we paid a visit to Madame Gagiotti Richards, and found her, more beautiful than ever, in the midst of her artistic occupations. The whole family entertain the most enthusiastic veneration for you, and this alone would make them dear to us; the personal attractions of the beautiful artist are enchanting.

At the present day nothing literary is permitted to

make its appearance, be it ever so peaceful and inoffensive, without giving rise to manifestation of priestcraft and zealotry. The little book could not escape the universal fate, and the author must expect to meet with many an offensive objurgation on this head. But she has had the good fortune *de manger son pain blanc le premier*, she has reaped the praises of your Excellency, and may now quietly leave the black bread of detraction untouched!

We mean to leave for Dresden on Monday, and hope to find your Excellency again in excellent health at the end of a few weeks!

With profound veneration and grateful devotion,
Your obedient   VARNHAGEN VON ENSE.

216.

HUMBOLDT TO VARNHAGEN.

BERLIN, *September 16th*, 1857.

AN inquiry about letters and packages of the 8th and 22d of August, gives me the gratifying certainty of your return to monastic Berlin, where (supplement to No. 215 of Tante Voss, Sept. 15) "God in History"* is accused of rationalism and sinful Romanism on account

---

* Title of a work by Chevalier Bunsen.

of a kiss extorted from M. Merle d'Aubigné, and not yet sufficiently explained, and where (what is much more refreshing) pastor Kind boasts of having been kissed on the shoulder by a young Italian chambermaid at Naples, with the warmth of semi-conversion to Evangelism. As my monotonous birth-day has already brought in more than three hundred letters and packages, I never know anything about the dates of arrival; but I well remember having received a letter with a black margin of the 15th of July, from your distinguished relative Adolfo de Varnhagen in Madrid, and also a fragment of his history. I shall thank him heartily. His history is not without interest. You know that an attempt was made to get rid of M. von der Heydt, whose independent activity is disagreeable to his colleagues, by the appointment of a commission of finance in the council of state. But the man has acted with considerable energy, and the King has adjourned the whole commission, which was the work of Niebuhr.

With heartfelt friendship,

WEDNESDAY. Yours, A. v. H.

My respects to your talented niece.

I believe "God in History" has acted unwisely in accepting the King's invitation, even after so many repetitions. I esteem him, but he will be accused of many things of which he is innocent.

217.

HUMBOLDT TO VARNHAGEN.

BERLIN, *October 14th*, 1857.
(WITH LETTER FROM GENTZ AND GARVE RETURNED.)

MY best thanks! I had already received the letters and enjoyed them. Nothing can add more to the glory of my brother. Strange that Ancillon could so long deceive so shrewd a man as Gentz.

A. v. HT.

Varnhagen's diary of Dec. 3d, 1857, reads as follows: "I called on Humboldt; M. von Olfers was just going, and told me that Rauch had died in Dresden. Next General Count von der Groeben took his leave; he was very cordial, and pleased with my offer to send him a man who will republish the poems of Schenkendorf. Humboldt was full of cordiality for Ludmilla and myself; told me about the King, about Schoenlein, about the Princess of Prussia, about Doctor Lassalle, whose work* he had read accurately in three nights, and of Friesen; spoke of the 'Kreuz Zeitung' with contempt, praised the Count von der Groeben as a man of honor, and von der

---

* The Philosophy of Heraclitus the Obscure of Ephesus.

Heydt for his determination to leave the cabinet. He had a letter from the Queen. The King wishes to see him, and he therefore drives to Charlottenburg. He is hale and hearty. I read much in Lassalle. Even the external appearance of so great and important a work excites reverence. On me it makes a peculiar impression to witness the downfall, one by one, of the stays and rivets by which my inveterate opinions have been upheld. Every one who has grown old has to observe and experience such things; but in our times the changes are quicker and more powerful than in former times, and I am peculiarly sensible to them. Even where the contents do not matter to me, where I do not lose in the matter, because the subjects do not belong directly to my province, the phenomenon is nevertheless somewhat disagreeable. Such is again my lot in regard to Schleiermacher; his work on Heraclitus was hitherto the last word, the final disposition of all questions relating to that philosopher; even Hegel's adverse hints had not been able to overturn this authority. One could rest upon it as on a downy pillow, when lo! a new critic comes, and snatches it from under us. True, Lassalle supplies its place with another, which is large and well stuffed, but still the change is uncomfortable. And yet I am pleased with this unrest of intellectual efforts, this ingenuity, learning, progress, which asks no fear or favor."

218.

HUMBOLDT TO VARNHAGEN.

BERLIN, *January 11th*, 1858.

REVERED FRIEND,—I, too, am a sufferer from the returning cutaneous affection, an unwelcome consequence of old age. You have, at least, unconditional freedom, and can attend to your comfort; to me there is no freedom granted; I am molested by all; most unmercifully and inexorably by the mail. The kind memento of Mrs. Sarah Martin is very honorable to me. I owe it, like many other things, to you. Suffer me to make you the interpreter of my gratitude and of my faithful reverence for the talented lady, and for her brother, so dear to me, Mr. John Taylor. The news from Livingstone interests me chiefly on account of his views of the susceptibility of the negro race to civilization, at a time when France on the one hand, and North America on the other, are most shamelessly subserving the capture of slaves in Africa, under the flimsy pretext of introducing free laborers. The political news from India, by Captain Meadows Taylor, was unimportant. Perhaps it is agreeable to you to add to your archives some original letters of Count Walewski,

Prince Napoleon, who goes to Egypt, son of King Jerome, Lord Stratford de Redcliffe, and a copy of a very finely-written letter of the Pasha of Egypt, the original of which I was obliged to present to Dr. Brugsch.

Dr. Michael Sachs could not be prevented from celebrating me in Hebrew.* Many kind greetings to the noble General von Pfuel, whom I shall visit as soon as possible.

Yours faithfully, always equally illegible,

A. v. HUMBOLDT.

219.

PRINCE NAPOLEON, SON OF JEROME, TO HUMBOLDT.

PARIS, *Oct.* 13*th*, 1857.

MONSIEUR LE BARON,—Mons. Mariette sent to me, only a few days ago, your letter of July, in which you speak of Dr. Brugsch, and of his having sent me a Demotic Grammar, which I have not yet received. I mention this, so that you cannot accuse me of negligence in answering you. To-day I do not feel the courage in me to speak to you even of science. Your heart and your mind must be much afflicted by the sickness of your sovereign and friend, who causes us

* A Life of Humboldt was written in Hebrew by Mr. Sachs.

great sorrow. I say us, because the few days which I passed at Berlin made me appreciate the eminent qualities of the King, and attached me very much to him. May God preserve his life! I wish it from my heart.

Receive, Monsieur le Baron, the assurance of my high esteem. NAPOLEON.

Varnhagen reports in his diary under February 18th, 1858:—"I went to Humboldt. With a wonderful presence of mind he immediately thinks of all the things of which our presence can remind him; he tells most flattering things to Ludmilla on her book, for the second edition of which (which he declares to be inevitable), he will give her a passage on Friesen,* which he had indeed intended to communicate to the 'Turners' of Leipzig, as an inscription on the monument intended to be erected in Friesen's honor, but which, after a preliminary inquiry, appears to have been forgotten by them. He is out of humor with the Grand Duke of Saxe-Weimar, who robbed him and the brothers Schlagintweit of some hours, by repeated visits; they soon found out that he did not want to inform himself about those things they had prepared for him, but that he only wanted to have spoken with them; he also gave to each one the Falkenorden.† About —— he made

---

* One of the founders, "der Turnkunst."
† Order of the Falcon.

the same excuse to Humboldt as he made to me, that noble birth was indispensable, which Humboldt thinks quite detestable, and moreover entirely in harmony with the personal prejudices of the Grand Duke; the father, he says, who also was not very remarkable, had at least concealed this sentiment, but the son expresses it openly; once, after a man who was not of noble birth had left the company, he had with great satisfaction given utterance to his delight, saying, 'Now we are among ourselves!' Another time, when some one observed that thirteen were at the table, he replied for consolation, that two among them were not nobles, and therefore did not count! and this he said to Humboldt in French, because, he said, these two would certainly not understand that! Humboldt complained bitterly of the mass of letters by which he was visited; he had to read at least 400 of them in one month; many commenced, 'Noble old man,' or, 'Noble youthful old man;' or also in this fashion: 'Caroline and I are happy; our fate is in your hands.'* He praised Princess Victoria, saying, that she was not pretty, but had pleasing simple manners, and an eye full of soul."

* Meaning "Caroline and I can get married, if you will help us to some money."

220.

VARNHAGEN TO HUMBOLDT.

BERLIN, *February* 19*th*, 1858.

You see, dear friend, that in spite of many little cavils of Mr. d'Avezac, who has learned to quote from Malte-Brun, your cousin does you much honor. But it is incomprehensible that Mr. d'Avezac knows nothing at all of the map of Juan de la Cose, of 1500, published by me in 1830, six years before the death of Colon, and of a work in large quarto, under the title "Geschichte des Seefahrers Ritter Martin Behaim, von W. Ghillany and Alex. Humboldt, 1853," where the origin of the name of "America" is discussed.

A. HT.

The ravages of a single night. The noble, youthful old man, Vecchio della Montagna.

Accompanying the book, "Considerations Géographiques sur l'Histoire du Brézil, Examen critique d'une nouvelle histoire générale du Brézil, par M. Francois Adolphe de Varnhagen. Rapport fait par M. d'Avezac, Paris, 1857-58."

221.

HUMBOLDT TO VARNHAGEN.

BERLIN, *March 7th*, 1858.

I PRESUME that you, dear friend, have not seen the indiscreet, almost talentless, book of Normanby. I shall not return it to Lady Bloomfield without offering it to you. Skip over it according to the index, and send it kindly back to me in four or five days. It depicts a badly played comedy.

My reverence to your amiable niece. Your most attached

A. v. HUMBOLDT.

SUNDAY NIGHT.

"A Year of Revolution. From a journal kept in Paris in 1848. By the Marquis of Normanby, K.G. London, 1857. 2 vols. in 8vo."

Varnhagen remarks in his diary, under March 8th, 1858: "Humboldt sends me, with kind lines, the book of the Marquis of Normanby on the revolution of 1848. He calls it an indiscreet book, and almost talentless. I call it stupid, and perfidious in its contents; it shows the evil results of meddling with diplomacy, particularly if unofficial, as was that of the Marquis at the time. Lamartine as well as Cavaignac gave far too much heed to him. He is one of the dullest and most tedious Englishmen ever heard of."

March 9th, 1858. Varnhagen adds this further remark on Normanby: "Read a little more of Normanby. He is a poor fool, but his bad book is good enough to expose the paltriness of Louis Philippe, the villany of Guizot, and the pernicious influences of sneaks and sharpers. His forte consists in the perfect success with which he flattens down to insufferable monotony the enlivening and exhilarating effects of the torrent of events."

222.

HUMBOLDT TO VARNHAGEN.

BERLIN, *April* 13th, 1858.

I AM touched by the kindness of your letter, and the souvenir from your talented niece, Miss Ludmilla. As Illaire called yesterday, I have made every preparation to be of use to M——, the esteemed clergyman of ——, in the acquisition of one of those toys, which, if they do not nourish, yet afford an agreeable diversion, like that enjoyed by the knights of old, who galloped over a course covered with obstructions, and the prospect of escape from the infernal regions of the fourth class.* I shall write to Illaire for the third class, but beseech you to jog my memory. ——'s title! I believe he does not preach—has even ceased to administer the little wafers which refuse to unite with the bread, their chemical kinsman. I believe, however, he is a Protestant power in ——.

For the benefit of your soul and Miss Ludmilla's, I inclose some phantasies on the antediluvian universal absence of rain in the Berlin world, and on the consuming fire, sure to be occasioned by a little forgotten potash, in the midst of innocent felspar of the granite formation, on the day of judgment: " de la géologie hébraïzante," as I have been imprudent enough to style it in " Kosmos."

Yours, A. v. Ht.

TUESDAY.

---

* *I.e.* of the order of the Prussian Eagle. The sentence reads thus: " Da gestern Illaire bei mir war, so habe ich alles vorbereitet, Herrn —— dem vielgeachteten Geistlichen in . . . . nuetzlich fuer eines der Spielwerke zu werden, welche zwar nicht naehren, aber eine augenehme Zerstreuung, *auch des spaet ausgefuehrten Reitens mit Hindernissen,* Aussicht zur Errettung aus der Unterwelt dervier ten Klasse gewaehren." As it stands, the clause printed by us in italics makes nonsense.—*Translator.*

("Thoughts on the first Rainbow, in connexion with certain Geological Facts." London: 1852. The author is W. Bateman Byng, but it was sent to Humboldt by Mr. F. A. Fokker, of Hamburg, a superannuated pilot captain.)

On the 24th of April, 1858, Varnhagen observes in his diary: "Humboldt was very droll yesterday, in speaking of the letters he receives. A number of ladies in Elberfeld have conspired to labor at his conversion, by means of anonymous letters, and have informed him of their design. Such letters are received from time to time. Somebody in Nebraska asks him what becomes of the swallows in winter. I suggested that this inquiry must be for ever on the wing. 'Of course,' he replied; 'I don't know any more than other folks, but,' he added, with jocose gravity, : 'I took care not to write that to the man in Nebraska, for it is never safe to make such admissions.'"

223.

HUMBOLDT TO VARNHAGEN.

POTSDAM, *June* 19*th*, 1858.

TEDIOUS on the whole, and full of internal contradictions, but still historical in reference to the mythical Americo-Germanism, and unfortunately too true. See

p. 76 to 80, and pp. 33, 35, 75. The charms of a language without genders. "*Fermez les lèvres et serrez les dents.*"* "Der" and "die" fell into lazy mouths, and lapses into "de," and this was corrupted into a neutral, lifeless "the."

Page 88 sets forth how my friend Froebel escaped being *Blumed*. A. HT.

There gloomy Potsdam has kept me too long from your side.

NOTE BY VARNHAGEN.—This letter accompanied "The German Emigration, and its Importance in the History of Civilization. By Julius Froebel. Leipsic: 1858." A copy sent by Froebel to Humboldt.

* "Close your lips and set your teeth." In the '*Anglaises pours rire*' there is a squib which says, "*Ouvrez la bouche et serrez les dents et vous parlerez anglais!*" Open your mouth and set your teeth, and you will speak English. Humboldt may have had this in his mind and have converted *ouvrez* into *fermez* by mistake.

Froebel says in page 35: "After all, the German and the English are but two different dialects, or rather stages of development. The English occupies the higher grade, for it is acknowledged that the attrition of grammatical form corresponds to a higher mental development." Opposite this passage Humboldt writes "Ah!"

On p. 88, Froebel alludes to the great mission of Austria in the future. Similar passages were to be found in a pamphlet of his, which appeared in 1848; they were pointed out to Prince Windischgraetz by an aide-de-camp, just in time to procure his pardon, while his colleague, Robert Blum, was brutally shot.

224.

HUMBOLDT TO VARNHAGEN.

BERLIN, *September 9th, at night,* 1858.

HEARTY thanks, my dear friend, for your affectionate missive. The thanks of the excellent .... is far from indifferent to me. No one here has had the politeness to inform me that my proposal has been accepted. As you and your accomplished niece, Miss Ludmilla, are fond of curiosities, and as my extreme old age has deadened all compunction at the exhibition of my own praises, I send you a letter from Queen Victoria, delivered by the Princess of Prussia, and requesting an autograph of some passages from the Views of Nature and Kosmos (poetical descriptions of nature), as well as a letter from the American Secretary of War, who has been accommodating to me for the traveller Moellhausen, the son-in-law of Seiffert, draughtsman of the two expeditions to the South Sea, and who, *mirabile dictu*, has dismissed all political animosity on account of my friendship for Fremont. The latter of the communications gives me the greater pleasure of the two, though it is unpardonably extravagant in the use of great names.

The regency, indispensable as it is to restore the wasted power of the country, is still, alas! in the clouds. I hope the Prince of Prussia will abide by his present promise, not to act further without being expressly invested with the title of Regent. But who is to make the first move, when the King is kept in such seclusion, that even I have not seen him since the return? If the Chambers initiate the matter, the Government stands convicted of pusillanimity. *Alea jacta*, and the sum of intelligence at stake seems to have been doled out by nature with laudable economy.

What knowledge have you, dear friend, of M. Iwan Golowin, whose impudence is so unprecedented as to admit of his photographing me before the public in the most dreadful *négligé de costume, même*, as I wrote him in great indignation, *en me dotant de deux fautes de français, venaient* instead of *viennent, pourrait* instead of *pouvait*. What will men not do to make tools of their neighbors?

I beg you to return me the three curiosities consisting of the copy of Victoria, the letter of the Secretary of War, and Rovira by Golowin, by Sunday morning, when I must go to Tegel with Baron Stockmar, the father.

My walk (*ma démarche*) increases lamentably in senile want of direction. Beware of my patience with life. Reputation keeps pace with imbecility, and the part of the "dear youth in age," of the "worthy Nestor of all living men of Science," *Vecchio della montagna*, becomes extremely irksome, though there be in the neighborhood of the Netze, a maiden whom the Nestor is to establish for life at Tegel, because the place is so near to Berlin, that on the slightest hint she can hasten to the city to close my eyes.

With the most faithful friendly esteem,
   Yours,
      A. v. HUMBOLDT.

My wicked friend Lasalle—Heraclitus the Obscure—has been expelled by the Prince of Prussia and Illaire,* in spite of all my intercession, and in spite of the promises made to me. They led me to hope that after a few weeks (the election being over) the Obscure would return to Pythagoras, the more obscure. What a dispensation of justice!

NOTE BY VARNHAGEN.—Iwan Golowin had asked Humboldt's permission to dedicate to him a Russian drama entitled Rovira, and when Humboldt assented in a hasty French note, he inserted a facsimile of the note into the book.

* Not quite exact, in so far as M. Westphalen, the minister, carried this point in the absence of the parties named, and, as afterwards appeared, without their knowledge.

225.

HUMBOLDT TO LUDMILLA ASSING.

BERLIN, *Oct. 12th*, 1858.

WHAT a day of agitation, of grief, of misfortune was yesterday. I was summoned by the Queen to Potsdam, to take leave of the King. He wept with deep emotion. Returning home at six in the evening, I opened your letter, my friend! He has departed from the earth before me, the man of ninety years, the old man of the hills! It is not enough to say that Germany has lost a great author, him who could most nobly mould our tongue to the expression of the finest sentiments—for what is the value of form in the presence of such acuteness, such pregnant force of mind, such elevation of thought, such knowledge of the world. What he was to me, to me who am now entirely isolated, is incomprehensible to any mind less refined, less beautiful than yours; I shall soon come to tell you,

Bowed with grief, yours,

A. v. HUMBOLDT.

Alphabetical Index

OF PERSONS ALLUDED TO.

The figures opposite the names refer to the numbers of the letters in which they are mentioned.

---o---

A.

ABERDEEN, Lord, 106.
Albert, Prince Consort, 124, 131, 132.
Alembert, d', 143.
Allan, 46.
Alvensleben, 46, 61.
Amerigo Vespucci, 36.
Ancillon, 22, 217.
Arago, Francis, 50, 68, 75, 76, 78, 153, 155, 157.
Arndt, E. M., 48.
Arnim, Achim von, 64.
Assing, Ludmilla, 213, 214, 217, 222, 224, 225.
Augustus, Prince of Prussia, 4, 87.
Auguste, Princess, 22.

B.

Baader, Francis, 145, 205.
Balzac, 75, 83.
Baudin, 128.
Bauer, Bruno, 60, 66, 94.
Baumgarten, 42.
Bavaria, Crown Prince of, 123.
Belgium, King of, 48.
Bettina, 43, 48, 51, 52, 63, 71, 75, 88, 120, 133, 144, 162, 178.
Bessel, 48, 111.
Beyme, 168.
Beust, 175.
Beuth, 11.
Bigelow, John, 192.
Bodelschwingh, von, 106, 107, 116.
Bollmann, 19.
Bopp, 48.
Bresson, 22, 75, 76, 78.
Brown, R., 76, 84.
Brunel, 75, 76.
Buch, Leopold von, 31, 41, 150.
Buchanan, James, 176, 208.
Buelow, von, 8, 48, 49, 61, 65, 69, 70, 71, 72, 97, 101, 103, 106, 111.
Bugeaud, Marshal, 27.
Bunsen, 11, 61, 68, 75, 159, 168.

C.

Cados, 80.
Canino, Princess, 116.
Canitz, von, 61, 74, 75, 126, 134.

Index.

Cardanus, 6, 7.
Carolath, 12.
Carlyle, Thos., 70.
Carrière, M., 70, 132.
Chasles, 62, 172.
Chateaubriand, 16, 36.
Cherubini, 63.
Christian VII., King of Denmark, 43, 44, 53, 76, 81.
Clanricarde, Marquis of, 41.
Columbus, Christopher, 28, 36, 61.
Constant, 163.
Cornelius, Peter, 142.
Cotta, 10, 16, 24, 35, 56.
Custine, 71, 73.

D.

Dahlmann, Prof., 48.
Delisle, 17.
Dohm, 64.
Duchess of Dino (Talleyrand), 75, 76.
Duke of Coburg Gotha, 168.
Duchess of Orleans, 27, 75, 76, 117, 119, 139, 148.

E.

Eckermann, 71.
Ehrhardt, 7.
Eichhorn, 48, 51, 60, 68, 75, 107, 133, 134.
Elsner, 11.
Encke, 74, 111.
Endlicher, 42.
Engel, 64.
Ettinghausen, 42.
Eylert, Bishop, 8.

F.

Fallersleben, Hoffmann von, 106.
Feuerbach, Ludwig, 94.

Fichte, 99, 196, 213.
Fillmore, Millard, 177.
Forster, 16.
Freiligrath, F., 62.
Fremont, 176, 177, 192.
Friedrich II., 64, 68.
Friedrich Wilhelm III., 8, 22, 35, 42.
Friedrich Wilhelm IV., 35, 40, 42, 45, 46, 49, 51, 52, 53, 54, 60, 63, 67, 68, 75, 76, 91, 92, 110, 134, 154, 156, 158, 168, 185.
Friesen, 213.
Froebel, Julius, 223.
Froriep, 159.
Fry, Mrs., 46.

G

Gagern, H., 134, 141.
Galuski, 125, 135, 147.
Galilei, 41.
Gama, Vasco de, 28.
Gans, E., 7, 25, 29, 30.
Gauss, 44.
Gay, Mad., 73.
Gay Lussac, 88.
Gentz, Fr., 36, 202, 217.
Gérard, 33, 83.
Gerlach, L. von, 68, 92, 159, 168, 183, 195.
Gerolt, Baron de, 177.
Girardin, Mad., 73.
Gneisenau, 159.
Görres, 41.
Goethe, J. W., 10, 43, 52, 71, 161.
Goethe, Ottilie von, 145.
Goetze, 28.
Golowin, 224.
Grand Duke of Tuscany, Leopold, 88.
Grand Duke of Weimar, Charles Alexander, 171, 179, 180, 181, 182, 183, 189, 193, 194, 200, 201, 202, 206, 207, 208, 209, 210, 212.

Index. 405

Grand Duchess of Weimar, 135, 183.
Grau, 149.
Gretsch, 41.
Grimm Brothers, 40, 48, 51.
Guhrauer, 106.
Guizot, 48, 49, 60, 62, 99, 106, 172, 221.

H.

Hanover, King of, 31, 40, 66.
Hansen, 81.
Hardenberg, Prince, 7.
Hedemann, 48, 193.
Hegel, 3, 7, 29, 30, 41, 54, 196.
Heine, 174, 177.
Helfort, Frau von, 75.
Hengstenberg, 68, 159.
Herschel, 75, 76, 82.
Hertzberg, Count, 64.
Heyne, 38, 64.
Hildebrandt, 186, 187, 191.
Hoeninghaus, 76.
Hordt, 64.
Hormayr, 60, 95, 101, 103.
Huegel, Baron, 42.
Humboldt, Wilhelm von, 10, 16, 18, 21, 27, 31, 33, 36, 64, 67, 70, 129, 133, 140, 152, 153, 154, 159, 167, 192, 217.

I.

Jacobs, Friedrich, 38.
Jaeger, 42.
Janin, 99.
Joburd, 190.
Itzstein, 97.

K.

Kamptz, 26, 76.
Kant, Immanuel, 33, 73, 107.

Klein, 64.
König, 41.
Kolowrat, 129.
Koreff, 2.
Kotzebue, 169, 170.
Kries, 38.
Kunth, 64.

L.

Ladenberg, 48.
Lafayette, Marquis de, 20, 151.
Laplace, 16.
Lasaulx, 195.
Lassalle, 217, 224.
Lavater, 6, 105.
Leist, 31.
Leo, 196.
Leonardo da Vinci, 52.
Liegnitz, Princess of, 35.
Lieven, Princess, 169, 170, 172.
Link, 68.
Liszt, 68.
Loeffler, 64.
Louis Philippe, 75, 139, 184, 221.
Louise, Princess, 33.

M.

Maltzan, 61, 68.
Manzoni, 114.
Marco Polo, 36.
Marheineke, 41, 68, 94.
Mary, Princess, 22.
Massmann, 110.
Melloni, 68.
Melgunoff, 41.
Metternich, 35, 42, 45, 68, 75, 76, 85, 98, 106, 122, 130, 137, 181, 185.
Meyerbeer, 88, 99.
Milner, 104.
Mole, 78.
Mueffling, 43.
Muller, A., 36, 202.

Muller, O., 16.
Mueller, Chancellor, 106.
Mueller, Privy Councillor, 28, 68.
Muenster, Count, 60.
Mundt, Theo. 19.

N.

Nacke, 39.
Napoleon I., 48, 71, 161.
Napoleon III., 141, 146, 147, 212.
Neander, 95.
Nesselrode, 187.
Nicholas, Emperor of Russia, 35.
Netherlands, Queen of, 22.
Niebuhr, G. B., 40.
Niebuhr, M., 154, 212, 216.
Normanby, 221.
Noroff, 208.

O.

Oersted, 44.
Oertzen, 26.
Olfers, 142.
Oltmann, 13.

P.

Palmerston, Lord, 48, 124.
Peel, Robert, 75, 76, 84.
Persigny, Fialin, 146.
Pertz, 160.
Pichler, 159.
Pierce, Franklin, 173.
Pourtales, Count, 176.
Prescott, 75, 76, 86.
Preuss, 105.
Prussia, Prince of, 74, 158, 168, 224.
Prussia, Princess of, 52.
Prutz, R., 90, 104, 100.
Pückler, Princess, 26.

Q.

Quinet, 43.

R.

Radowitz, 61, 68, 75, 142, 159, 168.
Rahel, 7, 9, 10, 24, 33, 36, 132, 133, 145.
Ranke, Leopold, 5, 68, 86, 105, 159.
Raphael, 52.
Rauch, 25.
Raumer, Charles, 41.
Raumer, Fred., 23, 64.
Raumer, Minister, 154, 168.
Récamier, Mad., 36, 75, 76, 87.
Redern, 88.
Reeden, 64.
Reimer, 70.
Reitmeyer, 64.
Reumont, 75.
Riess, 67, 68.
Rochow, 45.
Robert, 52.
Ruesel, 42.
Rothes, 75.
Rueckert, 59, 75, 113.
Ruehle, 25.
Rumohr, 68.

S.

Sachs, 101, 103.
Savary, 50.
Savigny, 68, 133.
Schelling, 41, 52, 54, 64, 75, 196.
Schiller, 2, 129, 169.
Schlagintweit, Brothers, 154, 212.
Schlegel, Aug., 55, 125.
Schlegel, Fr., 13, 14, 151.
Schleiermacher, 66.
Schlosser, 68.
Schoenlein, 197.
Schwerin, 61.
Seckendorf, 60.

Index.

Schumacher, 41, 81, 111.
Seiffert, 50, 173.
Sintenis, 41.
Spiker, 13, 55, 57.
Spontini, 68, 88, 91.
Staegemanns, 47.
Stael, Mad., 87.
Stahl, 159.
Stanley, 75, 76.
Steffens, 52, 65, 196.
Stein, 160, 168.
Stieglitz, 30, 33.
Stillfried, 176.
Stilling, 105.
Stollberg, 75.
Strauss, 64, 66.

T.

Talleyrand, 33, 78.
Therese, 133.
Thiele, 68, 107, 172.
Thiers, 48, 102, 115, 116, 211.
Thomas, 102, 115.
Tholuk, 65.

Tieck, 55.
Trubetzkoi, Princess, 73.

U.

Uhden, 158.
Uwaroff, 68.

V.

Varnhagen, Fr. A. 168.
Victoria, Queen, 124, 227.
Voigtlaender, 42.

W.

Wittgenstein, 5, 45, 88, 160.

Z.

Zeune, 16, 212.
Zinzendorf, Count, 6, 105.

CATALOGUE

OF THE

PUBLICATIONS

OF

RUDD & CARLETON,

130 GRAND STREET,

(BROOKS BUILDING, COR. OF BROADWAY,)

NEW YORK.

NEW BOOKS
And New Editions Just Published by
RUDD & CARLETON,
130 Grand Street,

NEW YORK (BROOKS BUILDING, COR. OF BROADWAY.)

N.B.—RUDD & CARLETON, UPON RECEIPT OF THE PRICE, WILL SEND ANY OF THE FOLLOWING BOOKS, BY MAIL, *postage free*, TO ANY PART OF THE UNITED STATES. THIS CONVENIENT AND VERY SAFE MODE MAY BE ADOPTED WHEN THE NEIGHBORING BOOKSELLERS ARE NOT SUPPLIED WITH THE DESIRED WORK.

NOTHING TO WEAR.
A Satirical Poem. By WILLIAM ALLEN BUTLER. Profusely and elegantly embellished with fine Illustrations on tinted paper, by Hoppin. Muslin, price 50 cents.

MILES STANDISH ILLUSTRATED.
With exquisite *Photographs* from original Drawings by JOHN W. EHNINGER, illustrating Longfellow's new Poem. Bound in elegant quarto, morocco covers, price $6 00

BOOK OF THE CHESS CONGRESS.
A complete History of Chess in America and Europe, with Morphy's best games. By D. W. FISKE, editor of *Chess Monthly* (assisted by Morphy and Paulsen). Price $1 50.

WOMAN'S THOUGHTS ABOUT WOMEN.
The latest and best work by the author of "John Halifax, Gentleman," "Agatha's Husband," "The Ogilvies," &c. From the London edition. Muslin, price $1 00.

VERNON GROVE;

By Mrs. CAROLINE H. GLOVER. "A Novel which will give its author high rank among the novelists of the day."—*Atlantic Monthly.* 12mo., Muslin, price $1 00

BALLAD OF BABIE BELL,

And other Poems. By THOMAS BAILEY ALDRICH. The first selected collection of verses by this author. 12mo Exquisitely printed, and bound in muslin, price 75 cents.

TRUE LOVE NEVER DID RUN SMOOTH.

An Eastern Tale, in Verse. By THOMAS BAILEY ALDRICH, author of "Babie Bell, and other Poems." Printed on colored plate paper. Muslin, price 50 cents

BEATRICE CENCI.

A Historical Novel. By F. D. GUERRAZZI. Translated from the original Italian by LUIGI MONTI. Muslin, two volumes in one, with steel portrait price $1 25.

ISABELLA ORSINI.

A new historical novel. By F. D. GUERRAZZI, author of "Beatrice Cenci." Translated by MONTI, of Harvard College. With steel portrait. Muslin, price $1 25.

DOCTOR ANTONIO.

A charming Love Tale of Italy. By G. RUFFINI, author of "Lorenzo Benoni," "Dear Experience," &c From the last London edition. Muslin, price $1 00.

DEAR EXPERIENCE.

A Tale. By G. RUFFINI, author of "Doctor Antonio,' "Lorenzo Benoni," &c. With illustrations by Leech, *of the London Punch.* 12mo. Muslin, price $1 00.

LECTURES OF LOLA MONTEZ.

Including her "Autobiography," "Wits and Women of Paris," "Comic Aspect of Love," "Gallantry," &c A new edition, large 12mo. Muslin, price $1 25.

EDGAR POE AND HIS CRITICS.

By Mrs. SARAH HELEN WHITMAN. A volume possessing many attractions and which has created considerable interest among the *literati*. 12mo. Muslin, price 75 cts

THE GREAT TRIBULATION;

Or Things coming on the Earth. By Rev. JOHN CUMMING, D.D., author of "Apocalyptic Sketches," &c. From the English edition. FIRST SERIES. Muslin, price $1 00.

THE GREAT TRIBULATION.

SECOND SERIES of the new work by Rev. DR. CUMMING, which has awakened such an excitement throughout the religious community. 12mo. Muslin, price $1 00.

ADVENTURES OF VERDANT GREEN.

By CUTHBERT BEDE, B.A. The best humorous story of College Life ever published. 80*th edition*, from English plates. Nearly 200 original illustrations, price $1 00.

CURIOSITIES OF NATURAL HISTORY.

By FRANCIS T. BUCKLAND, M.A. A sparkling collection of surprises in Natural History, and the charm of a lively narrative. From 4th London edition, price $1 25.

BROWN'S CARPENTER'S ASSISTANT.

The best practical work on Architecture; with Plans for every description of Building. Illustrated with over 200 Plates. Strongly bound in leather, price $5 00

THE VAGABOND.

A volume of Miscellaneous Papers, treating in colloquial sketches upon Literature, Society, and Art. By ADAM BADEAU. Bound in muslin, 12mo, price $1 00.

ALEXANDER VON HUMBOLDT.

A new and popular Biography of this celebrated *Savant*, including his travels and labors, with an introduction by BAYARD TAYLOR. One vol., steel portrait, price $1 25.

LOVE (L'AMOUR).

By M. JULES MICHELET. Author of "A History of France," &c. Translated from the French by J. W. Palmer, M.D. One vol., 12mo. Muslin, price $1 00.

WOMAN (LA FEMME).

A sequel and companion to "Love" (L'Amour) by the same author, MICHELET. Translated from the French by Dr. J. W. Palmer. 12mo. Muslin, price $1 00.

LIFE OF HUGH MILLER.

Author of "Schools and Schoolmasters," "Old Red Sandstone," &c. Reprinted from the English edition. One large 12mo. Muslin, new edition, price $1 25.

AFTERNOON OF UNMARRIED LIFE.

An interesting theme admirably treated. Companion to Miss Muloch's "Woman's Thoughts about Women." From London edition. 12mo. Muslin, price, $1 00.

SOUTHWOLD.

By MRS. LILLIE DEVEREUX UMSTED. "A spirited an well drawn Society novel—somewhat intensified but bold and clever." 12mo. Muslin, price $1 00.

DOESTICKS' LETTERS.

Being a compilation of the Original Letters of Q. K. P. DOESTICKS, P. B. With many comic tinted illustrations by John McLenan. 12mo. Muslin, price $1 00

PLU-RI-BUS-TAH.

A song that's by-no-author. *Not* a parody on "Hiawatha." By DOESTICKS. With 150 humorous illustrations by McLenan. 12mo. Muslin, price $1 00

THE ELEPHANT CLUB.

An irresistibly droll volume. By DOESTICKS, assisted by KNIGHT RUSS OCKSIDE, M.D. One of his best works Profusely illustrated by McLenan. Muslin, price $1 00.

THE WITCHES OF NEW YORK.

A new humorous work by DOESTICKS; being minute, particular, and faithful Revelations of Black Art Mysteries in Gotham. 12mo. Muslin, price $1 00

TWO WAYS TO WEDLOCK.

A Novellette. Reprinted from the columns of Morris & Willis' *New York Home Journal.* 12mo. Handsomely bound in muslin. Price $- 00,

HAMMOND'S POLITICAL HISTORY.

A History of Political Parties in the State of New York. By JABEZ B. HAMMOND, L.L.D. 3 vols., octavo, with steel portraits of all the Governors. Muslin. Price, $6 00.

ROMANCE OF A POOR YOUNG MAN.

From the French of OCTAVE FEUILLET. An admirable and striking work of fiction. Translated from the Seventh Paris edition. 12mo. Muslin, price $1 00

THE CULPRIT FAY.

By JOSEPH RODMAN DRAKE. A charming edition of this world-celebrated Faery Poem. Printed on colored plate paper. Muslin, 12mo. Frontispiece. Price, 50 cts.

THE NEW AND THE OLD;

Or, California and India in Romantic Aspects. By J. W. PALMER, M.D., author of " Up and Down the Irrawaddi." Abundantly illustrated. Muslin, 12mo. $1,25.

UP AND DOWN THE IRRAWADDI;

Or, the Golden Dagon. Being passages of adventure in the Burman Empire. By J. W. PALMER, M.D., author of "The New and the Old." Illustrated. Price, $1,00.

THE HABITS OF GOOD SOCIETY.

An interesting handbook for Ladies and Gentlemen; with thoughts, hints, and anecdotes, concerning social observances, taste, and good manners. Muslin, price $1 25.

RECOLLECTIONS OF THE REVOLUTION.

A private manuscript journal of home events, kept during the American Revolution by the Daughter of a Clergyman. Printed in unique style. Muslin. Price, $1,00

HARTLEY NORMAN.

A New Novel. "Close and accurate observation, enables the author to present the scenes of everyday life with great spirit and originality." Muslin, 12mo. Price, $1,25.

MOTHER GOOSE FOR GROWN FOLKS.

An unique and attractive little Holiday volume. Printed on tinted paper, with frontispiece by Billings. 12mo. Elegantly bound in fancy colored muslin, price 75 cts.

www.ingramcontent.com/pod-product-compliance
Lightning Source LLC
Chambersburg PA
CBHW050848300426
44111CB00010B/1183